A SHORT

HISTORY

OF

PENZANCE,

S. MICHAEL'S MOUNT, S. IVES,

AND THE

LAND'S END DISTRICT.

BY

REV. W. S. LACH-SZYRMA, M.A.,

VICAR OF NEWLYN S. PETER,

AND LATE VICAR OF CARNMENELLIS; M.A. BRASENOSE COLLEGE, OXFORD; EX TUTOR AND LIBRARIAN OF S. AUGUSTINE'S COLLEGE, CANTERBURY; LOCAL MEMBER FOR CORNWALL OF THE COUNCIL OF THE BRITISH ARCHÆOLOGICAL ASSOCIATION; AUTHOR OF "PLEAS FOR THE FAITH," "THE BISHOPRIC OF CORNWALL," ETC.

TRURO: LAKE AND LAKE, PRINCES STREET.
LONDON: SIMPKIN, MARSHALL & CO., STATIONERS' HALL COURT.
1878.

THE PENZANCE MARKET CROSS 1836.

To the

Right Reverend the Lord Bishop of Truro,

the following Sketches from the

History of a small portion of his Diocese

are respectfully Dedicated

By the Author.

PREFACE.

———o———

I PRESENT the following brief record of our past history with much diffidence, knowing how little time my numerous avocations have given me to do justice to such an important subject. I only hope that the following narrative, short though it is, may prove useful to residents, as speaking to them of their ancestors, and to visitors, as giving them an additional interest in this beautiful locality.

I may just mention :—

1. That I have striven as far as I can to avoid controversial topics of religion and politics, and to judge the past and the men of the past as far as I can without bias.

2. That to render the narrative more lively, I have, more frequently than is usual in books like this, employed the historical present.

3. That very many details of no general interest have been omitted for the sake of brevity.

I must also express my sincere thanks to the gentlemen who have given me information on local subjects.

AUTHORITIES.

————◆◆————

These works, marked *, contain further particulars on our local history. Those desirous of studying the subject may find in them interesting details.

————————

BANNISTER (Rev. Dr.)—Glossary of Cornish Names.
*BLIGHT'S Week at the Land's End.
    Churches of West Cornwall.
    Crosses of West Cornwall.
BOASE—Bibliotheca Cornubiensis.
*BORLASE (Dr.)—Antiquities of Cornwall, 1754.
    (W. C.) Nænia Cornubiæ.
        Article in Quarterly, 1874.
BOTTERILL'S Traditions and Hearthside Stories of West Cornwall.
CÆSAR—De Bello Gallico.
*CAREW'S Survey of Cornwall, 1602.
*COURTENAY'S Guide to Penzance.
    Cornish Provincial Dialect, 1846.
DAVY'S Life of Davy.
DIODORUS SICULUS.
DREW'S History of Cornwall.
*DUGDALE'S Monasticon Anglicanum.
FROUDE—History of England.
GILBERT'S (DAVIS) Parochial History of Cornwall, 1838.
GILES' History of the Ancient Britons.
GREEN—Short History of the English People.
HALLIWELL'S Rambles in West Cornwall.
*HALS' Parochial History (MS. in British Museum) 1685—1736.
*HARVEY (Rev. G.)—Mullyon.
*HUNT'S Drolls and Romances of the West of England.
*LAKE'S Parochial History of Cornwall.
*LELAND'S Itinerary.

LINGARD'S History of England, 10 vols.
LYSON'S—Magna Britannia—Cornwall.
MACAULAY'S History of England.
*MILLET'S Penzance, Past and Present.
    First book of the Parish Registers of Madron.
NORDEN'S Speculum.
NORRIS—Cornish Drama, 2 vols, 1859.
    Cornish Grammar.
OLIVER'S Monasticon Diœcesis Exoniensis.
PARIS (Dr.)—Mount's Bay.
    Life of Davy.
*PEDLER—Anglo Saxon Episcopate of Cornwall.
*POLWHELE—History of Cornwall.
PRYCE—Cornish Grammar (Tonkin and Gwavas ?)
*Records of Borough of Penzance.
    Borough of Marazion.
    Borough of S. Ives.
*Reports of Royal Institution of Cornwall.
SMITH (Dr. GEORGE)—Cassiterides.
STOKES—Life of S. Meriasek, "Beunans Meriasek."
    Cornish Drama.
TACITUS (Caius Cornelius) Annals.
TREGELLES—Haunts and Homes of the Rural Population of Cornwall.
WARNER'S Tour in 1809.
WESLEY'S "Journal."
WHITTAKER'S Cathedral of Cornwall.
WILLIAM OF WORCESTERS' Itinerary, 1478.
WILLIAMS'S Lexicon Cornu-Britannicum.
*WORTH—Cornish Mines.

CONTENTS.

PART I.—ANCIENT DAYS.

PART II.—THE AGE OF INDEPENDENCE.

PART III.—THE MIDDLE AGES.

PART IV.—THE SIXTEENTH AND SEVENTEENTH CENTURIES.

PART V.—MODERN TIMES.

INDEX.

—⚹—

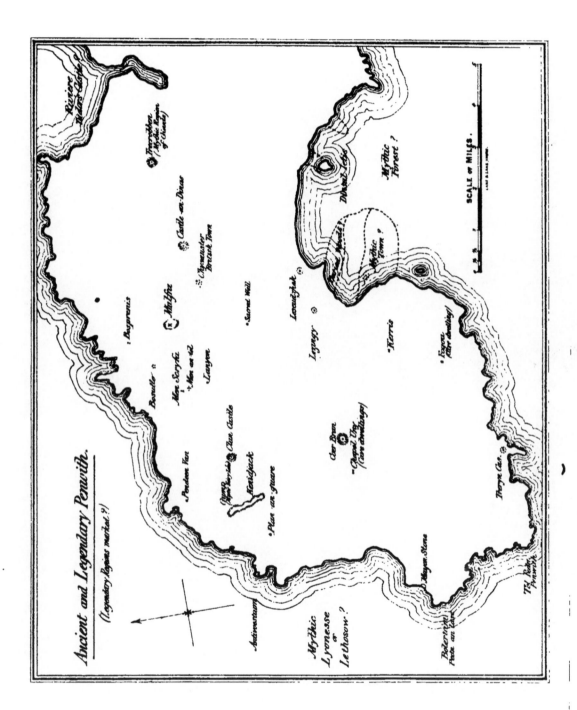

Ancient and Legendary Penwith.

(Legendary Regions marked ?)

SCALE of MILES.

Penzance, St. Michael's Mount, & Land's End.

AN HISTORICAL SKETCH.

PART I.—CHAPTER I.

THE PHŒNICIANS AND THE TIN ISLANDS.

*"Here the Phœnician, as remote he sailed
Along the unknown coast, exulting hail'd :
And when he saw thy rocky point aspire,
Thought on his native shore of Aradus or Tyre."*
Bowles.

THE inhabitants of that extremity of Britain which is called. Belerion both excel in hospitality and also, by reason of their intercourse with foreign merchants, are civilized in their mode of life. These people prepare the tin, working very skilfully the earth which produces it. The ground is rocky, but has in it earthy veins, the produce of which is wrought down, and melted, and purified. Then, when they have cast it in the form of dice-shaped cubes, they carry it into a certain island adjoining to Britain, and called Iktis. For, during the recess of the tide, the intervening space is left dry, and they carry over abundance of tin to this place in their carts. And there is something peculiar in the islands of these parts lying between Europe and Britain ; for at the full tide, the intervening passage being overflowed, they appear islands, but when the sea retires a large space is left dry,

A

and they are seen as peninsulas.   From them then the merchants purchase the tin of the natives, and transport it into Gaul, and finally, travelling through Gaul on foot, in about thirty days they bring their burdens on horses to the mouth of the river Rhone."   *(Diodorus, v. 2.)*

Such is the statement of Diodorus Siculus, who lived in the Augustan Age, not long before the birth of our Lord.   That it relates to St. Michael's Mount and the Land's End district, there is, at present, little doubt.   Other theories have been advanced in days gone by, *e.g.*, that St. Nicholas Isle, near Plymouth, or Mount Batten, or Looe Island, or even the Isle of Wight were meant, but all these are now, by more accurate geological researches, exploded ; and commonly the statement of our Parochial History that the account " must satisfy every one that St. Michael's Mount was the Iktis of that author *(i.e.* Diodorus,)" is accepted by men of science.   On this point Dr. G. Smith is most positive.*   " The Ictis of Diodorus is, undoubtedly, St. Michael's Mount."   Professor Max Müller—no mean authority in matters of criticism —accepts this view.   " The description which Diodorus gives answers so completely to what St. Michael's Mount is at the present day, that few would deny that if the Mount ever was a ' Hoar rock in the wood,'† it must have been so before the time of which Diodorus speaks—that is, at least, before the last 2000 years."

The statement of Diodorus about " the islands in these parts lying between Europe and Britain ;" that " at the full tide, the intervening passage being overflowed, they appear islands, but when the sea retires a large space is left dry, and they are seen as peninsulas," is remarkable, and deserves consideration.   This is true, not only of St. Michael's Mount, but of the Gugh of St. Agnes, in Scilly.   Nor is that a solitary instance.   Whether it is true of any other part of the European coast or not, in Scillonia it may be accounted a law.

But if indeed St. Michael's Mount be the Ictis of Diodorus, and if the Phœnicians really did come there for tin,—what follows as a conclusion from these premises ?   That there was a time when the region around Mount's

---

* *Cassiterides*, p. 79.   (See Mr. Pengelly's *Insulation of St. Michael's Mount, in Cornwall.)*
† *Chips from a German Workshop*, vol. iii., p. 331.

Bay was in advance of the rest of Britain in commerce, which means in wealth and civilization (of course, speaking relatively). While the rest of Britain was peopled by half-naked savages,* living on their flocks and herds— it may be only half emerged from the mere hunter state,—the miners of West Penwith may have been bartering their tin with the Phœnician merchants for clothes and pottery. When London was a primeval forest by the banks of the then blue Thames, peopled by the deer and wild bull and a few savages ; when Paris was merely two swampy islands on the Seine, covered by the wretched huts of the Lutetii ; when many a venerable mediæval city whose hoar antiquity strikes the stranger,—*e.g.*, Cologne, or Canterbury, or Rheims,— was a virgin forest, it may be with a few wigwams of half-naked savages ; about these hills of Mount's Bay already the cromlechs and the barrows may have been raised, while the Danmonian miners lived in their little beehive villages on the slopes.

But let us go further back still. "The Father of History," the first of secular historians, Herodotus, who writes 440 years B.C., is exceedingly frank on the subject when he says :—" Of that part of Europe nearest to the west, I am not able to speak with decision. . . . . Neither am I better acquainted with the islands called the Cassiterides, from which we are said to have our tin. . . . I have endeavoured, but without success, to meet with one who, from ocular observation, might describe to me the sea which lies in that part of Europe."†

Whether the Cassiterides was the only place whence the Phœnicians got their tin has been doubted. Herodotus, however, on this point, is positive. He says :—" It is nevertheless certain that both our tin and our amber are brought from those (*i.e.*, Cornwall and the North Sea) extreme regions." The tendency of modern critics is to think him right. Most, if not all, the tin of the old world did come from West Cornwall and the Scilly Isles. But what does that involve ? In the Bible even we have mention of tin. Ezekiel, speaking of Tyre, says : "Tarshish was thy merchant by reason of the multitude of all kinds of riches : with silver, iron, tin, and lead they traded in thy fairs."

---

* That the Ancient Britons were ordinarily in the primitive costume that Cæsar saw them in is improbable. They stripped to fight, and put on, perchance, *their* "*war paint*" for the occasion.

† Herodotus, *Thalia*, cxv.

Ezek., xxvii., 12. Could this tin be Cornish? If so, how it exalts one's estimate of Cornwall and Cornish mining; for no other country (except Spain in Romans xv., 24, 28) in Western Europe is referred to directly in the Bible. Nor is this the only place. In Num. xxxi., 22; Isaiah i., 25; Ezek. xxii., 18, 20, we find tin mentioned. If so, was it Cornish tin? If not Cornish, where could it have come from? We have seen what Herodotus says of the Tin Isles.

It is not easy to realize Mount's Bay as it was in those primeval days. Probably the hills were covered, to a great degree, save in the rockiest places, with a virgin forest. Here and there, about where Gulval and Marazion now stand, would be the clearings of the Danmonii around their beehive huts, of which Chysauster may be a type, suffered to remain through long ages,—circular wigwams on granite foundations, with now and then a large chief's hut, with its central court. The Mount was a mere granite pile—the Dinsul, the Castle of the Sun,—more of a peninsula than now; but about Gwavas Head, probably, one would then see a low-lying woodland, which, at every great storm, the ocean threatened to submerge, as it at last did.

Lo! to the south, ships are coming,—strange, quaint, beaked galleys, with bronzed Jewish-looking crews, in long Asiatic robes! They enter the Bay, and make for the Mount, the appointed emporium of their trade with the natives, who are jealous of the foreigners landing on the mainland. Out of the beehive huts now stream to the shore little crowds of the natives. They are a fair-skinned, bright-coloured people, and talk in a quaint Celtic language. Their dress is very queer,—"Long black cloaks and tunics reaching to the feet, girt about the breast," and they are "walking with staves" in their hands. They make for the Mount; and lead with them their hardy little horses, laden with blocks of tin. These they barter with the Jewish-looking merchants for money, clothes, and pottery.

Such may have been the scene presented at Mount's Bay some scores of times in ages long gone by. Let us, if we can, learn more about these aboriginal Penwith miners and fishermen. We cannot expect much, as it is so long ago; but perhaps we may learn a little by the aid of modern research.

CHAPTER II.

THE ANCIENT DANMONII.

"There raise their heads the isles Oestrymnides,
Lie loose together and in metals rich
Of tin and lead ; the men are very strong,
Proud in their minds, but in their conduct wise.
Their souls are ever on their traffic bent,
Yet, with no boats like ours, do they attempt
The wide, the boisterous, monster-breeding sea.
     *   *   *   *   *
There make their vessels with conjoined skins,
And range in leather o'er the wide-spread waves."
                Festus Avienus. (Translated.)

F anywhere we should expect to find ancient British antiquities it would be in Wales or Cornwall, for to them history and tradition alike affirm the Britons were driven before the Saxons ; and in Cornwall even more than in Wales, for there is reason to think that here (in spite of Cæsar's laudation of the Belgae) the most civilized British tribe —the Danmonii lived. Here, also, we have an advantage which is not usually offered in other parts of England. The common stone of the country is the almost indestructible granite. England may once have been covered with British antiquities, but, in most places, they have ages ago disappeared. In Cornwall, they remain, and, if let alone, will remain for centuries to come. The parish of Madron (in which Penzance has been built) contains more British antiquities than whole counties in other parts of England. The Lanyon Quoit, the Mên-an-tol, the Mên-scryfa, Mulfra, Chûn Castle, the British town of Bosullow, the Truen Menhir, represent a valuable collection of important Celtic antiquities. Few of our Midland counties can rival such a display of British remains.

But Madron is no exception. There is not a parish in Penwith which is not rich in antiquities. St. Just, with its circles of Carn Kenidzhek, the old mines near Botallack, the Plan-an-Guare, and Pendeen Vau; or Burian, with Bolleit, Boscawen Un, the Fogou, &c., &c., rival even Madron.

The crucial difficulty surrounding all Celtic researches in Cornwall is the great mystery about the actual date of the antiquities. If they were found in Kent, or Sussex, or Oxfordshire, the case might be more clear. They must be pre-Saxon, if not pre-Roman. Not so in Cornwall. The Britons were not entirely subdued here by the Saxons until the tenth century (in fact, little more than a hundred years before the Norman Conquest), and the Roman remains are few and unimportant, marking, perhaps, as we shall see, rather a nominal subjugation than actual colonization. The date of a Cornu-British antiquity, therefore, often cannot clearly be decided within a thousand years space. Native customs may have lingered on in Christian times.

Still, this does not altogether subvert our estimate of the importance of Cornish remains. Even supposing they were of the early Christian epoch, *i.e.,* the age of the independent Cornish princes (the probability is that they are much earlier), still they mark a "survival" of anterior customs. Mr. Wright sums up the case thus :—"Although some of the remains of antiquity may belong to an age more remote, the most probable view of the case seems to be that the mass of our British antiquities belongs to the age immediately preceding the arrival of the Romans, and to the period which followed."*

To collect and state all that is known about the ancient Danmonii, and all the antiquities supposed to relate to them, would be almost to write the history of the Ancient Britons, a task which I should certainly not think myself qualified to attempt, and which, in the present transitional condition of Celtic researches, no one ought, perhaps, to undertake. There are very many important problems in connection with the subject, to elucidate which more facts are needed. All that is required here is briefly to mention a few facts relating to our local remains.

According to classical statements, with which, as we find, local monuments tally (that is, supposing they are of the pre-Christian era, or, at least,

---

* *The Celt, the Roman, and the Saxon,* p. 83.

representatives of the state of things anterior to the Roman Conquest), the Danmonii were, by no means, "naked savages, scarcely above the Sandwich Islanders in the last century, who murdered Captain Cook" as they have been defined. Whatever Cæsar's account of the Kentish and Midland Counties may be, the Danmonii were certainly rather of the state of semi-civilization of the Aztecs, whom Cortez conquered, than of the Polynesian savages, whom Cook discovered. They had most of the signs of semi-civilization, as contrasted with mere barbarism.

1. They wore clothes,—long, dark, probably woven, tunics, "down to the ancles." These they may, indeed, have bought of the Phœnicians, and the shape of the tunic looks suspiciously Asiatic. But still they wore them, and the use of clothes (especially garments completely covering the body) is a distinctive mark that separates the civilized man from the savage.

2. They lived in houses, and if those remains we see of circular huts (formed on the Gallic model related by ancient writers), be really huts of the old Danmonii, they had almost reached the point of stone-houses. In this matter they were far advanced, not merely beyond the savage, but the nomade. The British bee-hive hut, if really anterior to the Roman Conquest, marks some progress in constructiveness; and so does the cromlech, especially the larger specimens, *e.g.*, Lanyon or Chûn.

3. They knew the use of metals,—if not iron, at least tin. The American nations, when discovered by Columbus, were very imperfect in their knowledge of metallurgy. The Cornish, probably, above 2000 years ago, were beyond any of them in this point.

4. They had boats,—something more than trunks hollowed out of trees, as canoes, *i.e.*, wicker and leather coracles.

5. They had tamed, it seems, the horse and the dog, both important steps in progress.

The whole inquiry is, however, at this moment, so utterly confused by the possibility of the influence of the Roman conquerors of Britain, and of the return, during their long struggles with the Saxons, to ancient Celtic habits, that it is difficult to decide, positively, the actual dates of any of these interesting remains. One thing may be considered as certain, *i.e.*, that, at a very

early age (certainly more than a thousand years ago) West Penwith was well peopled.   As Mr. Borlase truly says, we find " with these monuments of unrecorded misery " (*i.e.*, the ancient British castles and entrenchments), " the ruinous heaps of what were once the dwellings of a large resident population." *
It may have been so during the epoch of the visits of the Phœnicians ; it, probably, was so during the age of Constantine the Great.   Wherever we go, in almost every parish, we are reminded of the existence, at an early age, far anterior to the oldest of our cathedrals or baronial castles, of a numerous and not quite barbarous Celtic population.   These remains belong rather to archæology than history, so I shall merely give a list of the classes into which they may be divided, leaving my readers to refer to works specially devoted to the subject.   They are :—

I.   Sepulchral (or religious) remains, *e.g.*, 1. Cromlechs, *e.g.*, Lanyon, Chûn, Zennor.

2.   Kistvaens, *e.g.*, Bosavern Ros, in St. Just, Botrea, &c. ; and Barrows, Chapel Uny, Treryn, in Zennor, Tregiffian, Trevean (Morvah.)

3.   Menhirion, *e.g.*, Pridden-stone, in Buryan ; Tresvenneck, in St. Paul ; the Mên-scryfa (of which, hereafter.)

4.   Circles (possibly religious), *e.g.*, the Dans-mên (Bolleit), Tregaseal, in St. Just ; Rosmoddress and Boscawen Un, in Buryan.

II.   Forts or entrenchments.   1, interior, *e.g.*, Castle-an-Dinas ; 2, Cliffs, *e.g.*, Treryn Castle (near the Logan Rock.)

III.   Towns of hut-circles, *e.g.*, Chysauster, Bosullow.

IV.   Cave-dwellings, *e.g.*, the Pendeen Vau, the Fogau at Trewoofe, Chapel Uny Cave.

V.   Mine-works and streamings of the " old men."   Many of these (perhaps, most) are mediæval ; some, however, are plainly of great antiquity.

With all these remains, which still exist, we should remember that numbers more, even in human memory, have been destroyed, and that those we still see are merely the remnant spared by the avarice, Philistinism, and love of destruction, of many centuries.   Professor Max Müller's list of our ruined antiquities is a sad record of irreparable mischief wantonly committed.

* *Nænia Cornubiæ*, p. 257.

All this, however, tends to show that the excessive barbarism and ferocity of some of the ancient Danmonii, believed in by Camden and Carew, was much exaggerated. The verses, as he translates them, however, are worth giving, if only for Carew's fine old Shakespearian English :—

> "Whom beasts' raw hides for clothing served;
> For drink, the bleeding wound;
> Cups, hollow trees; their lodging, dens;
> Their beds, brakes; parlour, rocks;
> Prey for their food; ravine for lust;
> Their games, life-reaving knocks.
> Their empire, force: their courage, rage;
> A headlong brunt, their arms;
> Combat, their death; brambles, their grave.
> The earth groaned at the harms
> Of these mount harboured monsters; but
> The coast extending west,
> Chief foyson had, and dire dismay,
> And sorest fury prest,
> Thee Cornwall, that with utmost bound
> Of Zephyr art possesed."

And yet some such men as these may have given rise to the myths of the Cornish Giants.

For an account of the ancient sepulchral remains in Penwith, see Mr. W. C. Borlase's *Nænia Cornubiæ* (1872); also, Dr. Borlase's *Antiquities;* and Polwhele's and Drew's *Histories, &c.*

Chapter III.

THE POSITION OF THE OLD CORNISH IN THE FAMILY OF NATIONS.

"Me an' pref guyr a gousaf,
 Kyns ys dybarth."
"I will prove it true what I say,
 Before we separate."
Resurrexio Christi, 924-5.

HE title that we have here used may seem a strange one: The "Old Cornish in the Family of Nations;" but is not Cornwall a mere county of England? So it is, and so, in one sense it is not. There was a time, as we shall see, when not the Atlantic but the Exe, and afterwards the Tamar, was the border of England—that England, whose very name comes from the Angles, a Teutonic people of North Germany, who came, some fourteen hundred years ago, to settle in South Britain. Yes, Cornwall may be called "a county of Cornwall," and still the ancient Cornishmen were a nation of themselves*—a little nation, indeed, but quite distinct in language, in government, and in character from the rest of Europe. Perhaps there are yet some slight peculiarities about many Cornishmen: in ancient times, there was a great deal of distinction between them and the other races of Great Britain. There is nothing in all this of which we should not be proud. The Welsh are very proud of the memories of the old Cymri. Why should we not be proud also of the past independence of the ancient Danmonii? It is not every county in England that can share Cornwall's boast of having once been the *habitat* of a distinct race of men. In fact, Cumberland alone can claim the privilege with us.

---

* *Anglia et Cornubia* was a legal expression as late as Ric. III.

But who were these men?   The answer in some points, and within certain limits, is not very hard to give; but, before we attempt it, let us for a moment, to make the answer clear, glance at the present position of Ethnology, or the "science of the human race."   Speaking generally, the inhabitants of Europe and Asia may be divided into three great families :—

1.   The Semitic, including the Jews and Arabs, Assyrians, Phœnicians, &c., who have not much to do with our subject, unless it be the coming of the Phœnicians to buy tin at Mount's Bay and Scilly; and the legends of the Jews in Cornwall, of which, more hereafter.

2.   The Turanians, including the Finns, Tartars, Huns, Hungarians, Basques (?), Chinese, &c., who have still less to do with us, unless, indeed, we accept the rather attractive theory (very popular in many quarters) that the tribes of Finns originally settled in Europe, and were turned out of their homes and driven north by the Aryans, or Europeans.   If this theory was true, there might, in very ancient times, have been, even in Cornwall, some Finnic settlers—cavemen, perhaps, who used flint arrows, and such like rude weapons; but of this there is not much proof, and perhaps, for the present, till more research is made, "the least said soonest mended," by those who wish to state, as near as may be, ascertained facts.   Some think there is Basque blood in a few of our Penwith people.   It is not impossible, seeing how near Biscay is.   But the subject is very obscure.

3.   The Aryans, or Indo-Europeans, or, if we may use a Bible name for them, the "race of Japhet," from whom most of the nations of Europe (our own included) sprang.   These races predominate from the Ganges to the Land's End and Ireland; and, thanks to emigration, at present through most of America.   Of their characteristics we need not speak, for they are familiar to us everywhere in England and on the European continent.

By the science of language these races have been classified into different divisions, on the supposition (generally true, though, like most rules, it has its exceptions) that language is the best test of race.   Passing over the two great Asiatic divisions of this Aryan family, we shall confine ourselves to Europe. There we find, generally speaking, four great divisions, into which the European nations may be divided :—

1.   The Latin or Romance, including, perhaps, the Greeks and Wallachians, and certainly the Italian, Spanish, and Portuguese nations, with the French (in whom, however, there is a good deal of Celtic blood from the old Gauls, and some Teutonic blood in the northern departments.)   The chief languages of this family are the Latin, Italian, Spanish, Portuguese, French, Romansch, and perhaps Greek,—but that last point does not seem quite settled now, though our fathers thought it was.

2.   The Slavonic, including the Russian, Polish, Bohemian, and Servian nations and languages.

3.   The Teutonic, including the Germans, the Swedes, Norwegians, Danes, Dutch, Flemings (except the Walloons), and last, but by no means least, for they are the greatest of all, the Anglo-Saxons.   The chief living languages are the German, English, Swedish, Danish, Norwegian, Dutch, and Flemish.   The chief dead languages of this family are the old Gothic and the Anglo-Saxon.

4.   The Celtic.   This great division once peopled most of Western Europe. Its chief races now are the Bretons (of French Brittany), the Welsh, the Irish, the Highlanders, the Manxmen, and we may add, to a certain degree, the Cornish.   The principal languages now are the Welsh, the Breton, the Irish, and the Manx and Gaelic of the Scotch Highlands.   In olden times we might have added the Cornish and the Cumbrian, the language of the Strathclyde Gaels ; and, at one time, the Gallic of the old French Gauls.

This Celtic family of nations is usually divided into two sections :—

1.   The Gaelic, including the Irish, and the Gaelic and Manx (of the Isle of Man), who are supposed to have been the first settlers in Britain.

2.   The Cymrian, including the Welsh, Cornish, and Bretons.

Now, if we take language as the test of race, we shall be induced to divide the Ancient British tribes into two nations, *i.e.*, the Cymrian and the Gaelic. Of these, the Gaels are supposed, by Mr. Norris, to have been the earlier settlers, followed by the Cymri.   The Cornish language occupies an interesting position between the two classes of languages.   The Welsh is a caseless language, without any inflection at all in the noun ; the Irish, on the other hand, has a complete set of inflexions ; the Cornish was the *via media* between the two, containing, like our Modern English, one case only, the genitive or possessive,—but that was formed, not like our English by the addition of an *s*, but by modification of the root vowel, as it is sometimes in Irish. So Cornish is looked on, by Mr. Norris, as a sort of connecting link between the two families of British speech. "It is the only trace of a declension in the Cymric class of languages, and is decidedly opposed to the theory that cases were developed in Gaelic, after the separation of the two families. It impugns, also, the classification, which denies to the Cymric the character of an Indo-Germanic tongue, on the grounds of the supposed non-development of declension." On the other hand Mr. Jenner considers the Cornish genitive as apocryphal and rare.

Who were the people who originally spoke the old Cornish? The question is not easy to answer. It may be that Cornish was a mere development of the languages of the Danmonian tribes; but the probability is, as Mr. Norris puts it, "that the Cornish is the representative of a language once current all over South Britain at least." In other words, according to this theory, there was a time when a language like Cornish was spoken not merely in Devon and Cornwall, but by the Ancient Britains, who lived in—what we now call—Sussex or Kent, and in Hants or Dorset.

Probably, there was a time when, in the forests that covered the hills and dales where London now stands, old Cornish was spoken,—the ancestral and primitive language of the Southern Britons. If so, our remarks have more than a local interest,—in fact, become of importance to every educated Englishman.

Our chapter has been a short one, and we fear rather a dry one; but still, it is most important. Much of one's comprehension of Cornish history depends on one's knowledge of the laws of race,—on the grasping the scientific fact that the old Cornish race had more affinity to the Welsh than to the Anglo-Saxon. The Cornish people of the Middle Ages were a people who not only "spoke no English," but did not call themselves Englishmen. Even legal documents spoke of *"Anglia et Cornubia."* Happily, as time has progressed, the Cornish and Anglo-Saxon has amalgamated, but we should never forget that "the old men," as our miners call them, spoke a Celtic language, because they were of a Celtic race.

CHAPTER IV.

THE CORNISH HEATHEN MYTHOLOGY.

"Lowene dys du Monfras,
Me a vyn pesy the grays.
Kyn moys the guell."
"Joy to thee! God Monfras!
I will beseech thy grace.
Before my going to battle."
Beunans Meriasek, 2338-40.

EW subjects have proved so fascinating to Cornish antiquarians as "the Druids," and few, perhaps, have proved so dangerous to truth. Those venerable deceivers who deluded the Danmonii, or who, we suppose, did so, some 2000 years ago, had a posthumous power of deception over the antiquaries of the last, and even the present centuries, and led them to view Logan rocks as architectural achievements, rock basons as artificial altars, and make numberless other mistakes needless to relate here. The Druids are, therefore, very dangerous persons for a writer about Cornish history to deal with. I may be pardoned, therefore, in having very little to say about them.

The evidences of the influence of the Druids in West Penwith, if critically examined, are not above suspicion. Probability leads one to take it for granted that they did live here, and teach and sacrifice. Actual evidence of tradition does not exactly tally with the records of the classics.[*] If Druidism was the religion of the ancient Danmonii, it was either a particular form of that mysterious religion of the Celts, or else, which is most probable, the classical writers give us a one-sided, and partial description of the system.

---

[*] Messrs. Hunt and Bottrell both agree that the Druids are not mentioned in any Cornish legend before the Druidical antiquarian movement of the last century. *V. Nænia Cornubiæ,* p. 12.

If one might take local tradition, customs, and myths of an evidently heathen origin, in connection with the ancient Danmonian remains, some of which, though sepulchral, may still have a religious symbolism, one would be inclined to view the ancient heathenism of Cornwall as a form of Sun and Fire worship, rather than a system of floral symbolism, as Druidism was supposed to be. The probability is that the floral part of Druidic naturalism struck the classical writers, who did not notice the fireworship. They both may have been parts of the same system, the one dying out, the other surviving into Christian times, and, under innocent forms, being not quite extinct even in this nineteenth century, either in Cornwall or in Brittany. The West Penwith custom of dancing around fire at the winter solstice, or Christmas-tide, and passing between fires at the summer solstice (*i.e.,* Midsummer) is a manifest "survival" of the religious customs of a remote heathen antiquity. Little as they may think it, the children who this Christmas-tide have danced singing "round the candles" have been keeping up an ancient symbolism derived without doubt from pagan antiquity.* Still to this age (as it may have been when the Phœnician galleys came to Ictis for their tin two thousand years ago) the hills around Mount's Bay are lighted at Midsummer eve (*i.e.,* the solstice period) with the bonfire, and still the descendants of the old Danmonii wave the torch around their heads after the old, old, rite. Nowhere, perhaps, in England do the British mystical customs linger with such strange vitality as in West Penwith. Brittany may excel us on the continent of Europe, but Brittany witnesses also to the very same Celtic spirit of conservatism.

Whether the other half of the naturalism of the old Druidical system, *i.e.,* floral worship or divination may still be shadowed in the curious Helston Furry day, it would be hard to say. There is something very old-world and pagan about this curious custom, but it is out of Penwith, so we say no more of it.

The reverence for wells and springs, and superstitions about them, *e.g.,* Madron well, may not be merely mediæval but pagan. So, also, the belief in

---

* This custom appears now to have become peculiar to the Land's End district. A basket is filled with sand. A dozen candles are put in it, painted according to fancy. The candles are lighted and the basket put on the floor. The children dance around it, singing. The same custom exists in Brittany.

witchcraft, and in the "evil eye," still far more general in Cornwall than those who do not know the county may suppose. The "Drolls" of Giants and Fairies and "Knackers" are probably relics of it. But they do not belong to history, so we may merely refer our readers for them to the pages of Messrs. Hunt and Bottrell.

To sum up :—Druidism, if local customs or traditions of apparently pagan origin can throw any light on it, in addition to classical reports, would seem to be a system of Naturalism, not unlike the Brahmanism of ancient India— the oldest Aryan religion—a mixture of fire and nature worship, with a belief in transmigration of souls.

CHAPTER V.

THE GREEK AND ROMAN MERCHANTS.

" Your mind is tossing on the Ocean
There, where your argosies with portly sail,
Like signiors and rich burghers on the flood,
Or, as it were the pageants of the sea,
Do overpeer the petty traffickers."
Shakespeare.

CORNISH mines seem to have been treated by the Phœnicians as their monopoly for many ages. Dr. Henry says for 300 years, but in this matter accurate information is out of the question. Like the Dutch in Japan during the last century, they had the trade in their own hands, and meant to keep it there. Classical writers even say they frightened the innocent Danmonii from venturing over to Gaul on their own account, with dreadful stories, but it is possible that if Festus Avienus, in his poem, told the truth, the old Cornish canoes were very unfit for a voyage to France.

The first who broke in on the Phœnician monopoly (for tin was very valuable in those days) were the Massilian Greeks. Marseilles was in ancient times, as at present, a port of considerable importance, and the Marseilles sailors were, two thousand years ago, relatively more famous then even than now. Among the great navigators of that port was Pytheas. He resolved on a voyage into the Atlantic ocean. With a picked crew of brave Greek sailors he set off from Marseilles, passed the Pillars of Hercules (now the Straits of Gibraltar) and

C

pushed out, sailing northward, in his good ship, into the wide Atlantic. He seems, somehow, not to have easily made the Scilly Isles or Mount's Bay. Deluded, probably, by the false reports of Phœnician traders, and unprovided with maps, he got a great deal too far north, to the Orkneys, where he was much astonished at the length of the summer day. It appears, guessing his mistake, he sailed southward again, and at last found out the Cornish coast. The loss of his own account of his voyage is most tantalizing.[*] All we can now know of the adventures of Pytheas are very uncertain reports. He got home safely and published an account of his voyage.

Midacratus appears to have utilized the knowledge now acquired, and sailed to Mount's Bay and bought up some tin for the Marseilles market. How he got here, from France or through the straits of Gibraltar is not very clear.

According to Dr. G. Smith the Carthaginians did something in the way of the Cornish tin trade, after the decay of the Tyrian power. The probabilities are strong in favour of the theory, *e.g.*, the nautical activity of Carthage, the proximity of Gades, and their connexion with Tyre, but the direct evidence is not much.

The Romans came here as traders some time before they arrived as conquerors. The merchants preceded the legions, a point, by the bye, which common English histories usually omit.

The value of the tin trade at an early date struck them. A Roman ship was ordered to cruise outside Cadiz and follow any large Phœnician vessel which should appear to be sailing to Cassiterides. At first the plan seemed to answer. Shortly after a large Phœnician ship left the port and sailed north-west into the Atlantic. The Roman cautiously followed at a distance, but not losing sight of his pilotship. The Phœnician captain observed the foreign sails, and guessed why he was being dodged. The Romans were evidently seeking to track out the Tin Islands. To tack about and return was of course possible, but the Phœnician resolved on a stronger and more patriotic mode of action. Knowing well the Spanish coast, he was aware that there was a place near where the shoals were very dangerous. He made straight for the perilous spot. As he had hoped the Roman ship followed. In a few minutes both

---

[*] See Grote's *Hist. of Greece, XII.*, p. 620.

vessels were wrecked. The Phœnician crew took to their boats and saved themselves. Their captain was liberally reimbursed from the public treasury at Cadiz. The Romans, however, were not to be foiled. They did not admit of impossibilities. The Phœnicians had purposely falsified the map, and represented the Scilly Isles and Mount's Bay (or Ictis) as just off the northwest coast of Spain. Here the Romans sought for them, it is needless to say, in vain.

Among the Roman adventurers who sought for these "will-o'-wisps," the Cornish Tin Isles, was Publius Crassus, a rich brave man, who by his courage merited success. He boldly plunged into the Atlantic, sailing northward. At last the long broken line of the hills of West Penwith met his eyes, and he saw, nestled in its beautiful bay, the world-famed Ictis. Unlike the Phœnicians he was not satisfied with buying the tin the native Danmonii brought him. He landed and tried to make friends with them in their beehive huts.

Crassus went to see the tin mines. He was a man who knew something of mining himself, and so took a special interest in the subject. It is said he gave the Cornishmen some useful advice as to mining improvements, and recommended them to build ships and run over to France with their own tin, and not wait till Tyrian traders came to buy it.*

The kindly advice of Crassus does not seem to have been much taken. The Romans soon (we don't know how soon) came in a very different manner, and under different auspices, as conquerors, not as traders.

---

* For further particulars see Drew's Cornwall, vol. I, p. 295-329. Cassiterides. *Passim.*

CHAPTER VI.

THE ROMAN CONQUEST.

"Ithoff gelws costentyn
In Rome chyff cyte an beys
Emperour curunys certyn."

"I am called Constantine
In Rome chief city of the world
Emperor crowned certainly."
Bennans Meriasek. 2513-5.

T is strange that the evidence of the Roman Conquest and occupation of West Penwith should be so slender as it is. Tradition is silent. History is nearly so, or rather is very vague. Antiquities are not at all satisfactory. There are no Roman villas, no camps, no roads, just a milestone (?) at St. Hilary, and perhaps a camp at St. Erth. Coins are plentiful, but they do not prove much, except that the Romans bought tin of the Cornish miners and paid for it. To explain ourselves :— Piles of French sous and francs buried beneath the ruins of Brussels would not exactly prove to the mythical "New Zealander of the future" that Belgium was a French province. Still, it has been taken for granted that the Roman cohorts marched to the Pedn-an-las itself, and that the eagles, with the world-famed inscription S. P. Q. R., have been borne in proud triumph over the moors of Penwith. We may suppose so, but we cannot actually prove it. We suppose it because the Romans sought to conquer all Britain, and they never would have omitted the rich tin region that Crassus had found out in the West. The probability is that the Danmonii submitted to the legions without a struggle, and bought protection and peace by a liberal tribute, while the Roman officers saw nothing in the far west of Cornwall to attract them to a permanent residence. Perhaps some unfortunate centurion may occasionally have been sent here for banishment, but of the evidences of Roman civilization so common in other parts of England, in Penwith we have next to none.

Drew supposes that Cornwall was conquered by the Emperor Claudius, or rather, to put the argument in a more distinct form, was annexed without a serious struggle by Vespasian (then merely a general, but afterwards an Emperor). The fleet of Agricola which circumnavigated Britain (for military as well as geographical purposes) probably put into Mount's Bay, before sailing round (as it certainly did) the rugged coasts of Penwith.

To judge, however, from local remains, it would seem as if the Roman civilization took no such root in Penwith as in the rest of England. There is one point, however, which, bold though the theory may seem, I think may be worth suggesting, *i.e.*, whether the old Cornish mode of building is derived from the Romans, and whether the open air plan-an-guâre can ever have had any connection with the Arena? I make the suggestion with all diffidence, but still the consideration of it may not be worthless, even though it be said (and with reason) that these traditions of Roman civilization may have been continued in Cornwall, or introduced into it, by settlers from other parts of South Britain, who fled here from the victorious Saxons.

The Cornish mediæval mode of house architecture is stated by Carew to have been "to plant their houses low, to lay the stones with mortar of lime and sand, to make . . . their lights *inward to the court*, to set the hearths in the *midst of the room* for chimneys . . . . to frame the rooms not to exceed two stories."

This is not much like the English house-architecture of the period. The ideal of the old English manor was the hall roofed in, to which a solar was attached, and a kitchen, with the small chambers and offices in a court. Such houses are still familiar to us in many instances in other parts of England. But the conception of the Roman house, as still lingering in the old French *hôtel*, and as so admirably preserved to us in the remains of Pompeii, was that of a low square enclosing a court or *atrium*, into which the rooms opened. To which of these does the conception of the old Cornish house belong? Is it not rather the Roman than the Gothic ideal?

The *plan-an-guâre* also was, or seems to have been, rather a Roman than an English idea ; nay more, it is not distinctively Celtic.   There are traces of more such amphitheatres in Cornwall than in all the counties of England. How was it the Cornishmen got the idea?   It might have been original, it might have been Roman.   Without a doubt, with their strong conservatism, they stuck to their amphitheatre up to the Stuart period.

As for the remarkable abundance of seemingly Latin words in Cornish and other Celtic languages *(e.g.,* Welsh and Irish) there may be other ways of accounting for them, than by supposing them introduced by the legions.   Latin and Cornish are both sister tongues of the same Aryan family, or at least first cousins.   We should not be surprised if we occasionally notice a great likeness.   It may be an essential result of their common origin.   But still some of these very Latin looking words might have been introduced by the legions. Who knows ?

The occupation of the West, *i.e.,* Devon and Cornwall, Polwhele thinks was by the " *Legio secunda Augusta,*" which was stationed in these parts.   The Roman Geographers seem to have had some notion of these regions either from merchants or military officers.   Ocrinum, I am inclined to believe (with Polwhele) was the Lizard, and not St. Michael's Mount (which is no cape, and would not surely be put in a list of capes).   Bolerium was, without doubt, the Land's End.   No Roman town ever has been believed to have heen in Penwith.   Voluba and Cenio were in East or Central Cornwall, where it is needless here to enquire,—their sites are disputed.   Lostwithiel and Tregoney are possible localities for them.

The long period of Roman sovereignty is therefore, in our local history, almost a blank.   The references of Latin writers are to other parts of Britain, not to Cornwall, still less its extreme end.   Legend does not help us.   There are scarcely any local legends referring to the Romans extant now, but in the Middle Ages the legend of the Emperor Constantine's conversion appears to have had a powerful influence on the popular mind.   It is in such a distorted form, and so hopelessly irreconcileable with the records of Eusebius and other ancient writers, that one is inclined to doubt whether Constantine the Great has not somehow been confused with some other Constantine, *e.g.*, Constantine the British usurper, or Constantine the legendary Cornish king (from whom Constantine parish is said to be named), or Constantine of Brittany.

As we have said, Roman coins have been found in plenty in Penwith. In 1702 no less than 80 coins (on which the names of the Emperors Valentinian I., Gratian, and Arcadius, were made out) were found at Towednack. (Leland mentions a pot of Roman money being found at Treryn). At Ludgvan coins were found of Claudius (this is important as pointing to an ancient date, *i.e.*, that of the probable conquest), Nerva, Hadrian, Antoninus Pius, L. Verus, Lucilla and Faustina. In the same parish (near the coast) an urn of coins of Gallienus, Victorinus and the Tetrici. In 1789, in Morvah, near Chûn. Castle, another urn was found full of similar coins. In 1807 no less than 300 coins of Gallienus, Postumus, Victorinus and Tetricus were found, near the Land's End. From the small value of these coins, and their worn state, some have supposed they were soldier's pay, but might they not as well be miner's wages, or remains of a Roman counting-house, if the Roman coinage was once general here.

Chapter VII.

WHERE THERE JEWS IN WEST PENWITH?

> " Sufference is the badge of all our tribe :
> You call me misbeliever, cut throat dog,
> And spet upon my jewish gaberdine,
> And all for use of that which is mine own."
>
> *Shakespeare.*

HE tradition of the Jews in Cornwall demands a separate chapter not only from its intrinsic importance, but from the amount of learning in modern times expended in the investigation of the subject. The tradition assumes two distinct forms (not exactly irreconcileable with each other.)

A. That after the Destruction of Jerusalem the Jews were sent here as slaves by the Roman Emperors to work in the Cornish mines.

B. That King John and other English kings employed Jews to work in the Penwith tin mines; and sometimes treated them with great severity to make them disgorge their mineral wealth into the royal coffers.

Now the former legend certainly, though not at first sight improbable, has some suspicious points about it.

A. (1) It is an evident attempt to link Cornwall with Biblical history. The prophesies of the destruction of Jerusalem occur again and again in Holy Writ. Might not mediæval preachers have thought it edifying to their people to point to the Cornish legends of the Jews as evidence of their fulfilment.

(2) Though it is probable that Jewish slaves were "condemned to the mines" by the Roman Emperors, there is no evidence that Cornish mines were selected.

B.   King John is the favorite king of English mediæval legend, a sort of royal scapegoat to whom popular fun could be pointed.

I can quite assent to Professor Max Müller's able correction of the derivation of Marazion as having nothing to do with a Jew's market, still less "bitter Zion," without assenting to the theory that erroneous derivation has caused this strong Cornish tradition.   The connection of the name Marazion with the Jews is apparently modern, for in the middle ages it was supposed (inaccurately, perhaps) to mean Thursday's market.   Whether the case of Jew's houses being derived from the Cornish Chy repeated with the English word "houses" is not quite so clear.   To outsiders both would seem mere after-thoughts made to suit preconceived notions.

One very natural mode of acccounting for the strong Cornish legend spring-ing up in so many forms and places, is that, after all, this story of the Jews may mean the Phœnicians.   The vitality of tradition is remarkable.   In Greece, to this day, legends linger of the siege of Troy.   In Cornwall we have cus-toms plainly handed down from Druidism.   If the Phœnicians did frequent these shores, as there is reason to think they did for three centuries, *i.e.*, some ten generations, why need we assume that all tradition of their coming must be totally extinct ?   The event was very important to the people.   The coming of the Phœnician traders meant to the ancient Cornish people the renewal of their little comforts of civilized life, which they did not know how to make for themselves, but which they bought from these Syrian traders.   A Phœnician ship arriving in Mount's Bay must have been a happy event to the old Cornish.   May not the "old men" have talked about it by the hut fires to their children, and their children's children, and so by degrees from mouth to mouth the story of those Asiatic traders, bronzed strange men coming to deal in tin, have been handed down from age to age, until, in mediæval times, when the dipersion of the Jews, and the Crusades represented the Hebrews and Saracens as the only Orientals familiar to Western Europe, the tradition passed from the Phœnicians to their Arabic and Israelitish brethren, and gathered fixity in date around the destruction of Jerusalem (familiar from Biblical references and the Guâre) and

D

King John, the centre of English legend?   No one who has lived for years in the county, and noticed how wide-spread the tradition is, can suppose it a mere offspring of a false derivation.   There may be historical truth in it (in spite of all destructive criticism can say), but if not, in all probability it is a hazy legend from the remotest past, of the Semitic traders who came to the Cassiterides for tin.

CHAPTER VIII.

THE FABLED LYONESSE.

HE origin of the legend of Lyonesse is not difficult to discern. Let anyone stand on one of the hills of Sennen or St. Just, the Land's End, on Chapel Carn Brea, or on a clear, calm summer's evening, and watch the western sun sink into the bosom of the Atlantic, when, like hill-tops sunk in a vast deluge, the islets of Scilly just rise over the waves, and the fable of Lyonesse must dawn on his mind, even if he had never heard of it. The scene is entirely that of a submerged land whose mountain tops yet peer above the wave in the cliffs of Scilly.

Nor would closer examination, to the unscientific observer, dispel this impression. If he goes to those distant islands he finds the same formation as in the Land's End district,—it is only Penwith partly sunken in the waves. Nay, more, if he examines the islands he sees traces of the growing power of the waters, of a submergence not finished but going on. It is no wonder that in ancient times the legend should have arisen of a land fair and fertile, stretching from the Land's End to Scilly, buried in the sea by a great convulsion Even modern science half justifies the notion, in the novel theory, founded on recent deep-sea explorations, that the true Atlantic bed does not begin till many leagues west of St. Agnes.

The legend of Lyonesse or Lethowsow speaks of this great region as once celebrated for industry and piety. 140 churches stood on those strands now buried by the Atlantic billows. A large city lay where now the rocks of the

Seven Stones extend. Fishermen relate how even now they sometimes gather from the deep the wreck of the great catastrophe. The very date of the catastrophe has been fixed by antiquaries of the old constructive type. There was a great overflowing of the sea in 1029, *ergo* Lyonesse was then sunk into the deep. One man saved himself from the cataclysm. Trevillian is said to have ridden away before the surging ocean and reached Perranuthnoe in safety. Henceforth, in memory of this famed event,* the Trevillians have as their arms, in heraldry, *Gules, a horse argent, from a fess wavy argent and azure, issuing out of a sea proper.*

The Lord of Goonhilly, a proprietor of Lyonesse, is also said to have escaped, and built as a thank-offering for his escape, the Chapel Idne at Sennen Cove.

It is possible that there have been changes in the coast line of both Scilly and Penwith since the Christian Era. Strabo's narrative, if accurate, implies as much, but the legend of Lyonesse is as little accordant with classical records, as it is with geological research. The Scilly Isles may once have been part of England, as England was of the European continent, but if so, it must have been at a remote geological epoch.

Associated with the legend of Lyonesse are others of a similar nature, stories of sunken regions once fertile parishes, clad with woodlands and cottages, where the sound of evening bells rang in the peaceful air, now buried in the ocean depths, where beneath the blue waters the bass and mullet dart hither and thither amidst sea weed and naked rock. Such are the myths not only of Lyonesse but of the forest in Mount's Bay, and on the coast off Phillack. Both these stories may have some slender fabric of evidence, though the little truth has, without a shadow of doubt, been exaggerated into a gigantic error.

Let us take the Mount's Bay legend first. In the middle ages, or rather at the end of them, we find it in full vigour. William of Worcester calls St. Michael's Mount the "Hoar rock in the wood." "Le Hore Rok in the Wodd." This is supposed to be a translation of the Cornish name Carew gives it, "Cara clowse in cowse," which means "hoar rock in the wood." For this

---

* See Hunt, Drew, Polwhele, &c.

name another form, however, is given, " Cara cowz in clowze," " the old rock in the tomb," a translation of the Latin "*Mons in tumba.*" The legend about the six miles of forest around St. Michael's Mount is supposed by Professor Max Müller, with some probability, to refer to the other St. Michael's Mount (Mont S. Michel) in Normandy, with which, as we shall see, the Cornish St. Michael's Mount was intimately connected during the middle ages, being indeed a "subject priory" to it. Geologically speaking though, the sea may have made, and indeed has made, great encroachments around St. Michael's Mount ; yet it probably would take a period far more prolonged than that between us and the Phœnician visits to submerge so great an extent of country as is implied in the legend.

As for the submergence of a neck of land at the entrance of Gwavas Lake, the case is rather different. Leland, a cautious narrator, is, positive as to the tradition at his time (temp. Henry VIII). He says,—" There hath bene much land devourid of the sea betwixt Pensandes and Mousehole. An old legend of St. Michael speaketh of a tounlet in this part now defaced, and lying under the water."

Scientific observations at low tides are not unfavourable to the view of the submergence of land in historic times, near Newlyn and Wherry Town. In Larrigan Rocks remains of trees have been found. Between Chyandour and Marazion stumps of trees have been noticed at low tides.

A forest of beech trees is said to have extended from Gwavas head, and Gwavas lake was once a tranquil pool. It is even said that tithes were collected by the parsons of " St. Paul " from the land round the lake (it must have been well before William of Worcester's days). Newlyn is said to derive its name from its waters. Legend says the great deluge that ruined Lyonesse swept away church and forest and houses, and absorbed the lake into the great ocean.

It is possible that even in historic times there may have been some changes of the coast line in St. Ives Bay. The sands by Gwithian and Phillack and Hayle are ever shifting, and were far more so before the planting of the *arundo arenaria*, which has preserved so much land in these parts from destruction.

Gilbert relates that Upton Barton, a large farm, was suddenly overwhelmed in the last century, and then bared again in 1808. Even in more recent times two fields were covered with sand; and the buried church or oratory of Gwithian is a further instance of the encroachments of the sands. The legend of the buried castle of Teudar (the wicked pagan prince of the " Beunans Meriasek ") at Riviere, may not be a groundless fable; but the drowned city of Langarrow* (suddenly lost in the tenth century) is a manifest myth (though a pretty one).†

* Is not that founded on the same story as the drowning of Gwacleod (in Cardigan) by Seithenayn the drunkard? aud of Kaer-Is in Brittany Dahut mereh gradlon.

† *Vide Hunt's Series I,* p. 220.

CHAPTER IX.

THE OLD CORNISH LANGUAGE.

Mee a navidna cowsa sawzneck.
Cornish saying.

N explanation of our local names is the most practical and useful illustration of the old Cornish language, *i.e.* the modernized tongue of the ancient Britains of the South-west. A good deal has been done on this subject of late by the Rev. Dr. Bannister and others, so that one is not without a guide in the enquiry. The misfortune is, that in this, as in most cases of derivation, great vagueness exists, and numerous derivations have often been urged for the names of the same place, each equally plausible. In such case selection is difficult. But still, even though one may not be able to speak positively as to the origin of some of these names, yet the enquiry may not be without interest and profit to residents or strangers, who may thus trace the lingering relics of the old Cornish language on the lips of the people.

In this enquiry, I may say, I have scarcely ventured on any derivations of my own, doing little more than quote from others the explanations which appear most probable. A very few illustrations of the Cornish language, especially in its relations to some Penwith names, are selected almost at random. Those who wish to go deeper into the subject, can easily find help in philological works; for the general reader these illustrations will, I fear, be counted more than enough, and this chapter voted "very dry."

Among the most important words which enter into the composition of Penwith names are the following, which are selected as illustrations :—

Caer—a fortress, castle, Welsh, *caer;* Breton, *cear;* Irish, *cathair;* Hindu, *gurh.*

Carn—a pile of rocks, cairn (*e.g.* Tolcarn), W., Breton, Ir. Gael. and Manx, *carn;* Slav., *gora,* rocky hill.

Ros—a moor, a common (Ross, a name); W., *rhos;* Br., *ros;* Gael., *ros.*

Pol—a pool, pond (Polwithen); W., *pwl;* Br., *poull;* Ir., *pol;* Gael., *poll.* Manx, *poyl.*

Lyn—a lake or pond (Newlyn); W., *llyn;* Br., *lenn;* Ir., *linn;* Gael., *linne.*

Mor—Sea (Morvah, Lamorna), W. and Br., *môr;* Ir., Gael., and Manx., *Muir;* Lat., *mare;* Fr., *Mer;* Slav., morze ; Sans., miras.

Maur—great (Moor Anglicized) W., *mawr;* Br., *meur;* Ir., *mor;* Sans., *mâra.*

Tre, trev—place, house, township (Trewidden); W., *trêv, tre;* Br., *trev, tre;* Ir., *treab;* Germ. *thorp.*

Nans—vale (Nancothan); W., *nant;* Br., *nant* (Nantes).

Coid—wood (Nancothan); W., *coed;* Sans., *kâsta.*

Hal—marsh, moor (Halwyn); W., *hâl;* Br., *hâl.*

Gon, Un—a plain (Chywoon, Boscawen Un); W., *gwain;* Br., *geun;* Ir., *foun;* Sans. *pattan* (to extend).

Lan—*church, enclosure* (Lamorna) ; W., *llan;* Br., *lan;* Ir., *lann.*

ADJECTIVES.

Gwidn—widn, white (Trewidden) ; W., *gwynn;* Br., *gwenn,*

Du—black (Baldhu); W. and Br., *du;* Ir. and Gael., *dubh;* Manx., *doo.*

Lays—glass, green (Pedn-an-las, Borlase); W. and Br., *glâs;* Ir. and Gael., *glas;* Lat. *glaucus* (?)

Tol, Toll—hole (Mên-an-tol); W., *twll;* Br., *toull;* Ir., and Gael., *toll;* Manx., *towl;* Sans., *talla* (Talla).

Cornwall, Dr. Bannister gives as the "horn shaped land of the foreigner." This is the accepted derivation. Bp. Gibson suggests that it is "the stranger's (or Celts) land of carns." In Cornish, it is *Kernoes,* as in the modern name. Whether a land of *carns* or of *promonteries* would be the most natural description, I leave to my readers. The root *corn* for a horn runs through most Aryân languages, it is nearly universal. *Carn* also appears both in Celtic and Slavonic; the Slavonic word "Goraln" for a mine, would look very tempting, but is not the Celtic form.

Penwith is obscure. " Promontory of blood;" Pen-guit (blood) is suggested by Bannister. Carew thinks it "Head of Ash trees" (enwith). Polwhele, merely "the end," for Penwith. Another possible etymology is *Pen Gwith,* "the headland of protection," or the " guardian point."

Penzance. The accepted derivation is, as the arms of the borough punning represents it, "the Holy Head," or rather " headland." Pen-Head—Sans-Holy; Latin sanctus. Pryce and Tonkin, however, think it is " Head of the Bay." (Sans), and this is by far the most probable meaning.

Newlyn. Probaby merely New Lake. This would support the theory of the advance of the sea.—Lyn is Cornish for pool. Pryce suggests open lake for Noath-Lyn.

Chyandour—The house (*Chy, ty*) by the water (*dour*).

Pendre—The head (*Pen*) of the town *(dre, tre)*.

Lescudjeck—The field *(Les)* of blood, (*gudzhic. dj*), or the warlike [*cadic-cadjic*] field.

Poltair—The pool (*pol*) of oaks, (*dar*).

Madron—The Church of S. Paternus (?)

Lanyon—The enclosure (*lan*) on the down (*von*), or "the Church of [St.] John (*yon*)."

Men-an-tol—The stone (*mên*) of the hole (*tol*).

Tol carne—The holed (*tol*), or the high (*talas* in Madron), carne (*cairn*).

Men-scry-fa—The stone (*mên*) written on (*scryfa*—Lat. *scribo*).

Truen—For Trewen, contr. the white house.

Landithy—*digethi* (of piety) (?).

NAMES NEAR THE SOUTH COAST.

Trewarveth—The house (*tre*) upon the hill. (*monedh*).—(Price).

Ragennis, (near Mousehole)—Opposite (*rag*) the island (*ennis*) *i.e.* S. Clements Isle.

E

Halwyn, (near Mousehole)—The white (*gwyn*) moor (*hal*).

Kemyel, (near Lamorna)—Enclosure (*ke*) Michael.

La morna—Enclosure (*lan*) by the sea, (*morval ?*)

Rosemodris—The heath (*rose*) with the circle, (*moderuy*).

Dawnsmen—The dome (*dawns*) of stones (*men*)—Blight.   Possibly *dance* (qy.) stones *men*.

Boleite—The house (*bos*) of slaughter (*ladh*) or the clan (*leid*).   Pryce says of (*laid*) milk, and is probably right.

Trewoof, Trove—The place (*tre*) of blackbirds or rooks, (*moelh*) rookery.

Boscawen, (Lord Falmouth's name and place)—the house (*bos*) of the elder trees (*scawen*).

Carn barges—the carn of the kites (*bargus*).

Merthen point—The sea (*mor*) hill, or-castle (*din*), or Myrddin's [Merlin's] point.

Burnuhall, (legend of the Queen)—The well (*burne*) on (*yu*) the moor (*hal*).

Pen berth—The green (*berth* Lat. *viridis*) head (*pen*), or pen *porth* (creek).

Logan Rock—The logging rock or shaking rock (modern).

Tre reen—The house or place (*rhyn*)—*Tonkins* ; on the headland (*tre*).

Porth Curnow (or the " Porth of Cornwall "), (telegraph station)—The port (*porth*) with hornlike hills (*corn*).

But the vestiges of the old language are not only to be traced in Cornish names. It had a literature once, on which has been founded what little we know of the old tongue. The fragments of the old Cornish literature will be dealt with in another place, suffice it to say that the relics have been sufficient for Mr. Norris, in this century, and also in a past generation, for Lloyd and Pryce to found on them Cornish Grammars, not to speak of Zeuss's famous Grammatica Celtica, and also for Williams to compile his valuable and copious Lexicon Cornu Britannicum.   In fact, it is probable that very little of the old language is now totally lost, although the discoveries since 1869 show that even Williams' Lexicon is not an exhaustive treatise, and that more and more is being added to our knowledge of the ancient British tongue, of the southern tribes of old Britannia.·

This is scarcely a work for even an elementary treatise on old Cornish, so I shall confine myself to giving as a sample of it the Lord's Prayer; the numerals, with an explanation of their congeners in other Aryan tongues;* and the history of a few living Cornu-British words still in use among the fishing and mining folk of West Penwith.

LORD'S PRAYER—ANCIENT CORNISH.

An Taz ny es yn nef, bethens thy hannow ughelles, gwrênz doz thy gulasker. Bethens thy voth gwreiz yn oar kepare hag yn nêf. Ro thynny hithow agan peb dyth bara. Gava thynny agan cam, kepare ha gava ny neb es camma erbyn ny. Nyn hombrek ny en antel, mez gwyth ny theworth drok. Rag gans te yre an mighterneth an creveder hag an' worryans byz a venitha. An dellna ra bo.—(*Pryce*).

RELATIONS OF SOME OF THE CORNISH WORDS STILL USED IN PENWITH.

Bowjey—Cattlefold (*beuch*, cow; *chy*, a house); W., *buch, buchod;* Br., *bu*; Ir. and Gael., *bo;* Lat., *bos;* Gr., *boûs.*

Brave—Great, *brâs;* W. and Br., *brâs;* Ir. and Gael, *breas.*

Bucca—Spirit (bucca boo); W., *bwg;* Ir., *puca;* Gael., *bogan;* Slav., *bog.*, qy. *bogie.*

Cheeld veän—(little child), Vean, Bechan; W., *bâch;* Ir., *beag;* Manx., *beg;* Gael., *beagan.*

Clunk—(to swallow); W., *llyncu;* Br., *lonca;* Ir., *slugadh;* Gael., *sluig.*

Cager—seive, (cadar, a chair); W., *cader;* Br., *cador;* Ir., *cathaior;* Lat., *cathedra.*

Cowal—fish basket; W., *cwbyl.* Also kibble, a mine caldron.

Croggan, crogan—limpet (shell); W., *cragen, crogan;* Br., *crogen.*

Crou—A sty; W., *craw;* Ir., *cro.*

Fogau-Vau—cave (Pendeen Vau); W., *foc* (?)

Garrack—rock; W., *carreg.*

*Vide Appendix.

Gurgoes—old fences; W., *cwr;* Br., *cer;* Ir., *curr.*

Hoggan—Pork pasty. W., *hwch* (a sow). Br., *houch.*

Huel, Wheal—A mine, a work. W., *chwyl.* Br., *kouls.* Manx, *queeyl.*

Keggas—Hemlock. W., *cegid.* Br., *cegit.*

Mabyer—Mab, son, child. W., *mab, mâp.* Br., *mâb, mop.* Ir., and Gael. *mac.* Manx, *mac.*

Maber—Yar, hen. W., *iar, giar.* Br., *iar.* Ir. and Gael., *ceare.* Manx, *kiark.*

Miryon, Murryan—Ants. W., *mor, morion.* Br., *merien.* Ir., and Gael. *moirb.* Lat., *myrmex.*

Padzepaw, a Lizard, *Paj* four—*Pow* foot. W., *pawen.* Br., *paô.*

Par, or Porth-Cove—W., *porth.* Br., *porz.* Lat., *portus.* Manx, *purt.*

Plum—Soft, *pluven-*feathers. W., *pluo, plam.* Br., *plû.* Ir., *clumh.*

Scaw —Elder tree. W., *yswagen.* Br., *scaô.* Lat., *scobies.*

Scaw dour, Figwort—(*Scaw* elder, *dour* water, v.)

Tummals—Quantity, (tomals). W., *talm.* Ir., *tamal.* Manx, *tammylt.* Lat., *tumulus.*

Such are just a few of the still living Cornish words, whose connection can be traced. A comparative dictionary of recent Cornish, is a work yet to be done, and one which would prove in the county of great interest, and in philological circles of some importance. Williams' Lexicon, however valuable for the old Cornish of the dramas, hardly touches the Cornish words embedded in the modern dialect.

It is to be hoped that something more may be done in this matter.

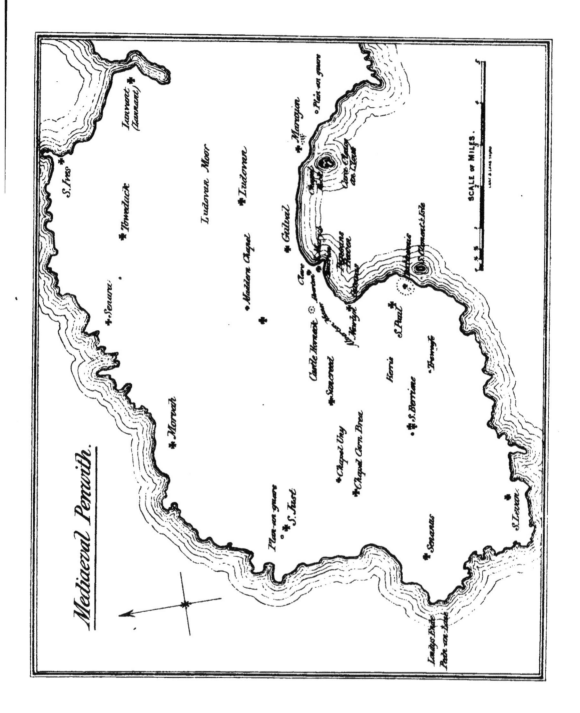

Mediaeval Penwith.

PART II.—THE AGE OF INDEPENDENCE.

CHAPTER I.—CORNISH SAINTS.

Omma ythese tregys
　　Avel Hermyt in guelfos
In le ov delles ourlyn
Purpur pannov fyn certyn
　　Lemen me a wesk queth los
In ov nesse hevys ruen
Ny eve cydyr na gwyn
　　Na dewes marnes dour pur
Hag erbys an goverov
A veth ov bos thum preggyvov.

" Here have I been dwelling a hermit in the desert. Instead of silk raiment, fine purple clothes, now I wear a grey garment. Next me is a horsehair shirt. I drink no cider nor wine, nor any drink but pure water, and herbs of the brooks are my food for my meals."—BEUNAN'S " MERIASEK," 1663-72.

S the traveller passes through Cornwall he constantly, at almost every turn, meets with the names of Saints of whom he never, however familiar with general hagiology, heard before, and whom he is never likely to hear of anywhere else, save perchance in Wales, or Brittany.

Who were these mysterious personages, around whom this halo of reverence has hung from remote ages? The reply to the question in full, *i.e.* as far as our materials enable us to detect their biographers, would not be without great interest; but at present we must confine ourselves to the consideration of a few names intimately connected with the history of the Land's End district.

With regard to the parishes skirting Mounts Bay, there is something highly probable in the theory of the Rev. G. Harvey—"The probability of Mullyon being none other than S. Malo is heightened by the fact of the frequent intercourse which, without doubt, existed about that time (*i.e.* the sixth century) between the inhabitants of this part of Cornwall and those who dwelt in the north of Brittany; and while many of our parishes preserve the names of Saints of Irish extraction, almost all those which skirt Mount's Bay are dedicated to persons who, under similar circumstances to S. Malo, retired into Brittany, particularly that part of it which is now called *Côtes du Nord*.*

According to this theory, we should infer that the parishes along the south coast are named after Breton missionaries, who either came over about the sixth century from Armorica to convert to Christianity the still heathen fishing folk, miners, and husbandmen of the country round Mounts Bay, or passed through this part of Cornwall on their road to Brittany; while on the other hand those on the north are of Irish hermits, who came over somewhere about the same time on probably a similar mission.

About the *S. Paul* of the parish containing the western shores of Mounts Bay, there is great uncertainty. On one point only is everyone agreed, that is that he was not the Apostle, but some later Saint.

a. Some attribute it *e.g.* to S. Paulinus, Archbishop of York, who shortly after the landing of S. Augustine, in Kent, was sent to preach the Gospel in Yorkshire, and founded the "Northern Province."

b. Another theory is that of S. Paul de Leon. He was an eminent Breton Saint, and Bishop of Leon. The Cathedral of S. Pol is named after him. He was cousin-german with S. Malo, of S. Sampson, Bishop of Dol, (in Brittany.)

c. But there seems to be a third claimant—the famous British Pawl-Hên, the founder and abbot of Whitland, in Carmarthen, and one of the most eminent theological teachers of the ancient Welsh. Among the contending claims with Mr. Harvey I prefer the second—the Breton S. Pol de Leon as the most probable.

The S. Clement, of S. Clement's Island, to whom the ancient chapel and hermitage were dedicated, was most probably not the S. Clement, first Bishop of Rome, the eminent writer of the religious works bearing his name (*e.g.* S. Clement's Epistle, &c.), but S. Clement or Clemens, a Christian king of Cornwall, the father of the famous S. Petrock, (of Padstow and Bodmin).

* Mullyon, p. 23.

Saint Levan is, however, supposed to have been an Irish prelate, in the age when Ireland was (amidst the irruption of barbarism on the European continent) the refuge of civilization and Christianity. He became famous for his successful missionary labours among the Flemish tribes (then in a state of barbarism and heathenism).

Local legend describes him as a hermit who supported himself by fishing near Pedn-mên-an-mere. The two accounts are not necessarily irreconcileable. An Irish ecclesiastic might have devoted himself to an anchorite's life in West Penwith, aud when his example and precept had produced a satisfactory result on the Cornu-British fishermen of S. Levan, have felt a call to proceed further in search of heathens to convert, and thus have taken ship for the Belgian coast.

There are, for those interested in the marvellous, some curious mediæval legends extant about S. Levan, one of which is very similar to that of S. Neot, *i.e.* the legend of the one fish only suffered to be caught by the hermit.*

S. Levan obtained the crown of Martyrdom November 12, A.D. 656, (according to the hagiologies). The local parish "feasten-tide" is, however, kept at S. Levan on October 15.

It may be worth remarking that one of the most eminent personages in in early Cornish ecclesiastical history, was Bishop Living, or Livingus, the chaplain and adviser of King Canute the Great, Bishop of Cornwall and Devon, to whom, as we shall see, the union of the two dioceses was due.

Saint Burian is said by Leland to be named after an Irish woman. "S. Buriana, an holy woman of Ireland, sometime dwelt in this place, and there made an oratory. King Ethelston (Athelstan) going hence, as it is said, unto Scilly and returning, made *ex voto* a college where the oratory was."

Another and less poetic theory has been, however, founded on the legend of the battle of Bolleit, *i.e.* that it was so called by the Saxons, from the burying of their dead there. The coincidence of the two names, Burian and Burying is rather curious, and in history one does not like to pass over coincidences where there is no positive evidence that they are purely accidental.

---

* The account of them may be found in Messrs. Hunt and Botterill's works, *in loco.*

However, Leland is pretty positive that S. Burians was so called before Athelstan's time, and perhaps he is right,

Saint Sennan, or as some suppose St. Sininus, was also an Irishman; at least, according to Leland, and the tradition of his period (not easy now to correct or criticise at present). This tradition relates that he was a friend and companion of S. Patrick, and came over from Ireland to Cornwall, at the same time as Saint Breage. S. Sennan's feast, or at least that of the parish is Advent Sunday, or the Sunday nearest S. Andrew's day.

Hals raises a doubt on the theory that Sennen means the Holy Valley—*san,* holy; *nan,* valley. Modern criticism seems opposed to this. There is no valley, nor any special region of sanctity at Sennen.

S. Just Church is usually supposed to have been dedicated to S. Justus, the Roman, the companion of S. Augustine, in his missionary journey to England, (596), who was consecrated bishop of Rochester in 604, and succeeded S. Augustine in 616 as Archbishop of Canterbury. He seems to have been generally respected and honored as a faithful prelate by his contemporaries. He died in November, 627. The "feasten-day" of S. Just parish is the Sunday nearest All Saints' Day, November 1. S. Just's proper feast was November 10.

The dedication to this S. Just, who though by birth an Italian, was strictly speaking, an Anglo-Saxon Saint, points to a Saxon dedication, not a Celtic for S. Just parish. S. Just himself was in all probability never in or near Cornwall (any more than the Justus surnamed Barsabas, mentioned in Acts). So the story of his adventures* with S. Keverne are mere Celtic myths, probably of the heathen period.

S. Morwetha is said to have been the patroness of Morvah (though by the bye, Morvah means a place by the sea, in Cornish, no inaccurate designation of the parish), as well as of Morwinstow in North Cornwall.

The dedication of *Madron* is doubtful. The usually accepted theory supported by Dr. Oliver, the Exeter antiquary, is that its patron was Paternus, (the old Cornish, like other Celtic nations, were rather weak on the distinction between " P's," or " B's," and " M's "), the Bishop of Avranches in the

---

* Vide Hunt ii—5.

sixth century. The accounts are very contradictory, however. Hals supposed it was Madan.

Gulval is supposed to be S. Gulval, who though born in Wales, became Abbot of Plecis, and thence came into Cornwall, and preached the gospel in these parts. From thence. he went to Brittany, and succeeded S. Malo (the patron of Mullyon as Bishop of Aleth). Thus the two parishes at the mouth and inside of the bay are connected with two holders of the same Breton see. S. Gudwal died early in the seventh century.

S. Uny and *S. Hya*, (of Lelant and S. Ives), are supposed to have been sisters according to tradition. Leland thus shortly narrates the story :—

"The parish church is of Iva, a nobleman's daughter, and disciple of S. Barricus. Iva and Elivine, with many others, came into Cornwall, and landed at Pendinas. This Pendinas is the peninsula and stony rock where now the town of S. Ives stands. One Dinan, a great lord in Cornwall, made a church at Pendinas, at the request of Iva, as it is written in S. Ives legends." She was afterwards, it seems, slain by the heathens around Hayle, with S. Elwyn (after whom S. Elwyn's church, Hayle, is now called).

There is also a tradition about S. Ives, Cornwall, S. Ive (near Liskeard), and S. Ives, Huntingdon, that they were dedicated to a certain Persian bishop called Ivo, who came from the east to Britain, and preached the gospel. The link between the British and Oriental churches are thus partly explained. Leland's story, however, is more probable

Such are the meagre and unsatisfactory statements that we can make about the Cornish Saints of Penwith. It might have been easy out of the conflicting claims to have selected a pet theory as to each, but really our knowledge of the subject is too slight for one, with a consideration for truth, to select a particular view and work it out. All we can say in apology for the vagueness of this chapter, is the old Cornish proverb :—

Ex kez? ez, po neg ez ; ma sêz kêz
Dro kêz ; po negez nêz, dro peth ez.

F

Chapter II.

PENWITH UNDER THE OLD KINGS OF CORNWALL.

" Me yv duk in oll Kernow,
In della ytho ov thays
Hag vhel arluth in pov,
A Tamar the Pen-an-lays."
BEUNAN'S " MERIASEK," 2205-8.

" Duke in all Cornwall am I ; so was my father; and a high lord in the land from Tamar to
the Land's End."

T is difficult to realize that there was a time when the Cornish formed a separate and independent little nation, with their own dynasty of native kings, their own government and army, their own language, their own national church, in fact were quite independent of the rest of the world, save an occasional friendly alliance with the Welsh princes. Yet all this certainly was the case. Nay more, if we may take tradition as an authority, there is reason to think that West Cornwall itself was once a separate state under its native princes, independent of, and even at war with the eastern regions, where the ancient princes reigned at Castle-an-Dinas, in Pydar (*i.e.* the Castle-an-Dinas near S. Columb), and at " Dundagel by the Cornish sea."

Of this most interesting epoch, however, unfortunately we know no more than of the native Cornish branch of the Brito-Celtic church then prevailing here. The densest Egyptian darkness rests over the whole of this era, a period lasting, be it remembered, some five centuries, *i.e.* as far as that which severs us from the England of Geoffrey Chaucer; and what a chasm in manner, thoughts, and institutions lies between the England of the Canterbury Tales and the England of our own age of telegraphs and railways ! The very names of the Cornish kings are almost lost, for the authority for these lists is not worth much. Carew has saved the tradition of a few, and we may make out a little hazy sketch of the old Cornish dynasty, not nearly as clear as of some dynasties of ancient Egypt. Perhaps the so-called kings or earls of Cornwall were merely head chieftains, like Brian Boru, of Ireland, or Mac Cullum More in the Gaelic Highlands. It will be no harm to give the list, which the reader may accept *cum grano salis*. One wishes one could tell something of the lives and adventures of these Cornu-British chiefs ; perhaps their records might be more charming than any historical romance. But it is no use wishing.

Cador is said by Carew to have conquered Childeni. Blederic, another Cornish king, with the Welsh princes warred against Ethelfred, and at the head of the Cornish, won the victory. Ivo, son of Alan, king of Brittany, is said to have reigned over Cornwall, Devon, and Somerset, and to have kept peace with the Saxons, thus securing his possessions. Bletius, under Roderic, the Welsh king, defeated Adelred, king of Wessex, when he invaded Cornwall, and drove out the Saxons. Such are the statements of Carew, which may or may not be fact. They read probable, and for lack of better, are worth recording. We also read of Solomon, king of Cornwall, of king Cuby, and king Constantine (to whom we shall hereafter refer again). Constantine is said to have led an evil life, and then repented and abdicated.

We must not, however, dwell too long on the mythic records of East Cornwall, our subject is Penwith. Here comes before us in the dim past, the shadowy memory of the struggle of West with East Cornwall, as shadowy as the hazy Cornish battle of the Land's End, imagined by the poet laureate :—

"Among the Mountains by the winter sea ;
Until King Arthur's table. man by man,
Had fallen in Lyonness about their Lord."

Dim and uncertain rises that vague tradition. The story of the heathen chieftain Teudor, of Hayle, (or Tudor, a name linked with memories of later greatness, when the offspring of a Celtic prince reigned over both Celt and Teuton, and founded a name ever shining in the history of the world), who lived at a castle at Riviere, close to Hayle, now buried in the waters, meets us in many forms. His cruelty to the Christian missionaries is the theme of Cornish drolls, and the mainspring of the plot of the *Beunans Meriasek*, the ablest drama of Cornish literature. The legend relates how not merely was Meriasec driven from Britain by him, but that SS. Ia and Elwyn fell victims to his rage. A west Cornish kingdom seems a very small affair in this age of great empires, but we should recollect that even still there is a principality of Monaco, and that till lately as the train rushed on through Germany, one might often ask with propriety " What state is this?" or " What government are we under now?" At any rate, the prince of West Cornwall had no doubt larger territory and more subjects than the prince whose contingent to the federal armies was fixed, it is said, at "four soldiers and a drummer boy."

If historical records be silent about these "dark ages" of local history, antiquities are not absent, evidencing a fairly abundant population, a comparative civilization. It should be remembered with regard to the latter point that the ages after " the irruption of the barbarians " on the continent, and the Saxon conquest of England, was an age of relapse into a savage state for most parts of Europe. In whole counties of England, in whole departments of France not a relic remains of this dark epoch. The ages of Roman rule, and of Mediæval feudalism leave every where abundant traces; but this, the intervening age, is a blank. Not so in Cornwall, especially in West Penwith. A large portion probably of our Celtic antiquities, belong to this epoch. The Cornish crosses of our moors and roadsides were perhaps reared mostly by the Cornu-Britons of the old Brito-Celtic church. The Mên-Scryfa recording the resting place of Rialobran, the son of Cunoval (Cymbeline), belongs to this epoch, so possibly does the tomb of Silus* in S. Just Church. Who Rialobran was we cannot say, nor who his father Cunoval, but probably they were Cornish chieftains, whose names were honored by their countrymen, and not improbably, as the legend says the Mên-Scrifa marks a battle field, and perchance Cunoval was the founder and endower of Gulval church.

Legendary lore is rich about this epoch as we shall see. It was the age of the Cornish Saints of S. Leven, S. Sennen, S. Hya, S. Breachan, S. Piran, and a host of others, of whom we speak elsewhere.

The state of society in this epoch it is of course impossible now to know. Probably the miners, and fishers, and husbandmen were formed in little

---

* There is some doubt about the inscription. It may be Silenis ; who Silus was no one knows.

village communities, near their mines, fishing grounds or fertile oases (in the deserts of forest and moor), where all were equal, and the motto "one and all," of equality and fraternity were realized in time of peace; but when assailed by Saxon or Dane, they banded together under the native princes (first of West Cornwall, or Riviere, then under the kings of all Cornwall, whose castles were Tintagel, or Castle-an-Dinas in Pydar). This would explain the coincidence of two apparently opposite principles in Cornish tradition, a democratic spirit of "one and all," with a personal devotion to the Sovereign. It may be it also explains the absence of any tradition of descent from the native Cornu-British chieftains among the leading county families. Many boast of springing from the Norman followers of William the Conqueror, none from the native Cornish chiefs. Is this any evidence that the clan spirit of the Highlands and Irish was not true in Cornwall, and the Cornu-British lived in democratic village communities, such as Sir Henry Maine so ably describes in his "Early History of Institutions."

As to the state of civilization of the Cornu-Britons it not improbably was a survival of Danmonian customs, and modes of building with a thin veneer (apparent rather than real) of Roman culture. May we not use the Mên-Scry fa as the type of this state of things, a Celtic Menhir with two Cornish names graven in Roman letters upon it, and one Latin-word abridged? This perhaps represents the state of Cornwall in the mythic age, glorified in European romance by the legends of the mythic Arthur.

CHAPTER III.

FOREIGN CONQUERORS.

"The long mountains ended in a coast
Of ever shifting sand, and far away
The phantom circle of a moaning sea.
There the pursuer could pursue no more,
And he that fled no further fly the king;
And there, that day when the great light of heaven
Burn'd at his lowest in the rolling year,
On the waste sand by the waste sea they closed.
    *   *   *   *   *   *
And ever and anon with host to host
Shocks, and the splintering spear, the hand mail hewn,
Shield-breakings and the clash of brands, the crash
Of battle axes on shatter'd helms, and shrieks
After the Christ, of those who falling down
Looked up for heaven and only saw the mist."

                                    TENNYSON.

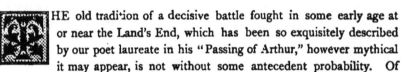

HE old tradition of a decisive battle fought in some early age at or near the Land's End, which has been so exquisitely described by our poet laureate in his "Passing of Arthur," however mythical it may appear, is not without some antecedent probability. Of course the modern mythologist will affirm that the myth arises from the apparent suitableness of the battle field of natures' forces for the scene of human strife. But this will hardly account for the force of Cornish tradition, even after a thousand years, nor for that tradition having gained fixity.

Dismissing Arthur and Modred from the domain of history to that of romance, or rather regarding the former as the representative of almost, so to speak, the personification of the struggle between the Cornu-Briton and the Saxon, is there any probability that once at least in the history of Cornwall

"The pursuer could pursue no more,
   And he that fled no further fly the king."

And that the Cornu-Britons may have been driven like a stag at bay to a last final fight, in sight of the Pedn-an-lase? The probability is considerable, the evidence is not by any means strong of a great battle in Buryan.

The visits of the Danes or Norsemen rather (for as is now known, but a small portion of our Norse pirates came from Denmark proper) to West Penwith are robed in mystery. A moment's consideration will show that in any case this was to be expected. The annals of the little Cornu-British kingdom, as we have seen, have well nigh all perished (if they ever indeed were written); and as to the Vikings themselves they were not strong in literary attainments. So as scribes did not abound in either part, it is no wonder if no one had recorded to us the adventures of the Vikings in Penwith.

This, however, is no evidence at all that there were no Danes in Cornwall, nor that Penwith may not have been often visited, either as friends or foes, by those pirates of the ancient seas. If ethnological characteristics were allowed to be considered, one would say that there are not a few persons in Penwith in whom the Scandinavian physiognomy is perceptible, mixed with the Celtic. The accusation of springing from "the red-haired Danes" may be counted as an insult, but some would think it a compliment. There is nothing to be ashamed of in the being born of those gallant Norsemen, from whom spring some of the bravest and wisest of the human race. The blood of the Scandinavian is mingled with the Saxon and Celts in the population of our Eastern and Northern counties. The race that produced a Snorro Sturleson and a Canute, a Gustavus Vasa and Gustavus Adolphus, a Linnæus and Thorwaldsen, a Nelson and a Charles XII, to which in its purest form belong some of the most civilized populations of Europe, is not to be despised. To be sprung from the "red-haired Danes" is a compliment instead of an insult, above all when the beloved Duchess of Cornwall is a Danish princess. Much of the nobler characteristics of the coast population of Penwith may come from Scandinavian ancestry. Those Newlyn fishermen, who sailed in 1856 in an open boat to Australia, were perchance no unworthy descendants of the Vikings, whose name was dreaded even in Sicily and Constantinople.

It is unfortunate, however, that false derivation and strained antiquarianism should have striven to find by theory unreal evidences of Danish settlements.

Castle-an-Dinas, in all probability, was never a castle of the Danes, but a mere translation and repetition of the word Dinas—a castle; Treryn was more probably an old Danmonian than a Danish fortress. The battle of Vellan Dreath is little more than a legend. The tradition of a Danish settlement in Penwith is not overturned by this. Nothing is more probable than that the Cornish, pressed by the superior numbers of the Saxons, did seek help from the brave Norse pirates, that that aid was given, and probably well paid for; that the brave fair-haired Danish warriors did charm the dark-eyed daughters of the Cornu-Britons, especially when they came as defenders and friends; that the coves of Penwith were comfortable ports for Danish ships. All this may be likely, it cannot be asserted as historically certain. The visits of the Danes may therefore be claimed as one of those historical statements, which are supported strongly by tradition and indirect testimony, but are not actually capable of proof. The change of the conduct of the Danes rest on much the same testimony. Plunder and power were the sole and darling objects of the Danes. "By degrees," says Dr. Borlase, "they came to use the Cornish as bad as the rest of the kingdom, so that Cornwall is supposed to have been at last utterly ruined by them." Hence the bitterness of the charge of springing from a "red-haired Dane."*

* Vide Borlase. Drew, pp. 421, 433. Hunt II, p. 65.

CHAPTER IV.

THE ANCIENT BISHOPS OF CORNWALL.

"An bara-ma kymereugh
Theugh lemman yn kettep pen,
Hag anotho ol dybreugh,
Ow corf yv re'n oferen."
The celebrated passage in the Passio Christi.

MONG the many mysterious and yet interesting subjects connected with the religious history of England, none has a greater fascination than the Brito-Celtic Church. We know so little of it that we may imagine anything about it; and thus writers, according to their bias, have seized on it as a peg on which to hang their theological controversies, or their philosophical theories. Every one views it from his own standpoint. To one it appears a marvellous witness from Apostolic times, an anticipation by some seven centuries in England of the work of John Wycliffe, or Hugh Latimer; to others it is a mere hazy tradition of the half barbarous teachers of quite barbarous Celtic tribes, who clung on dimly to their traditions; to others it is a totally worthless speculation, and they would be too glad to cast its memories, if they could, into the mystic shroud of Arthur and the Round table, and lodge the Welsh and Cornish Saints of the Dark Ages on the mythical shelf with the magician Merlin.

And yet there are facts which even a hypercritical and sceptical student can hardly deny. There was, from the fourth to the ninth century at least, a native Brito-Celtic Church in Great Britain; its foundation was anterior to S. Augustines mission, or indeed to his birth or S. Gregory's; it was independent of the Church of Rome, and remained so formally for ages; it differed

G

from the Papal system in certain important matters, *e.g.* the observance of Easter, the form of the Cross, the ideal of Episcopacy and Church Government, which it did not surrender till it was forced to do so.   There is then a remarkable non-Roman early Christian tradition in Cornwall, and when controversialists talk about "The Church of our Fathers," one is inclined to ask "which Fathers?"   The Cornishman of A.D. 677, nay, perchance of A.D. 877, was no more a Roman Catholic in the sense now attached to the word by Ultramontanes, than is the Cornishman of 1877.   He and his religious teachers rejected the authority of the Papacy, rejected many usages of the Roman Church; nay, even did not keep Easter or Lent at the same time as the Romans did.   I do not of course say he was an Anglican, or a Methodist, I only deny that he was what we now call a Roman Catholic.   He was a professing Christian, of the native form of the old Brito-Celtic Church.*

The records of the Brito-Celtic Church are very few and give us little information.   Most that we know of it is from its foes, rather than from its friends.   As for its work in Cornwall we can learn next to nothing, save from vague tradition and untrustworthy statements.   A good deal of the religious life of Cornwall came from Ireland.   Thence, legend affirms, came both S. Petrock and S. Piran, as well as our local Saints, S. Sennan, S. Buryan, S. Uny, S. Ives, S. Elwyn.

The ancient Irish Church was very peculiar in many of its customs.   It professed to have received its traditions from the Apostle S. John rather than from S. Peter.   Hence in some cities it retained the custom (founded on the seven Churches of Asia, in the Apocalypse) of having seven churches, and, what is stranger still to our notions, seven bishops.   But the Irish idea of episcopacy was very different from the Roman, or that which we have derived from the Mediæval Latin Church.   The bishops were in some parts merely regarded as church officers for ordinations and other episcopal duties, but not for governing the church, which was ruled by presbyters.   A bishop had therefore no more right to rule a diocese than a precentor had.   The presbyters governed everything, merely keeping a bishop for his special work.

---

* For a statement of one side of the subject, see Rev. W. Haslam's and Rev. C. P. Collins's curious books, 'Perran-Zabuloe.' Even on their Sacramental teaching, the quotation given at the head of our chapter shows a tradition of teaching very different from that accepted usually in the Middle Ages, and implying consubstantiation.

Thus curiously episcopacy and presbyterianism were combined, *i.e.* episcopal orders and presbyterian government. This peculiarity may explain many difficulties about the obscure history of the Cornish episcopate. Was the Silus or Silenis, whose tomb is at S. Just, such a bishop? or is the supposed Pastoral and Cross a mere *chi r'ho* of a Primitive Christian.

The early history of the Cornish bishopric is shrouded in obscurity. Some old writers, from a passage in William of Malmesbury, were led to suppose it was founded in 904, by King Edward, or Edward the Elder, and that the first bishop, Athelstan, was consecrated at Canterbury, by Archbishop Plegmund.* Mr. Pedler and others have thrown doubts on this theory, and considered it of a much earlier date. Leland mentions eleven bishops buried at S. Germans.

"That a see of Cornwall once existed, and flourished for some generations, there cannot now be a shadow of doubt. The Registry at Canterbury, the Manumissions in the Bodmin Gospels, the Charters of our kings, the concurrent testimony of ancient chroniclers, the universal decision of modern local historians, prove the fact without dispute. Polwhele (the local historian) narrates the names of twelve such Cornish Bishops, seven of whom he thinks lived at Bodmin, and five at St. Germans; but now critics reduce that number to eight, and consider that the Bishops may have alternately lived at St. Germans and Bodmin, the latter, being used as a see for West and Central Cornwall (then thinly peopled and perchance only nominally under Saxon rule), and St Germans being the capital of the Eastern portion. The history of the foundation of the see is obscure."—*The Bishopric of Cornwall, p.* 6, 7, (1869).

Now the dream of so many ages is realized, and we see Cornwall among the bishoprics of England, not indeed as in the days of Archbishop Cranmer, as a mere suffragan, but as a regular See.

The history of the See belongs rather to the annals of Truro or of Bodmin than of Penzance. The Bishops of Cornwall may or may not have had much influence on the early religious history of West Penwith. If the "clan theory" is to hold good, if the tradition of a king of West Cornwall be worth any

* William of Malmesbury, bk. II, cap. 5.

thing, and if the Brito-Celtic Church here held the same position as in Ireland ;—and be it remembered, much of West Cornwall appears to have been converted by Irish missionaries, who, doubtless, would bring with them Irish theories of the episcopate, as merely *primus inter pares*, the first (even if so much as first) of the presbyters,—it is quite possible that West Cornwall was not really much affected by the Bishops of Bodmin or S. Germans, or more correctly, " Cornubiensis ecclesie episcopi ;" for never, till now, strange to say, do the Cornish bishops appear to have called themselves after a cathedral city. It is probable, as Mr. Pedler supposes, that until the Saxon Conquest, the bishops of Crediton had authority over the small part of Cornwall, annexed by the Saxons, and that afterwards the old Brito-Celtic bishopric was adopted into the Saxon system, and brought into subjection to Canterbury. The semi-independence of the Cornish Christians is a very curious subject ; the business of a bishop of Crediton was "to visit the Cornish race to extirpate their errors, (independence of the Roman Church I suppose being meant by this) for they had previously, to the utmost of their power, resisted the truth, and not obeyed the apostolic (by which was meant the papal) decrees." So even a thousand years ago the Cornish had their spirit of independence.

The honor or dishonor of abolishing the Cornish bishopric may be shared between Leving, or Lyving, the friend of Canute the Great, a wonderful pluralist, being bishop of Cornwall, Devon, and Worcester, and his successor, Leofric, bishop of Cornwall and Devon, who moved the See to Exeter, by decree of Edward the Confessor, in 1050, owned the two Sees. Bishop Benson is the next bishop.

The following is a list of the old Anglo-Saxon Bishops of Cornwall, anterior to Bishop Living, and was given by Mr. Pedler :—

	NAMES.	EPOCH.	WHERE MENTIONED.
1.	Conan.	(925-940)	Leland.
2.	Æthelgar	(946-955)	Petrockstowe Records.
3.	Comœre	(959 about)	Petrockstowe Records.
4.	Æthelstan... ...	(966 about)	A Charter of 968.
5.	Wulfsige	— —	Petrockstowe Records.
6.	Ealdred	(978-1016)	Four Charters, 993-997.

7.	Æthelred (?)	...	— —	...	...	Charter 1001.
8.	Burhwold...	... (1016-1035) ...		...	...	Petrockstowe Records. Charter of 1018. Florence of Worcester. William of Malmesbury.

Of this early epoch which is so utterly unrepresented in the antiquities of most parts of England, and of Europe, we have probably many remains. The granite crosses of Penwith belong mostly, it is thought, to this epoch, *i.e.* the Brito-Celtic, or the Anglo-Saxon age. In them we are brought into contact, it may be, with the earliest forms of British Christianity, the form so often ignored in our common histories, which preceded the landing of S. Augustine in Kent. The usual Greek form of the Cornish cross, with its equal arms, points, it has been said, either to a period when the traditions of the Primitive Church were still living, or to the Oriental missionaries, who founded the early Cornish Church. The theory must not be carried too far, only it certainly tends to confirm the non-Roman and non-Italian origin of the ancient church of Cornwall. The Latin crosses, though we have many of them, are not the majority in the Penwith crosses, the cross of even arms, as the Greek Church in Russia and the East still accepts, is the prevailing form, on a shaft and with a "glory" or circle around it. In many cases, *e.g.* at Zennor, S. Burian, S. Levan, Rosemorran, S. Erth, Church Town, &c., a rude figure of "our Lord" is inscribed on one side of the cross.

Among the chief Latin crosses are the following :—

1. Boscathnoe, near Madron Church (in a field).
2. Tremethick, Madron.
3. S. Paul Down.
4. Ludgvan Churchyard.
5. Escalls in Sennen
6. Sennen Green.
7. Higher Drift, on Land's End Road.
8. Trevilley, Sancreed (a crucifix).
9. Brane, Sancreed.

All these are probably mediæval, but it by no means follows that the following Greek or Celtic crosses are so. At the recent visit of the British

Archæological Society to the West, the general opinion was that even San-creed Cross, which would appear to be one of the most recent of them, was anterior to the Norman Conquest, or to the annexation of Cornwall to the See of Exeter. It is within the verge of possibility that some might be coeval with S. Augustine, or as ancient as the Mên Scryfa.

The chief Greek crosses are

Penzance—The Market Cross, one of the most interesting antiquities in the borough. It was removed from the centre of the market-place in 1829. Its arms are equal—a Greek cross with " glory," on the reverse was found the inscription *hic procumbunt corpora piorum.*

Madron—1. Parc an Grouz.   2. Trengwainton Cairn.   3. Trembath. 4. Madron Churchyard.

S. Paul—Churchyard (with a figure).

S. Burian—1. Churchtown Square (very fine).   2. Churchyard. 3. Crowzan-wra.   4. Boskenna.   5. Trevorgance.

S. Levan—1. S. Levan Churchyard.   2. Rospletha.

Sancreed—1. Churchyard, very fine, with many ornaments, symbols of passion, 7 ft. 7 in. high.   2. Churchyard wall.   3. Trenuggo.

S. Just—Pendeen.

Gulval—Rosemorran.

Lelant—1. Churchyard.   2. Roadside cross, between Lelant Church and S. Ives.   3. Trecoven Hill.

Zennor—Vicarage garden.

Such are some of the crosses which still remain in the district, not a few of which may be rude relics of the old Brito-Celtic Church, of the early efforts of the Cornish people to express their faith on the all enduring granite. We may not have in West Penwith ancient buried churches, dug out from the sands in which, like old Nineveh, they have been buried for ages, such as are at Perranzabuloe and Gwithian, but we have crosses to mark the piety of the early Christians of old Cornwall.

CHAPTER V.

THE PLAN-AN-GUARE.

" Evugh oll gans an guary
Ny a vyn agis pesy
A luen golon.
Pybugh menstrels colonnek
May hyllyn donsia dyson."

BEUNAN's " MERIASEK."

" Drink ye all with this play, we beseech you, with full heart.   Pipe ye hearty minstrels, that
we may dance forthwith."

T is a very curious fact that the Drama—now so generally ignored in the county, and hardly represented in a single town in Cornwall—which, by a large portion of Cornishmen, is now held to be an unholy and evil thing, should be almost the sole subject of the little Cornish literature that is still extant.

Cornwall is a strange mixture of an intense conservatism and, at the same time, of an utter revolution of thought. The Baal fires of Midsummer Eve may be, and probably are handed down from, if not Phœnician, at least pre-christian times.   The customs and legends of the county point back to primitive Aryan days, the mythic age of the heathen Danmonii: the thoughts, habits, and traditions of the people are very "old world"; and yet in few of the rural (or rather non-urban) parts of England have modern inventions produced such a change to every class as in Cornwall.

The utter revulsion of public feeling in Cornwall on the subject of the Drama, if we examine it closely, is no symptom whatever of fickleness on the part of the people ; nay, it may he held as a partial resultant of their conservatism.   The Plân-an-Guare, or old Cornish play, was a very different thing

from the Drama of the London or Plymouth stage in this latter half of the
nineteenth century.   It was a Miracle-play, a religious representation of sacred
subjects, somewhat in the style of the Passion-spiel of Aber-Ammergau, which
during the last few years has excited so much discussion.

Of all the Cornish Dramas that we meet with, not one is secular, and except
"St. Meriasec" all are, more or less, scriptural in subject.   They have far
more resemblance then to the Methodist Sunday-school recitation (if we can
find a nineteenth century parallel) of, say "Joseph and his Brethren" or
Gideon, than to the popular dramatic performances of the London stage.

In their arrangements, like the old Greek theatre of the days of Sophocles,
and the common run of Miracle-plays in the Middle Ages, they were per-
formed in the open air.   The Plân-an-Guare at St. Just was the most famous
in the Land's End region.   Now—enclosed with houses and with the stone
seats of the little amphitheatre removed—it is hard to conceive how it might
have been employed for this purpose in its palmy days.   Here, from all parts
of Bolerium, the Celtic miners of the fifteenth and sixteenth centuries gathered
to see the Miracle-play, or Guare, which combined to them the attractions of
a revival and a fair,—a strange combination of amusement and devotion, with,
at the same time, a chance of seeing old faces and meeting old friends from
distant parishes.   There may have been a something national also in those old
Cornish gatherings,—something of the clannish "one and all" spirit,—a
mingling together of the men of the moors and the heath and the distant
rocky coves to hear, in their own tongue, their own old Cornu-British tongue
—a dying and a doomed language (and, perchance, they knew and felt it,)—
the mysteries of religion proclaimed.

The Plan-an-Guare of St. Just was a truly Celtic, a truly Cornish place for
proclaiming religious mysteries.   It was not unlike the spots where, a thousand
or two thousand years before, the Druids may have celebrated before their
ancestors the mysteries of the nature-worship of Druidism.   There was no
lack of background.   Far away stretched the glorious Atlantic, ever shifting,
ever changing in tint and colour ; now blue in deepest tints, now almost the
purple sea of Homer, now sheeted in white foam, now running the shifting
changes of the neutral tints,—an Atlantic, then, weird in mystery, for who

knew what was beyond those Scilly Isles, what " Atlantis," or " Garden of Hesperides," or what not? And, on the other sides, there were the wild, bleak, brown moors of strange, weird legend,—the fairy region of the Gump and Carn Kenidjack, the scene of so many wild Celtic myths.

After all—say what we may,—there was a certain grand old world poetry about those rough Cornish tinners who dug out the Plân-an-Guare. Art, perchance, did very little ; nature did very much indeed for the spectacle of their Miracle-plays. It was then in Cornwall, as now in the Bavarian Highlands, only nineteenth century influences have refined the carrying out of the idea.

In other respects, also, the rude Plân-an-Guare had its points of interest. We Westerns—above all, we English—have generally failed to enter into the spirit of the amphitheatre, the arena, the palæstra of the spectacles of classic times. It is most un-English, most un-Teutonic. The climate of the chilly, variable North is against it. Our English Miracle-plays were celebrated on carts in the streets, or else in Churches. The English peasant did not take his spectacular amusements *sub Jove*, in the open amphitheatre. He left it for the children of "the sunny South." But, in Cornwall, the instinct for open air spectacle, *i.e.*, for the amphitheatre, was developed, perchance, not by a spirit of foreign imitation (for of this the Cornishmen knew probably little, and cared less) but by climate. The open amphitheatre of the Plân-an-Guare may have had something to do with the mildness of the climate,—that climate so equable that the hardier flora of the Mediterranean shores can flourish beneath this sky. By this perchance, as a concurrent reason (with others that have been urged) we may account partially for the absence of the Plân-an-Guare in East Cornwall, where the climate was not quite as equable as in the far West.

Whether Dr. Borlase's suggestion that the Plân-an-Guare was used as an actual palæstra, where "the Britons did usually assemble to hear plays acted, to see the sports and games," may be doubted.

Dr. Borlase's description of the Plân-an-Guare at St. Just is interesting as illustrating the real condition of the amphitheatre above a century ago, and probably little more than a century after the last time it was used. " It was an exact circle of 126 feet diameter : the perpendicular height of the bank,

H

from the area within, is now seven feet; but the height, from the bottom of the ditch without, ten feet at present, formerly more. The seats consist of six steps, fourteen inches wide, and one-fourth high, with one on the top of all, where the rampart is, about seven feet wide."

It is a pity that this very curious relic of past ages and a past state of society was not preserved with more care. It was, in some senses, unique of its kind. (Perran Round differs in some points. The Plân-an-Guares at Redruth and Marazion have been quite destroyed.) The destruction it met is irreparable.

How the stage-directions were carried out, what the "scenery" was (save the noble background of sublime nature, pointing "from Nature up to Nature's God"), how the attiring was managed, it is difficult now to conceive ; and we have no records nor even tradition to aid us in solving the mystery. Perhaps it is better that we have not ; the fact might greatly shock our nineteenth century notions of propriety. Considering that the most sacred mysteries of the faith were represented on the stage, that the most holy personages and most sacred scenes were there attempted to be represented, the short-comings would, probably, create a grating sensation on the nineteenth century minds. And yet there was no intention of irreverence. All was *bonâ fide* and well meant, doubtless. Perhaps some of the rude tinners and fishermen were even edified and instructed by rough representations of the Gospel history, which, to our ideas, would be simply "shocking."

I cannot agree with the strictures which have been brought against the Cornish Drama. There is a certain boldness, an angularity it may be, a pre-Raphaelite quaintness (if one may apply the term of a sister art to Dramatic subjects) which pervades the Cornish Drama, that gives it, even under altered circumstances, a certain characteristic power. In it one may see, in a mediæval form, some of the better modern peculiarities of the Cornish character,—a passionate personal love for the Lord Christ, an enthusiastic reverence for Scripture, a rude eloquence, an elaborate and, in some respects, vivid detail.

The character of Pilate, in both the plays of *The Passion* and *The Death of Pilate*, is powerfully drawn, with something of an Albert Durer coarse vigour, and an utter disregard for difference of time and space. Pilate is an ideal unjust judge, coarse, brutal, but cunning,—a thorough Judge Jeffreys. He is such a man as Cornish legend describes Tregeagle. It is to be feared that, in the Middle Ages, there were but too many samples of such a character.

What the teaching power of these old Cornish Dramas were it is difficult now to decide. We should remember that the people for whom they were composed were ignorant and illiterate,—a people who could neither read nor write, and who knew no one probably who could either read or write, except their "parson" (I like that Cornish word, retained from the old Latin,)—a people who not merely never left their county, but who had never in their lives been even near a great town (for in those days there was no city nearer than Exeter, an immense distance for Cornish miners or peasants). Literature was closed to them (even such literature as England possessed then) not merely by their inability to read, but by their not understanding English, if it was read to them. How could these people be taught the Scripture history,—the narratives of Genesis or the Gospel? By either pictures or dramatic representation. All the Bible Societies (had such existed) would never have explained these things to people who could not read.

One thing is certain, that the influence of the Guâre over the West Cornish people was such that the Reformation could not, for some time, abolish it in Cornwall, as it did in other parts. Carew, who probably himself had been a witness of the Guâre, in 1602 writes of it as still existing and still a part of the local usages of the far West. "The Guâry miracle," he says, "in English a Miracle-play, is a kind of English interlude compiled in Cornish out of some Scripture history. For representing it, they raise an earthen amphitheatre in some open field, having the diameter of his enclosed playne some 40 to 50 foot." This latter remark supports our opinion that in many other places besides the Plân-an-Guare at St. Just, they might have been acted *e.g.* near the parish churches at the Church-feast. "The country people flock from all sides, many miles off, to hear and see it; for they have therein devils and devices, to delight as well the eye as the ear."

That it lingered even after Carew's time, is plain, from the fact that Jordan's *The Creation of the World* with *Noah's Flood* were written evidently with the intention of being acted, and containing stage directions as late as 1611, *i.e.*, far on in the reign of James I.

Scawen, on the other hand, who wrote soon after the Restoration, speaks of the Plân-an-Guare as if the use of them " was long since gone." The term " long since " is, however, very vague. It might mean only some twenty or thirty years. Mr. Pedler supposes that, early in the seventeenth century, an effort was made to revive the Cornish Drama, as a means of revitalizing the expiring Cornish language ; and that Jordan's work—the last book possibly written in Cornish—was an evidence of this attempted reaction. Certainly, it appears that the Plân-an-Guares of this period were larger than in former times.

The stage directions of the later plays *(e.g.,* the *Life of Saint Meriasek* and Jordan's *Creation of the World)* would lead us to think that these dramatic spectacles must, in their rude way, have been far more imposing than one would have expected. The number of actors must have been very large, and not merely men but horses were brought on the scene, so that some of the spectacles must have been a sort of rude Astley's,—a point in which the Cornish Guare had the advantage over the legitimate drama of the present day. The horses were not pasteboard, but real. In *St. Meriasek*, Prince Teudar has fifteen and the Duke 20 "streamers." Constantine's threatened massacre of the children must have brought a great number on the stage. In the *Origo Mundi*, both David's and Solomon's parts may have given occasion for scenic displays.

The arrangements, however, must have been very coarse compared with modern drama. Carew says that the players " are prompted by one called the Ordinary, who tolloweth at their back with the book in his hand, and telleth them softly what they must pronounce aloud. Which manner once gave occasion to a pleasant conceited gentleman of practising a merry prank ; for he undertaking (perhaps, of set purpose) an actor's room was accordingly lessoned (beforehand) by the Ordinary, that (what) he must say after him. His turn came. Quoth the Ordinary, ' Go forth man, and shew thyself.' The gentleman steps out upon the stage, and, like a bad clerk in Scripture matters, cleaving more to the letter than the sense, pronounced those words aloud. 'Oh !' (says the fellow softly in his ear) 'You mar all the play.' And with this his passion, the actor makes the audience in like-sort acquainted. Hereon, the prompter falls to railing and cursing in the bitterest terms he could devise; which the gentleman, with a set gesture and countenance, still soberly related, until the Ordinary, driven at last into a mad rage, was fain to give over all." This little joke, though Carew says it gave the spectators "a great deal more sport and laughter than twenty such Guáries could have afforded," perhaps was a hastening cause of the destruction of the failing institution. What is made ridiculous, if already declining, cannot long retain public respect.

Whether the Cornish Drama was a desirable mode of teaching religious truths, is a question which we cannot conclude this chapter without, for a moment, considering. In this matter, it would be most unwise and unphilosophical to judge the Cornish tinners and peasants of the Middle Ages by the criteria of the nineteenth century. As we have said, the mass of the people could neither read nor write, and a Bible Society distributing copies of Holy Writ to them (if it had been practical before the invention of printing) would have been attempting a "work of supererogation," It was by the eye and ear alone the people could be taught, and to these means the Cornish "parsons" of the period turned for help. Perhaps they were wiser in their generation than some of their successors of the eighteenth (not to mention the earlier portion of a later) century, who hoped to instruct and edify the Cornish miners by reading them elaborate essays in the form of a literary English not "understanded of the people." As for the plays themselves, their backbone was (as we shall see) quite Scriptural, with occasional *addenda* from Apocryphal sources, not so very far removed from the strict interpretation of the Biblical narrative. At the least, their tone was far more close to Holy Writ than most of the English Miracle-plays of· the same date, and breathe a healthier and more primitive tone of Christian thought than usually pervades the Townley or Chester mysteries.

As for the abstract theory of the Miracle-play, though our prejudices are against it at this moment, it is scarcely possible to predicate (with the experience of the admiring criticisms of Aber-Ammergau,) that it will always remain so.   There are a few, an extremely small minority (but small minorities are not invariably in the wrong) who think that Mendelssohn's *Elijah* might be even more effective if sung " in costume, with scenery," than by gentlemen in evening dress, and ladies attired after the latest Parisian fashion, with a background of blank wall.

Of course, tastes differ, but it may be most philosophical (in spite of current prejudice) to hold a suspended opinion on the subject ; and although at present in the nineteenth century the drama is invariably devoted to secular objects, and not unfrequently is, as is commonly owned, a teacher of irreligion and immorality, our forefathers (especially the " old men " of West Cornwall) were not so hopelessly deluded in thinking it might (with its wondrous and matchless power of appealing to the passions and sentiments of mankind) be a useful teacher of religion and morality.   Perchance the twentieth century may hold that neither the prejudices of the nineteenth nor the fifteenth century were quite right nor quite wrong ; and that the religious drama, though, in olden times shamefully abused, was not an unmitigated evil.

PART III.—THE MIDDLE AGES.

CHAPTER I.

THE NORMAN LORDS OF ALVERTON.

"This worthy family hath flourished here,
Since William's conquest full six hundred year."
Arthur Levelis's epitaph in Burian, 1671.

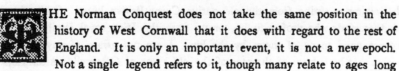

HE Norman Conquest does not take the same position in the history of West Cornwall that it does with regard to the rest of England. It is only an important event, it is not a new epoch. Not a single legend refers to it, though many relate to ages long anterior to Arthur and the ancient Cornish saints, and even to the Roman Emperors (*e.g.* the legends of the "Knackers" and of Constantine in "Beunan's Meriasek"). The fact was that the Cornish were by this time hardened to foreign conquest. In less than a century and a half thrice had the country been conquered by alien foes. The old fishermen or tinners of Penwith who had shuddered when they were children, and hid their frightened little heads in their mothers' laps when the stern thanes and warriors of Athelstan marched to the extreme border where sea and land met in Burian and Sennen, may have lived to hear the terrible news that Sweyn, king of the "Red-haired Danes" had landed in East Cornwall, and that he was master of Exeter after a long and memorable siege; that king Ethelred had fled England. The children that listened and heard by the winter's fireside the old men's stories of the cruel days of Athelstan and the Danes, and had imbibed in their young hearts a hate of the conquering Saxon, now in turn conquered by the Dane, may have lived to hear in their old age that world-famed story of Harold and of the field of Hastings, and the last struggle of the brave "men of Kent" against the chivalry of Normandy. A third conquest was at hand. At the time of the battle of Hastings the Earl of Cornwall was Condorus (or Cadocus, as some say) a prince of the old royal British line, a descendant of the native kings. In the disturbances of the Saxon monarchy he gained a real if not a nominal independence. Exeter rose against William the Conqueror, and its siege by the Normans is one of the great events of English history. The policy of Condorus is not quite certain, it most probably was one of sympathy with the men of Devon. At any rate William was resolved neither to spare Saxon or Cornu-Briton, and by the "right of might" deposed Condorus, and appointed as his successor his own half-brother Robert, earl of Moreton, who henceforth became earl of Cornwall. Thus ended the last relic of the native kingdom of Cornwall, and with Condorus, it would seem, the royal line. It is curious that among all the old Cornish families there should not be any that claims to spring from the old native Cornu-British kings. While there are thousands who profess to be sprung from the Irish royal families (there were a good many of them, by the bye), I am not aware of anyone who boasts that he is born of the race of the old kings of Cornwall. After Condorus we lose sight of them.

After the nomination of Robert to the earldom of Cornwall, came the usual sweeping schemes of spoliation and confiscation. Robert himself received 288 manors of land, with the castles of the old Cornu-British kings.

A curious record of Cornwall, as indeed of England in general, as it was in the reign of William the Conqueror, is contained in the far-famed Domesday Book, in which the king caused to be recorded the extent of the estates of the landowners and other particulars.

Alwaretone is supposed to have been our Alverton, including the sites of Penzance, Newlyn and Mousehole, i.e. the land on the south-west shore of Mount's Bay. If so, Domesday says that in the reign of King Edward the Confessor it was in the possession of Alward (from whom its name may be derived?). The arable land on the estate was sixty carucates, perhaps some 6,000 acres (though the size of the carucate varies.) In the Domain were

3 carucates—300 acres, eleven bond servants (a sad memorial that once on our free soil of Penzance something like slavery must have existed) and 35 "villains" (not villain in the modern but in the ancient sense of labouring men not in bondage) with their families, and 25 borderers. This, altogether, might represent a probable population of about 300 persons (women and children being included) connected with the estate. The pasturage in 1085 was two miles long and one wide. The value to the Earl in 1085, was £20, *i.e.* double that of Sheviock, Rame and Antony (near Plymouth) put together. Certainly Alwareton was one of the most valuable estates in Cornwall, according to Domesday. The Earl of Moreton, its first lord after Alward was turned out, had a goodly possession in it.

There are no doubt other estates in Penwith mentioned in Domesday, but the verification is not beyond doubt, and consequently the very basis of any argument founded on the names is very dubious. Eglosberry seems to have belonged to the Canons of Burian (S. Berrione as it was then spelt). In later Saxon times this estate was free, but the Earl of Moreton, after the Conquest, comes in here also for his share of spoil. Only a dozen families seem to have lived on it.

Now let us consider two of Earl Moreton's successors.

I.—HENRY POMEROY.

Among the friends and admirers of Earl (afterwards king) John, there was a certain west-country nobleman called Henry de la Pomeroy, Lord of Berry-Pomeroy Castle, in Devonshire, and of Tregony, in Cornwall, and what is more to our purpose, it seems, Lord of Alverton (*i.e.* Penzance Manor), who may have had a certain blood relationship of an unrecognizable kind with John, being a grandson of an illegitimate daughter of King Henry I. In consequence of De la Pomeroy's intrigues with John, (or as Hals insinuates for private reasons of his own), Longchamp, Richard's vice-regent, sent a herald, or sergeant-at-arms to Berry-Pomeroy Castle, to arrest the Devonian lord. De la Pomeroy, warned of his danger, stabbed the messenger to the heart, and knowing the consequences of so daring a deed, fled

I

from his castle to Tregony.   But, though he held twelve knights'-fees in Cornwall, none of his castles were strong enough to protect him, and Henry had to consider what he could do to secure himself.

Now among the ladies who lived at the nunnery at S. Michael's Mount (whether she was a professed nun, or only a lady staying there for protection, as was common in those troublous times, is not quite certain) was a sister of Henry de la Pomeroy.   What more suitable than that, now he was in West Cornwall, for Henry to visit his sister and make his offerings to the convent. Along the hills to the east of Marazion might be seen, one day, a procession of pious pilgrims, wrapt in their pilgrim cloaks, wending their way slowly to the Tumba S. Michaelis.   They pass through Marazion.   As the tide is low, they cross to the Mount, and, respectfully, the chief of the party asks admission to see his sister, and worship in the holy place.   Who can refuse the admission of a brother moved by fraternal love, especially if laden with rich offerings? It is not the usage of the abbey to refuse hospitality to such guests.

Henry enters, and with him his fellow pilgrims.   Their cloaks are no longer needed; they cast them off and appear armed *cap-à-pie* for war.   In loud voice Henry declares that he takes the Mount in the name of John, Earl of Cornwall, and threatens any who should dare to impugn his authority. He commands the Prior to deliver him the keys, and to find accommodation for his retainers.   The Prior submits *nolens volens*, though the monks complain that the soldiers are ousting them from their best rooms.   The soldiers hastily fortify the place, and think it is made impregnable.

For some months it seems Henry de la Pomeroy lived "in great pomp and triumph" at the Mount.   He was wealthy, and had many friends in Cornwall. No one in West Penwith dared to oppose him; so he was a feudal baron in all his might, or rather a petty sovereign, for King Richard he defied, and Earl John probably was quite willing to give him his full tether.   Whether he used his illgotten power well, history does not record.

However, times change.   After many months' imprisonment, King Richard is ransomed from the Austrian prison, and returns to London.   John, alarmed at Richard's power, flees to France, and ultimately throws himself on his brother's mercy. Still Pomeroy holds out ; he can expect no forgiveness.

When greater matters are settled, Richard remembers S. Michael's Mount. Revell, the sheriff of Cornwall, is ordered to assist Archbishop Hubert, then Chief Justice and Lord Chancellor of England, to reduce the rebellious fortress. An army marches to Marazion, and prepares for the siege ; the summons is sent to Pomeroy to surrender. Alarmed at the sight of the numerous army (perhaps the largest army ever seen in West Penwith), the rebellious baron surrenders to the archbishop.

Henry de la Pomeroy did not survive this misfortune. The mode of his death is veiled in mystery ; some say he died of a broken heart ; others, that, dreading the penalty of treason, he caused himself to be bled to death.

King Richard restored to the prior and monks their monastery and revenues, but to avoid the recurrence of such an awkward accident (the probable result of leaving a place so strong, by nature, undefended in troublous times), placed in de la Pomeroy's fort a small garrison of soldiers, to secure the Mount from any sudden surprise.

Such (as near as we can make it out, and as Hoveden, Carew, and Hals state it) is the history of Henry de la Pomeroy's achievement. Mrs. Bray has founded on the story a very pretty novel, which, however, is rather deceiving in many points (as not a few historical romances are), for :—

1. There is no reason to suppose any love affair. Henry de la Pomeroy appears to have been an elderly married man, with a grown-up son, and his sister was probably a lady of mature years.

2. The murder of the messenger occurred before, and was the cause of the adventure at the Mount.

3. Henry held the Mount for some months, and not for a few hours.

II.—RICHARD KING OF THE ROMANS.

"Richard, Earl of Cornwall, King of the Romans." The epithets appear so incongruous, so mysterious, so marvellous ! How could a Cornish nobleman be a king of the Romans? And how could a king of the Romans be Earl of Cornwall? Was he a successor of the Tarquins, or of Numa Pompilius, or of Romulus? If so, why was he Earl of Cornwall? Or did he, a brave Cornish chieftian, a second Arthur of fable, conquer Rome? Dreams of antique splendour surrounding the Cornish chieftian rise to one's mind. But stay, we must deal with history and not with dreams. A very few words will solve the riddle, and, as Richard had a certain influence on the history of West Penwith, and once seems to have been Lord of Alverton, *i.e.* Penzance and Newlyn, we may be excused in saying them.. This riddle, when explained, is exceedingly simple, like many of its class.

Now we suppose some of our readers are not aware that, in theory at least, the Frankish sovereign, Charlemagne, monarch of France and Germany, was supposed to be a successor of the old Roman Cæsars—of Augustus and Constantine. That which we or our ancestors called the German Empire, or the Western Empire, was considered by German legists to be the Roman Empire. Thus monarchs, like Otho the Great, Frederick Barbarossa, Rudolph of Hapsburg, though really merely emperors of Germany, held themselves to be the legal heirs of the Cæsars, of Trajan, of Marcus Aurelius, of Theodosius. They were not, but that does not affect their claim, which, indeed, has always to be kept in mind in trying to understand the politics of Europe during the Middle Ages. The emperor elect was therefore called King of the Romans, a proud title, and a rather vain one. The old German Empire was supposed to have been done away with for ever, with many other old things, by the French Revolution. But "not so fast!" We live in the age of "revivals" of many a mediæval institution; and so there is now-a-days, in 1877, at Potsdam, or somewhere else in Vaterland, a certain aged sovereign, who is often called "Der neu Kaiser Wilhelm," and who is not exactly a shadowy sovereign, for he has a few hundred thousand bayonets, and some parks of Krupp cannon always ready to deal with anybody who says that he is not the true Emperor of Germany. So the German Empire is not yet an old-fashioned thing which is only remembered in musty old books.

However, after this little digression and explanation, let us return to English and Cornish history.

For a long time (*i.e.* until the birth of Edward I., heir-apparent to the English crown), Richard, Earl of Cornwall, son of King John assumed an almost regal position in the English Court.* His friendship with his brother-in-law, the great Frederic II. (Hohenstauffen), Emperor of the West, brought him intimately into connection with European politics. In union with the chivalry of France and Germany, he set off on the Crusades, where his military ability and energy were crowned with brilliant successes. We have, in *Matthew Paris*, an account of this Crusade in a letter from Richard himself (or at least purporting so to be) to Rivers, Earl of Devon. It was the last gleam of brightness over those sad annals of crusading enthusiasm. Probably numbers of Cornish knights and soldiers followed their great earl on his chivalric expedition. Leland also speaks of an attempted Cornish Crusade in 1322.

Richard, by the favor of his brother, was given the care of the Jews, whom he, learning from his father King John, knew well how to squeeze. This, and the Cornish mines, combined with his great financial ability, caused him to be the richest man in Europe. The unsettled state of Germany led the electors to look for a foreign prince. No German could satisfy all parties. A Frenchman would not do. Germans even did not then like the French. They have not changed their opinion yet. Who so fit as the rich Cornish earl? "The money cries, 'It is for my sake that Cornwall is married to Rome,'" as was said.

With all his foreign adventures, Richard did not neglect his Cornish earldom. He probably did more for his county of Cornwall than any member of the Royal Family, before or since. Many of our Cornish towns, besides Marazion, owe their charters to Richard's favor.

He loved Cornwall, and seems to have realized fully that property confers its responsibilities,—a theory which it would be well for all our Cornish landowners ever to keep in mind. His eastern journeys did not prevent his looking after Cornish interests. He, probably, was in West Penwith, and visited Alverton and St. Michael's Mount; at any rate, Marazion owes to him its first charter, or, at least, the first charter of which we know anything. It is so quaint in its language, that though such legal documents are usually too

---

* For Richard's history, from a contemporary, see *Matthew Paris*. Materials may be found for a good-sized volume on the biography of our great Earl Richard, as related there and elsewhere.

dry for ordinary readers, we think it worth quoting. It may be translated thus :—

" Richard, by the grace of God, king of the Romans, and always Augustus, to the bishops, abbots, priors, earls, barons, and to all holding free tenures, and to others his lieges in the county of Cornwall, health and every good.

" May you all know that we, by this our present confirmation, have granted and confirmed to the prior of the blessed Michael in Cornwall and to his successors, that they may have and hold, and for ever possess, the three fairs and three markets on their own proper ground in Marchadyon, near their Barn ; which three fairs and three markets they have hitherto held by the concession of our predecessors, kings of England, in Marghasbigan, on ground belonging to others (here follows the dates of the three fairs) ; provided that these fairs and markets may not cause any damage or injury to other fairs or markets, in conformity with the laws and customs of this kingdom of England.

" In witness of all which things we have thought fit to certify this present confirmation with our royal seal."

It was not only Marazion and Burian that are connected in history with this singular prince. St. Paul parish is linked in its memories to him, as being so long subject to his Abbey of Hailes. Part of Paul, *i.e.* Newlyn and Mousehole then belonged to Alverton Manor.

There are two more scenes of Richard's life we must not pass over, though of European rather than local history.

The first is that scene on Ascension-day, A.D. 1257, at Aachen (or Aix-la-chapelle, as we often call it). The chivalry of Germany is crowding into the city. Princes of the empire, counts, barons, prelates in all the glory of mediæval pomp, with banners and trumpets, and minstrelsy, throng the venerable capital. That ancient cathedral,—the most ancient of the great cathedrals of Northern Europe,—is brilliant with splendid pomp, ecclesiastical and martial. Who is the centre of all this ? In whose honor is it ? Who is to be crowned by archbishop Conrad, the new Emperor of the West ? Who is the King of the Romans, successor of the Cæsars ? Richard Plantagenet, Earl of Cornwall, Lord of Alverton, patron of Paul parish ! It would seem as if Merlin's prophecy were no dream—that a second Arthur, champion of Christendom, the Earl of Cornwall, should be the Sovereign of the West; that the dreams of Camelot are no dreams in the crowning of the Royal Crusader at Aachen.

But the glories of the Cornish earl's reception by the Germans, did not end at Aachen or Aix-la-chapelle, as it is usually marked on our maps (though that name is not the correct one, being a French name for a German town). He went thence to his friend, Conrad's palace, at Cologne. Here he was received with splendour; nor here only. As the Cornish tourist travels, in summer or autumn, through the fair Rhineland, on the bosom of the beautiful German Rhine, he little thinks of the Cornish earl, who once was welcomed as sovereign of Germany, with splendour, in those mediæval Rhenish towns whose architecture now delights him.

Yes! Once upon a time a Cornishman—or, at least, an adopted Cornishman,—was owned as monarch in that fair region. Boppart, Wesel, Maintz, (*alias* Mayence) opened their gates to him, and were enriched by his largess, drawn from Cornish mines. The city of Oppenheim owned him as king. Even imperial Frankfort accepted Richard. He went further still. Worms and Spires (so famous in later European history) acknowledged him. Those pageants of the rich Cornish earl in the fair Rhineland read like a dream, or an old myth. Well, they were little better than dreams. "There is many a a slip 'twixt cup and lip." The Empire of the West was not easy to buy even for the rich Earl of Cornwall.

Another scene.—A paralytic old man lies dying at Kirkham. He is broken-spirited, broken-hearted. The Germans wanted not the Cornish earl, but Cornish treasure. Richard has spent and been spent in following a vain dream. His empire has proved a splendid phantom. The body of the broken-hearted old man is soon laid in Hailes church, by the side of his son, and Henry Plantagenet, *alias* King Henry III, soon follows his brother and nephew to the grave. "*Sic transit gloria mundi!*"

CHAPTER II.

THE DEANS OF BURIAN.

"Darber th grays
    In keth chyma pup seson
    May fo prest an Dreusis Fays
    Inno enoris dyson."

"O provide Thy grace
    In this same house each season
    The Father's Trinity always
    Therein be honored!"
                    Bennan's Meriasek, 992-5.

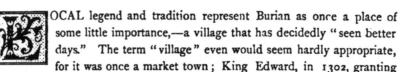

OCAL legend and tradition represent Burian as once a place of some little importance,—a village that has decidedly "seen better days." The term "village" even would seem hardly appropriate, for it was once a market town; King Edward, in 1302, granting a market on Saturdays to the Dean and Canons, beside a fair at Martinmas (November 11). A fair was likewise held at the parish feast, May 29. Burian, therefore, might claim to be, at one period, the westernmost market town in England, a claim which now belongs to St. Just, and which Leland, in the time of Henry VIII, gives to Penzance. The latter ruthless demolisher of local legends (Leland) rather shelves the tradition of Burian's greatness. He speaks of it thus, in 1538 :—" There lieth between the south-west (point) and Newlyn, a mile or more from the sea, S. Buryan *(sic)* a sanctuary, by which, close to the church, are not above eight dwelling-houses ! There belong to S. Buryans a dean and a few prebendaries, who scarcely ever are there. And S. Buryans is some four miles from the very south-west point." (Tol-pedn-Penwith or the Land's End ?)

The two accounts seem conflicting, and yet may be reconciled. Burian may have been, in the middle ages, when it had its full rights of sanctuary, its market, &c., a place of some local importance,—a sort of miniature cathedral city for West Penwith ; and then, when its ecclesiastical privileges were taken from it, may have sunk to the low state in which Leland found it. The "king's antiquary" may have been right, and yet our local tradition not wholly wrong. The number of influential families in the parish, most of which have long since either died out or left the neighbourhood, seem to point to better days for Burian, independent of tradition. The Boscawens, the Vyvyans, the Noyes, the Pendres or Penders, the Levelises or Lovels, the Tresilians, the Tresiders, and others, all once resided in this parish. It was the aristocratic resort seemingly of Penwith,—the Penzance of the period, only not exactly a watering-place, for the mediæval gentry did not care so much for sea-bathing and sea-views as they did for safety and "church privileges" (taking the term in a very wide sense), and those Burian offered. The sanctuary (still remembered by "Sanctuary field") was very convenient, no doubt, on certain occasions.

The Royal Peculiar is supposed to have been founded by Athelstan as we have seen, but the first Dean of Burian of whom we know anything, was a man who may have exercised more influence on European politics than any of the "parsons" of West Penwith before or since. Arnold, protonotary and favourite of Richard, Earl of Cornwall, King of the Romans, was presented to the Deanery of Burian by his august majesty, the Emperor-elect, in July, 1259, *i.e.*, two years after the coronation of Richard by Conrad, Archbishop of Cologne, at Aix-la-chapelle. Whether Arnold (was he an Englishman or a foreigner ?) resided at Burian, or was non-resident like many of his successors, is uncertain. If the former case, quiet little Burian may have seen strange scenes in its day.

But we must not imagine too much. The probability is the courtly Dean Arnold did not live at Burian at all, nor give his suitors the trouble to travel so far west.

Ten years after, *i.e.* in 1269, Stephen Hayme, another favourite of King Richard (of German, not English royalty), was nominated to the Deanery.

J

Was he one of Richard's new subjects? At any rate he seems to have been a pluralist.

On the death of Edmund, Earl of Cornwall (the son of Richard, King of the Romans), King Edward I, claimed the Deanery for the Crown, as a royal free church, and gave his first presentation to his chancellor, the Dean of York, Sir William de Hameldon, another wealthy pluralist. As Dean Hameldon had "many irons in the fire," he could not keep a residence. The Bishop of Exeter, however, did not admire his neglect of Burian by the Dean who was handsomely rewarded for this work, and certainly ought to have done it. Bishop Bytton's conduct, in 1291, was an example which it would have been well for West Cornwall if his successors had always kept in mind. A suit was opened in the King's Court, which dragged on its weary length till after Bishop Bytton's death in 1307. Whether the grant of the market by Edward I, in 1304, to Burian had anything to do with this controversy is not clear.

In the next reign, the dispute assumed more serious proportions. Queen Isabella, the wicked wife of poor weak Edward II, thought fit to thrust into the Deanery a foreigner,—John de Medinta, *alias* John Maunte. He seems thoroughly to have neglected his duty. Probably, the air of the Court suited him much better than the rough breezes of the Cornish moors. Bishop Stapledon did not like the appointment. Bishop Grandisson, who took an especial interest in West Penwith, called him to order for his neglect of duty. John de Maunte took the matter cooly, so the Bishop of Exeter resolved on the last act of ecclesiastical censure. In 1328, the Bishop formally excommunicated him at St. Michael's Mount, with Richard Vivian and others of his friends.

Bad times were in store for Dean Medinta. In July, A.D. 1336, West Penwith witnessed possibly the grandest succession of ecclesiastical pageants that it ever has known. John Grandisson,* the bold and active Bishop of Exeter, the wealthiest and most powerful prelate perchance that ever held that see,† anxious to make his power and authority felt to the furthest

---

* For Bp. Grandisson's life see Oliver's "Lives of the Bishops of Exeter," pp. 75-89.

† "He became the wealthiest Lord Bishop that Exeter had hitherto possessed." Oliver p 80.

limits of its diocese, made a visitation-tour to West Penwith. From the records we have it would seem that either there were many arrears of episcopal duties, or else that a good deal of work was made for Bishop Grandisson. No less than four parish churches were consecrated in a few days, *i.e.* more in one week than either before or after.

Madron must have been very gay that July morning. We can fancy the picturesque mediæval scene. The granite walls fresh from the mason's hand, looking bright and clean. The gay banners floating from the towers. A large portion of the crowd are in quasi highland costume, barefoot and barelegged. The knights and ladies in the fashionable attire of the period, with their fine horses and trappings (the ladies by the bye ride without side-saddles). Above all is seen the Vicar of Madron (was it Rev. Arthur Tyntagel?) all anxious and busy.

Expectancy increases. Up the hill now is seen waving the banner of Peter, the arms of the Diocese of Exeter. A long cavalcade is there, knights and gentlemen, soldiers and clergy, the chaplains, the officers of the diocese, and last of all, attired in the robes of his office, on a sleek and ambling palfrey, the Lord Bishop of Exeter. He is a tall man in the prime of life, just 44. A grave and dignified prelate,[*] one loved by Cornishmen, for his mother is one of their race, Sybylla de Tregoz; but he is a proud prelate, and his own cousin, Hugh Courtenay (the Earl of Devon) has been blaming him for it, and his love of grandeur and dignity.

The Lord Bishop dismounts as he reaches the church. The service begins according to the use of the diocese of Exeter. John Grandisson is very jealous about the liberties of the Church in Devon and Cornwall. He will not be dictated to by even the Archbishop of Canterbury. The Primate Walter de Mapes cannot put him down. After all uniformity is not unity, and why should the Church in Cornwall be forced into the groove of Canterbury? Why should not the "West countrie" have its independence.

After having dedicated Madron Church, the Bishop of Exeter, unwearied by the long service, remounts and pushes on over the Cornish moors and wastes,

---

[*] For Bishop Grandisson's portrait on his seal, see Oliver. He seems to have been a rather handsome dignified man.

amid stream works and rough bridle-paths, to St. Just. Here, close to the
Plân-an-Guare, he again consecrates a Parish Church, and gazes, perchance with
pride, on that mysterious Atlantic Ocean which alone bounds his diocese.

Bishop Grandisson's visit produced a great effect on the Burian people. The
great gentry of Burian seem to have taken Dean Medinta's part against
the Bishop, hoping for favour at court. But now their hearts soften to their
great Cornish Bishop, of whom the county is so proud. So they ask him to
forgive them, and Bishop Grandisson in full state rides over to Burian, and
gives them a good sermon on the text, "Ye were as sheep going astray, but
are now returned to the shepherd and Bishop of your souls," and forgives
them their rebellion.

But this is not all, S. Paul Church was also consecrated ; and Ludgvan also.

Why were there so many churches to consecrate that July? Had there been
a building enthusiasm, or had the Bishops of Exeter objected to the long
journey to West Penwith, and so left heavy arrears of work? The latter I
think more likely.

On August 15th, Dean Medinta had to give in and make his peace at Clyst
in Devonshire, so Bishop Grandisson got the best of it.

There was one Dean of Burian during the Reformation struggle of Henry
VIII and Edward VI, and he probably was a courtly temporiser, Dr. Bagh,
who must have been the Dean of Leland's time. He got a pension of £25
per annum (a much larger sum, it is needless to say, then than now), at the
suppression in 1553. Thus ended the Pre-reformation history of Burian
Deanery.

Besides the Dean, there seems to have been three Prebends at Burian, Tre-
thyny, and Respewell, with a minor stall. At the Reformation, there were
four clergymen on the staff, besides the Dean.

It is probable that the Deanery-house and the Canons' residences formed
a kind of square at Burian around the open space, of which the present outer
cross was the centre. A sort of cathedral close would thus be formed. On
Sundays and great festivals, probably, "Burian Churchtown" has been the scene
of many a bright *cortége* of knights and ladies coming from the surrounding

ing country to join at the quasi-cathedral service of the collegiate church.* To modern minds, the rich endowment of such a remote spot might seem a waste of power, and practically the Deanery of Burian generally, in ancient and modern times, seems to have been a source of scandal, until in an age of Church reform like this, it, some 10 years ago, was "reformed off the face of the earth." And still it need not have been a scandal, nor, we hope, always was so. The idea of a church, with all appointments and full means, where, day by day in full dignity the song of prayer and praise should rise, some few miles from nature's most glorious spectacles, Treryn, Tol-pedn-Penwith, and the Land's End, has in it a something poetical; and the idea is not less striking if we suppose (as our ancestors certainly did and, I think, rightly) that the last struggle between the Saxon and the Cornu-Briton was fought out on that very spot.

A Gradgrind would not see the motive of Burian; a Tennyson or a Neale would probably admire it. Let us hope Burian has still bright days before it and its restored church, although its mediæval glories cannot be restored.

---

* During the Wars of the Roses, Buryan was for a time, it seems, separated from direct crown patronage. Under Henry VI. being annexed to King's College, Cambridge, and by Edward IV. being attached to the Collegiate Church at Windsor.

Chapter III.

PENZANCE, NEWLYN, AND MOUSEHOLE DURING THE MIDDLE AGES.

"Whatever Market-jew pretends,
Upon some musty old record,
For noblest hearts and truest friends
Penzance shall ever have my word;
No little town of like account,
On this side or beyond the Mount."
FREEMAN (A.D. 1614).

HE early history of a town is always difficult to trace, and especially when, as in the case of Penzance, it has more than one name, or rather has sprung, as is usually supposed, from a congeries of some four little hamlets, which have coalesced in modern times, *i.e.* Alverton, Burriton, S. Clare and Chyandour.

The name Burriton is supposed to refer to a fortified place, but the little fort near the headland may cover this meaning, and not the old baronial "Iron" castle. Some think, like Mr. Courtenay, that Lescudjack may have been the fort.

Of Castle Horneck, the old castle of the lords of Penzance, an edifice peculiarly interesting therefore to all Penzance people, two vestiges are believed to remain. The one is a thick wall built into the back part of the present Castle Horneck House, the mansion of the Borlase family; the other is the locally famous rude archway at Trewoofe, supposed by some antiquaries to have once belonged to Castle Horneck It is very rudely carved in granite, and has been figured by Mr. Blight in his "The Land's End District."

It is curious as the oldest specimen of work from a West Penwith mansion extant.

Richard, Earl of Cornwall, King of the Romans, seems to have been succeeded in Alverton Manor, by Terric le Tyes, who thus obtained the Manor for his family, and was succeeded again by his nephew Waleran. Mr. Millet reminds us of the interesting fact of how the elsewhere rare name of Sybylla, the lady of Alverton Manor, and wife of Waleran le Tyes, long remained frequent in the parish of Madron, as witnessed by the Parish Registers. Three Henry le Tyes held the manor, the second of whom was first Baron Tyes, the last was beheaded in 1321, as a rebel. His sister Alice succeeded him.

It would seem that about 1284, Sir Henry le Tyes, Lord of Alverton, founded a chantry to S. Mary (query, is it hence that we get the original name of St. Mary's Church, Penzance), at a distance from the parish church of two miles and a half (one must not be too particular about measurements in old records), and gave it an endowment of £4 out of his Alverton Manor.

The first thing of importance about Penzance, the foundation of its future prosperity, is its market. Naturally, Penzance is designed for the chief market of West Penwith. Its position is fairly central, it is easily approachable, not hemmed in by hills as Mousehole, nor perched on a table-land as Burian, nor placed in a corner like S. Ives. Fishing and the market are the sources of the early prosperity of Penzance. As the records of the borough in the seventeenth and eighteenth centuries to a great extent relate to the markets and pier, so in the earlier times we find the market a leading feature in Penzance's meagre annals.

Markets in olden times were royal prerogatives, and granted by kings. Penzance or rather "Alverton Market" was granted by Edward III, in 1332, to Lady Alice de l'Isle, wife of Warren de l'Isle, sister of Lord Tyes (who as we have seen was beheaded for rebellion), whom Penzance people may remember as the foundress of their town. The market day was Wednesday, now it is Thursday. A fair of seven days was also granted at the feast of S. Peter (June 29). This is the first appearance of Penzance in authentic history. The merry-making at Peter-tide is a vestige of this old fair.

In 1404 Henry IV renewed the grant of the market to Thomas Lord Berkeley, husband of Alice de l'Isle's great grand-daughter, who was heir of Alverton, through his marriage with the de l'Isles. Three fairs of two days each were granted. The produce, therefore, of West Penwith to a great extent must have collected into Penzance market, which seems before the early part of the next century to have quite absorbed the business of Burian and Mousehole markets, so that Leland on his visit in 1538 does not refer to their ever having existed.

The early history of Penzance in some points reminds one of the rise of Brighton, its more successful fellow watering-place. Nature has done far more for Penzance, but proximity to London has been the making of Brighton. Both watering-places during the middle ages were mere collections of poor fishermen's cottages; in Penzance probably a very small and humble collection close to the promontory, which some affirm gave its name to the present town. In the centre of these huts, at the end of the fourteenth century, stood S. Mary's chapel, which Bishop Edmund Stafford licensed in 1397, some sixty years after the market was founded, and probably on the site of S. Mary's chantry. It would seem that, like Mousehole and Newlyn, the village rapidly increased, for in 1429 another chapel was built and licensed by Bishop Edward Lacy, possibly near the end of Barbican lane. This chapel, in the license, is dedicated to "SS. Gabriel and Raphael the archangels." It would seem that in S. Mary's chapel at least, the men and women were accustomed to sit apart, until 1674.

There was, besides these, a third chapel, S. Clare's, at the top of St. Clare street, in the north of the town, or rather to the north of it, for it is not likely to have extended so far inland. It stood near the high-road between Madron and Penzance, but is now destroyed.

As Mr. Millet says "Not a trace of this chapel now remains above ground, though its foundations were to be seen as lately as the latter part of the last century, in a field used as an archery and cricket ground, occupying the most elevated site within the borough, and probably some remains of them are still beneath the sod. They stood at the south-west corner of the field which adjoins the highroad between Penzance and Madron, and were near the borough stone."

Penzance must have had a humble sort of pier during the latter part of the middle ages, for although it may not be mentioned at an early date, Leland speaks in his time of "a forced pere or key" there but "no socur for botes or shyppes."

Of the three mediæval chapels at Penzance it would seem that Leland noticed only one (S. Mary's). Whether he accidentally passed over the other two, or whether they were disused in his time is not certain. The latter is the more probable conjecture.

Davies Gilbert briefly sums up the mediæval aspect of Penzance as "a small village occupying the promontory now dedicated to S. Anthony (?), the patron of fishermen, which in all probability (?) gave it the name of Pen-zance, or the holy headland, and it seems further that the new church or chapel-yard may have been an ancient fortress for the protection of the place," (v. III, p. 71). On this point Mr. Courtenay says, "If it ever existed this last named is the most probable situation, as it commanded the whole of the town, and was consequently the best adapted for its protection. We have at this day the Barbican and Barbican Lane in the neighbourhood, but whether they have reference to the present battery (which, however, we think is far too modern to have given such a name) or the fort in question cannot be deter-mined." (Guide to Penzance, p. 6, note).

The mediæval memories of Penzance must have been intimately connected with the Crusades. As patrons of Madron church, the Knights Hospitallers must have been often spoken of and often seen by the old fishermen of ancient Penzance. The dark martial cloak and the white cross of the Knight of S. John must frequently have been seen along the rude bridle-paths round old Madron Church, at the gates of Landithy, and at "the Holy Head," where S. Anthony's chapel was a marked object among the low huts of the Penzance fishers.

Now it was to this military order that Henry Pomeroy made over the pat-ronage of Madron. King John seems to have disputed the bequest. An enquiry was instituted in 1206. A jury of twelve Madron men was sworn in,

K

to enquire into the case of the advowson of the church "*Sancti Maderi de Runeri.*" The Knights of S. John gained their cause, but parson Thomas de Chimelly then rector of Madron, by the nomination of the crown, was allowed to retain his benefice.

The Knights do not seem to have appropriated the benefice to their house of S. John's, Clerkenwell, till 1278, when John de Metingham was nominated vicar "to the church of Saint Madern in Cornwall at the presentation of brother Joseph de Chaucey, Prior of the Hospital of Jerusalem, in England." Metingham's successor was Arthur Tyntagel who was probably the rebuilder of the church and vicar at the time of Bishop Grandisson's consecrating of it. Arthur Tyntagel's predecessors had to provide lodging for the prior or brethren, or procurator of St. John at Jerusalem, but Arthur agreed with them to yield a portion of his glebe.

The vicars of Madron do not seem to have, at this period, often died at their post, possibly it was looked on as a step to higher preferment. William of York in 1344 exchanged Madron for Redruth; Stephen Reswalstes, only 5 years after, resigned Madron; so did the next vicar, Ralph Boskastel, in 1363. This looks suspicious, as if Madron was not considered by the "parsons" of the period as a very favoured spot.

Of Ralph Redon, the next vicar, whom Prior Paveley nominated, we know nothing, but John Miledert, his successor, died at his post, so may Lawrence Trewythgy (a decidedly Cornish name). Under Lawrence Trewythgy S. Mary's chapel, Penzance, was rebuilt and enlarged in 1367. Again, the two next vicars, John Burdet and Richard Acton, seem to have been glad to leave Madron. The latter got the London church of S. Matthews's, Friday street.

From this time (1430) till the Reformation the vicars of Madron, *i.e.* Ralph Drew, Robert Pascho (Pasco), Benedict Trengoff (Trengove), John Jackes, seem to have died at Madron. Thomas Mabiston was the last appointed by the prior in 1536. He resigned for a pension of £16 13s. 4d. John Landre succeeded him by private patronage. The next vicar, Edmund Pouter, was a nominee of Queen Elizabeth. Thus the Knights Hospitallers yielded up Madron, and practically died in England, though still a Masonic order retains nominally their title.

The Madron Church which was consecrated by Bishop Grandisson, in 1336, was not the present Church, nor the only one. It would seem as if Madron had been three or four times partially rebuilt. At the last visit of the British Archæological Congress, the remains of no less than three distinct Churches were traced in a small piece of wall at the east end of the Church. The present Church is later pointed, probably of the end of the fifteenth century, built soon before the Reformation.

NEWLYN.

If William of Worcester had been asked which of the four towns on the shores of Mount's Bay, *i.e.* Penzance, Marazion, Newlyn, or Mousehole was likely to be the chief, he would possibly as soon have answered Newlyn as any other. His remarks on Gwavas lake, put in modern English are " The chief road of the bay for seamen that come this way is called Gooveslake (Gwavas-lake.)" Again Leland says, " In the bay to the east of the same town (Mouse-hole) is a good road for ships called Guaves Lake." Again, " A bay from Newlin *(sic)* to Mousehole called Guaver Lake." Polwhele says, " Here is the greatest depth of water throughout the whole bay, and the gun boat which is now (1804) stationed to guard the bay lies here ; while the general depth from Penzance to the Mount upon an ebb tide is only 6 fathoms at high water. But the fishery in this part of the sea was given to the Church of the parish of Paul, a church here standing high upon the hills, and a parish extending along the sea from the north of Newlyn to the south of Mousehole ; went at the appropriation of the rectory to the abbey of Hayle in Gloucestershire ; and was very valuable." It would therefore seem that at Gwavas lake most of the vessels lay in the middle ages, and along the shores of the lake in its inmost part by degrees the cottages of the fishermen clustered into the town of Newlyn.

In the reign of King Edward the Confessor, as we have seen, Alverton estate, which then included Tolcarn, Newlyn Town, and Street-an-Nowan, or rather the sites on which the houses are now built, belonged to Alward, probably a Saxon thane, who obtained possession of the estate after king Athelstan's conquest. From him it is supposed by some (the derivation is greatly disputed) that Alverton in Penzance is called.

After the Norman Conquest William the Conqueror transferred the lordship of Alverton manor to the Earl of Moreton. It then had 11 bond servants, 35 "villains," and 20 borderers.

The lords of Newlyn and Penzance lived then at Castle Horneck, the Iron Castle, in the Middle Ages a fortified place, the chief baronial castle of the Land's End district. Two markets were held by the Lords of Castle Horneck, one on each side of Newlyn, *i.e.* at Mousehole and Penzance, at least in the later Plantagenet period.

Newlyn was till 1848 a part of S. Paul parish. Thus its mediæval history, like that of most Cornish towns, is connected with the famous Richard King of the Romans, who made over the rectorial tithes, as we have seen, to his celebrated Abbey of Hales, which held them until the reformation. Richard was Lord of Alverton as we have seen, and therefore of Newlyn, *i.e.* if any village existed here in Henry III's reign. It is not improbable that the foundation of the little "fisher town," as Carew calls it, was not unconnected with the Abbot of Hales, who was especially interested, by his fish tithes, in the finny denizens of Mount's Bay.

The first debût of Newlyn as a township on the field of history was in 1435, a generation before Penzance or Pensants (as such, not as Buriton or Alverton) makes its public appearance on historical record. The importance of a little harbour of refuge in Mount's Bay was felt then as now. The storms raged with as great fury doubtless in the fifteenth as in this our nineteenth century. The smacks of the fishers and the ships of the merchants needed somewhere to flee to when caught by a gale on the rock-bound Cornish coast. What part of Mount's Bay would be so suitable for a place of refuge as the inner part of Gwavas-lake, sheltered on the west and south-west (the prevailing winds) by the high hills of S. Paul, and on the north by the ranges of the Madron highlands? But who should undertake the enterprise? Then as now capital does not seem to have abounded at Newlyn. Joint stock companies had not yet come into fashion, and "Limited Liability" was not dreamt of. How should the Newlyn fishermen get their pier, and how maintain it when got? was a question in the early part of the fifteenth as it is now in the last quarter of the nineteenth century.

The way was characteristic of the period. In the Middle Ages there were two great powers ruling society, the Church and the State. If the State would not help an enterprise the Church might. Now it does not seem that the State did care at all about Newlyn pier, so the fishermen had to turn to the Church. How they pleaded their cause history does not record (but probably the vicar of S. Paul did the part of an intermediary for them), in any case they somehow managed in 1435 to interest Edmund Lacy, then Bishop of Exeter, in their cause, at the same time as the Mousehole question was taken up. An episcopal pastoral was issued. The money was raised it seems, and the pier built. Contributions were procured "towards the repairing and maintaining of a certain key or jetty at Newlyn in the parish of Paul." Whether there had been a pier before is uncertain. At any rate the Newlyn pier question is 440 years old.

Of old Newlyn, *i.e.* the Newlyn of the Middle Ages, probably nothing remains except the foundations of the houses. We have in Newlyn Town dwelling-houses of the seventeenth century, but probably none anterior to the burning by the Spaniards in 1595. The old chapel of which Leland speaks, and which was probably mediæval, has disappeared, and its very existence not to say its site, is forgotten. There are records of three chapels in Paul parish, connected apparently with Mousehole, S. Mary, S. Edmund, and S. Francis.

One of them might have been the lost Newlyn Chapel. Newlyn is treated as a suburb of Mousehole. "Newlin *(sic)* is an hamlet to Mousehole." Now perhaps visitors regard it rather a suburb of Penzance. "A bay from Newlin *(sic)* to Mousehole caullid *(sic,* no spelling bees in those days) Guaverslake (Gwavaslake)."

MOUSEHOLE.

Unimportant though the little fishing town of Mousehole now may appear, with a population not half that of Newlyn, and hardly a sixth of Penzance, these was a time when it promised to be the chief town of the Land's End district, and perhaps when it really rivalled any other place in West Penwith in prosperity and wealth.

Its Anglicanized name of Mousehole was probably a mere corruption of an earlier Celtic form, though it was also commonly known among the old Cornish by the descriptive term of Port Ennis or the Port of the Island (referring to S. Clement's Island close to it). The fanciful derivation of Mousehole in quaint satire on the large cave close by, does not hold good with the old spelling in 1414 of Mosal, or of Mose hole in the charter of Ed. I. Some suggest "maid's river," others "sheep moor" as its derivations, but the safest conclusion is to say the subject is obscure.

A market, as it appears, was granted by Edward I in 1292 (the year after the great taxation, so memorable in the history of West Penwith parishes) to Henry Lord Tyes, the then owner of Alverton, a manor which in those days included the country where Penzance, Newlyn, and Mousehole now stand, though it is not very clear that any of those towns except Portennis as yet existed. This market was to be held on Thursdays, and must have been the westernmost in England, as S. Just was not yet established, nor for the matter of that of Penzance either, which it seems had not a market till 1332, *i.e.* 40 years after. The Port-Ennis market and fair was probably the commercial centre of West Penwith, under the later Plantagenets (or the house of Anjou as it is now the fashion to call them).

Port Ennis market was renewed by Edward II to Alice de L'Isle (Lord Tyes' sister) in 1313. A grand fair of seven days at S. Bartholomew tide (August 24) was also granted to the town.

The religious wants of the inhabitants were not neglected. S. Paul's church being considered too far, S. Mary's chapel was erected for their convenience, under the later Plantagenets; the exact date is uncertain. This chapel was built, it seems, too near the sea and was demolished in a storm. Hence the appeal of Bishop Stafford in 1414, "As the chapel of Mosal, formerly built in honor of the Blessed Virgin, and situated near a port or creek of the sea, is now by the force of the sea entirely thrown down and demolished; which while it stood was a mark to the seamen, and which, if re-built, might still be the means of the preservation of many sailing into this port or creek of the sea, and as the revenues of the said chapel are by no means sufficient. " . . .

A quay must have been established some time before, for we read in 1435 that Bishop Lacy offered (a quaint mode of carrying out commercial enterprize) a 40 days' indulgence to those who would repair and maintain it.

Towards the end of the middle ages it would seem that Mousehole was, with Marazion, the chief town on Mount's Bay. Probably the trade was more varied then than now. Land-carriage was difficult, so all the comforts and luxuries the Penwith people needed would be brought to these towns in ships, which returned laden with tin to the ports from which they came. However, old Mousehole has passed away, and only one house (and that of the Tudor period) remains.

The idea, I will not call it a tradition, that there are traces of Spanish descent in the aspect and names of some of the families of the fishermen of Mount's Bay, is worthy of consideration. *Per se* there is nothing improbable in the idea of Spaniards settling here. This is the nearest part of England to Spain. In Mount's Bay Medina Sidonia arranged that the "Invincible Armada" should reassemble in case of being scattered by a storm before reaching the English coast. Even to this day, not a few of our fishermen can talk of their adventures in Spain, and of what they have seen there, of the Carlist wars and of its ravages. But history does not speak of any Spanish settlement, or of a wholesale migration of Spaniards. Nor, in all probability, was there ever any such. Spain has seen many wars, and many persecutions, and many deeds of wrong which might well drive Spanish families across the Pyrenees into France, or, if that were impracticable, across the Bay of Biscay to Cornwall. The Spanish refugees would have found less attractions in the mining districts of the Cornish hills than in the agricultural and fishing regions of the coast, where they might well have settled. It has been suggested that possibly the Moors of Spain, great dealers in metals, may have traded to

Cornwall, and in a few cases have married and settled here, which may partly, though I think very insufficiently, account for the legend of the Jews in Cornwall, and for the Oriental, almost "Arabian Nights," type of some of our Cornish Drolls. Be it as it may, I am inclined to think that many of our fishermen, could they prove their lineage step by step as our old nobility can, would find that from Christiania in the North to Cadiz on the South, from the "Red-haired Danes" or Vikings to the "Spanish Dons," as well as from the old Cornish, comes their mingled race, the Iberian and the Basque mixing with the Dane and the Norseman, the Celt and the Saxon. Mixed races are often conquering races. The English, the Prussian, and the Yankee, are very mixed races, so the Mount's Bay people should not despise the idea of being of a mixed race.

THE RISE OF ST. IVES.

The early history of St. Ives, like that of most towns, is obscure. It makes its debut on the records of the past, however, before Penzance. There is a legend that once Pendinas was a tidal island like St. Michael's Mount, but in historic times became connected with the mainland by the influx of the sands. Even if this were true (which it cannot well be proved to be) it would not constitute any claim for Pendinas to be Ictis, since it is all but certain that the Phœnicians did not trade for tin on the north coast of Cornwall, with those dreadfully dangerous Penwith promontories to get round. S. Hya, or Ia, the Irish virgin saint, may have landed here. Legend relates that she died at Hayle.

Trenwith belonged in Edward the Confessor's day to Sitric, Abbot of Tavistock. The Earl of Cornwall got possession of it after the Conquest.

Hals says S. Ives was part of Luduham, or Ludgvan Manor.

We do not read much of St. Ives parish during the Plantagenet period. There was a Thomas Baillie who lived at Tregenna in 1371, whose son called himself Trenwith, but this does not speak for the town. It probably was merely a few fishermen's rude huts close to the sea. These huts, however, as time advanced, grew more and more numerous under the Plantagenets. It is not as much as mentioned in the taxation of 1294.

The first appearance of St. Ives as a town (and then probably a very humble one) was in the reign of King Henry IV, when "As it had pleased Almighty God to increase the town inhabitants, and to send down temporal blessings most plentifully among them, the people to shew their thankfulness for the same, did resolve to build a chapel at S. Ives," as the borough records declare. The wording of this statement would lead one to suppose that the increase of the town was very recent, possibly towards the end of the prosperous reign of Edward III. In 1408, appreciating the inconvenience of having to go to Lelant Church for divine service, baptisms, churchings, and funerals, the St. Ives people petitioned Lord Champernowne Lord of St. Ives to obtain a license for their proposed chapel. The license was obtained in 1410. The Church was not, however, consecrated until 1428, in the reign of Henry VI, by Bishop Lacy, a prelate, who seems to have taken some interest in Cornish fishing towns, for as we see, both Mousehole and Newlyn were indebted to him for their piers. The Church must thus have been many years in building, probably from difficulty about funds. When they had got their Church the S. Ives people aspired further—to get a market. Till then, they had to go to Lelant to do their marketing. Lelant market was very ancient, one of the oldest in West Penwith, dating from the reign of Edward I, 1295, and was held every Thursday. But S. Ives was resolved to have a market of its own. In 1487, Sir Robert Willoughby afterwards Lord de Broke having inherited S. Ives manor by right of his wife, the heiress of Lord Champernowne, obtained a charter in 1488 for the town to have a market on Saturdays, from Henry VII, as well as two annual fairs. A market house was built in 1490 (it remained till 1832, when the present one was built) and Lord Broke erected a fort for the protection of the town, which he armed with cannon.

St. Ives in the period of the Wars of the Roses may have had many aristocratic visitors. Part of the parish, *i.e.* Trenwith, then belonged to the Beauforts. John de Beaufort, son of John of Gaunt and brother of Henry IV, owned it. If he attended to business, possibly he may have visited S. Ives. The

L

Beauforts held it until Edmund Beaufort Earl of Somerset was attainted in 1471, by Edward IV, the Yorkist sovereign, and beheaded.

The S. Ives people seem to have been very good at church-building during the middle ages. Not satisfied with building their parish church, they erected no less than four chapels in their town and parish. (1) S. Leonard's chapel was close to the old quay. Here prayers were said for the fishermen before they went to sea. (2) S. Nicholas Chapel, of which there also are remains on the top of Pendinas Point. (3) Higher Tregenna Chapel. (4) Brunian Chapel.

In the reign of Mary I, *i.e.* 1558, S. Ives was promoted, as we shall see, to a borough, sending Members to Parliament. It still retains the privilege, and is the sole borough with Lelant, returning a representative of the House of Commons in Penwith.

> " If any discord 'twixt my friends arise
> With the borough of beloved S. Ives,
> It is desyred that this my cup of love
> To everyone a peacemaker may prove :
> Then I am blest to have given a legacie,
> So like my harte into posteritie.
>   *Francis Basset* (A.D. 1640,)

Chapter IV.

MEDIÆVAL HISTORY OF S. MICHAEL'S MOUNT.

"Who knows not Migell's Mount and chair,
　　The pilgrims' holy vaunt;
　Both land and island twice a day,
　　Both fort and port of haunt."—CAREW.

"Seven days I drove along the dreary deep,
　And with me drove the moon, and all the stars;
　And the wind fell, and on the seventh night
　I heard the shingle grinding in the surge,
　And felt the boat shock earth, and looking up,
　Behold, the enchanted towers of Carboneh—
　A castle like a rock upon a rock,
　With chasm portals open to the sea;
　And steps that met the breaker."—TENNYSON.

HE early history of S. Michael's Mount, like the early history of most other places, is linked with much of legend and tradition. The story of Iktis, in Diodorus Siculus, has been already considered. Some hint that the Mount was in olden times dedicated to the Sun. Perhaps so, it was a place well suited to the naturalism of the of the old Celtic worship. In the Landaff Book the Mount is called Dinsull, the Castle of the Sun, or perhaps merely High Hill. But who knows? Derivations are very vague. Christian legends then supersede heathen myths The apparition of S. Michael the Archangel hardly belongs to the pages of XIX century history. The date of the apparition of S. Michael is given as A.D. 495. There is a similar legend of an apparition at Mount Garganus and at Mont S. Michel, in Normandy.

S. Keyne, legend saith, was one of the first who made a pilgrimage here at the end of the fifth century. This saintly princess, with the characteristic zeal for her sex of a strong minded lady of the period, bestowed a blessing on any lady who should sit on the famed Kader Mighel, before her husband, similar to the charm of S. Keynes well, in east Cornwall.

> " If the wife should drink of it first,
> God help the husband then!"

So S. Keyne was a zealous champion of woman's rights in the good old times.

S. Cadoc, her nephew, made a pilgrimage here soon after, and found his aunt here. In spite of her strong mindedness she was persuaded to return with him to Wales.

It appears that the Church and Benedictine Monastery of S. Michael's Mount were erected and endowed by our great Saxon king, Edward the Confessor.

The charter of the Mount is as follows (translated from the Latin) :—

"In the name of the Holy and Indivisible Trinity, I, Edward, by the grace of God' king of the English . . . . have delivered to S. Michael the Archangel for the use of the brethren serving God in that place, Saint Michael, which is near the sea (*Sanctum Michaelum qui est juxta mare*) with all its appendages, that is to say, with its towns, castles, lands, and other appurtenances." To these the king adds the grants of Vennefire, and the harbour of Ruminella, with fisheries. "And that the authority of our donation may be held the more truly and firmly hereafter, I have, by confirming it, underwritten with my own hand, which many also of the witnesses have done."

Signed   REGIS EDWARDI ✠.

The witnesses are the signs of " Roberti Archiepiscopi Rothomagensis, Herberti Episcopi Lexoviensis, Roberti Episcopi Constantiensis," and three others.

This charter of king Edward was renewed and amplified after the Conquest by Robert Earl of Moreton, whom William I. made Earl of Cornwall, but at the same time he made over the rule of S. Michael's Mount to the Norman monastery, the church and monastery "Sancti Michaelis in Periculo Maris," *i.e.* Mont St. Michel, near Avranches, in Normandy, so strikingly similar in position to the Cornish "Mount," that it has in legend been confused with it.

At the Norman Conquest the priory had two hides of land, but the Earl of Moreton disposessed it of part of this.

In 1085, Leofric, the then Bishop of Exeter, formally granted a charter to free the "ecclesiam Beati Michaelis, Archangeli de Cornubiâ"—(the Church of the Blessed Michael the Archangel of Cornwall), from episcopal jurisdiction.

In 1135, William Warlwast, Bishop of Exeter, with the assistance of Bernard, Abbot of Mont S. Michel,* in Normandy (the real superior of the Cornish S. Michael's Mount), solemnly consecrated the church. Thirteen monks were established there. It seems that a nunnery was also founded on the island, as we shall presently see, though the particulars of the foundation are not clear. The Cornish prior was bound annually to visit Mont S. Michel as a token of obedience, and pay a tribute of 16 marks.

In 1155, Adrian IV. confirmed to S. Michael's Mount all its possessions.

Among the most recently discovered facts about S. Michael's Mount is the Charter of the reign of Henry II., found by J. Rogers, Esq., among the title deeds of Penrose.

This charter probably refers to S. Michael's Mount in Normandy, and not to the Mount in Cornwall.

But let us proceed from these dry details to one of the Romances of History.

The second capture of S. Michael's Mount is an episode of the wars of the Roses, one of the few cases in which that dread tempest of destructive civil war touched West Penwith. The story, if we may trust its mediæval narrators, is a romance of history, more like a story of Sir Walter Scott's novels, than a serious record of historic fact. As if the narrative itself were not enough, Cornish legend has brought in the supernatural into the story which we may introduce, though to be taken *cum grano.*

Sir Guy Saint Aubyn married Alice, daughter of Sir Richard Serjeaux, a knight, of Colquite, in the parish of S. Mabyn. Sir Guy Saint Aubyn died not very long after his marriage, and the dashing widow was wooed and won by Richard deVere, the eleventh Earl of Oxford, the representative of one of the noblest houses of mediæval England.† Persuaded, either by her husband, or by affection for her children by the second marriage, she was induced to make

---

* A curious history of "Mont S. Michel" in Normandy is written in French by the Abbé,

† For an account of the De Veres see Macaulay's History of England, vol.

over the property of Sir Guy Saint Aubyn from his child to her second husband, the Earl, and to his sons. A blessing, as Cornishmen would perhaps say, did not rest on these young men. The illgotten wealth seemed to bring a curse.

The eleventh earl, Richard, dying, his eldest son succeeded him as Earl of Oxford, but died a traitors' death with his son Aubrey, in 1462 (after the battle of Towton). John de Vere, his second son, succeeded (as thirteenth earl) to the title, with its responsibilities and its perils. Like his brothers, he warmly took up the Lancastrian side, *i.e.* that of King Henry VI.

The story of 1471 is probably familiar to my readers. How Edward IV. (just before this a fugitive in Holland) landed with an army at Ravenspur, (where Henry IV. formerly landed); how he advanced to York, and after a series of successful military operations, met the Lancastrians, commanded by the Earls of Warwick and Oxford, on Easter Eve, at Barnet. There was fought in a dense fog one of the fiercest battles of mediæval England. The brave Warwick fell, and De Vere, whose badge of "a sun with rays," was very like king Edward's, unluckily was mistaken for him by the Lancastrians in the fog. De Vere, seeing the battle was lost, fled, and after a series of adventures, took ship at Milford Haven and sailed for Cornwall, with a few resolute retainers; he landed in Mount's Bay in disguise. Remembering, probably, the story of Henry de la Pomeroy, he resolved with his comrades on a penitential pilgrimage to S. Michael's Mount. The pilgrims say that they have come from a distant part of the kingdom to perform a penance at the Archangel's Mount. The monks welcome them into the Abbey fortress. Did they forget Henry de la Pomeroy, or were they in the secret? Each of yon pilgrims conceals beneath his cloak a sword and a dagger. In a moment, at a signal the cry of the Red-Rose of Lancaster is raised, and their swords flash forth with the threat to slay all who resist King Henry the VI.

The little garrison surprised, cannot resist. The monks make a virtue of necessity. The Lancastrians master S. Michael's Mount and solemnly take possession of it in the name of King Henry the Sixth. John de Vere has succeeded in his project.

But the day of retribution comes. Swift over the Cornish moors ride messengers to King Edward the Fourth. A proclamation is issued declaring John de Vere and his followers traitors. The king orders Sir John Arundell, his Sheriff of Cornwall, to arm his *posse comitatus* and besiege the Mount. Sir John at this time resides at Trerice. Legend says once on a time he had lived at Efford, near the sands, but had moved from thence to Trerice, because of an evil prophecy which a man whom he had imprisoned had uttered :—

> " When upon the yellow sand,
> Thou shalt die by human hand."

Sir John perhaps forgets the warning, or dares not disobey king Edward. In spite of his precautions, he raises the forces of Cornwall and marches towards Marazion. He encamps near the sea, and sends a herald to the Earl of Oxford, with a summons to surrender to King Edward IV. (the Yorkist sovereign). The Earl of Oxford refuses point blank to do anything of the kind, nay that he would die sooner than yield. Sir John orders his troops (who now amount to a respectable little army) to storm the fortress. They try it, but fail, defeated at every point. They have a trained general to deal with in John de Vere. He uses his advantage. He does not wait for a second storm, but makes a sally. The raw recruits of the Cornish moors and vales, the rough tinners and peasants prove but sorry opponents to the veteran Lancastrian soldiery, seasoned in a score of hard fought fights. They yield to the trained troops, in spite of their numerical advantage. Sir John Arundell is slain in the melée, and dies on the sands, at the foot of the Mount. The prophecy is fulfilled.

Edward IV. hearing of this repulse to his troops, nominates John Fortescue, Sheriff of Cornwall. The siege is renewed, but for a long time with the same result. The Cornish militiamen cannot storm that rocky fortress, nor drive from it the veteran Lancastrian soldiers. King Edward is angry. He accuses the Cornish of being more Lancastrians than Yorkists, and calls the county of Cornwall "the back door of rebellion." Force being in vain, Edward at length thinks of conciliation ; he agrees to pardon the earl if he surrenders the fortress. As elsewhere the Lancastrian cause looked hopeless, De Vere accepts these terms. He receives a free pardon, and yields the Mount to Fortescue. The earl is sent a prisoner to Ham (though he had been promised liberty by the king).

Days of prosperity, however, come for brave John de Vere. In 1485 he joins the Earl of Richmond in his invasion of England, and witnesses the final triumph of his party at Bosworth field, and the coronation of the Tudor King Henry VII. He is a favorite of the new monarch, and becomes sponsor at the font to Henry VIII.

The Mount, however, soon after receives another visitor, equally famous, but a far less dangerous personage.

The father of Cornish tourists—a long list, among whom Dean Alford and Messrs. William White, Wilkie Collins, Alphonse Esquiros, are later representatives—was William Bottoner, *alias* William of Worcester, a quaint and eccentric old English gentleman who lived, so to speak, ahead of his times, and who seems to have anticipated the days when thousands of his countrymen should for pleasure sake run over the civilized world, and when they see anything to strike them, "rush into print," communicating their adventures and observations to the public. Such English gentlemen were very rare in those days. Travel was much less agreeable than now, and not nearly so safe (in spite of all our complaints about railway accidents), and the period after the wars of the roses, when at last Edward IV. settled " by right of might " on his undisputed throne, would not appear to be especially favorable to tourists. However, William had a penchant for travelling, and among other places was bold enough to ride over into Cornwall.

As a literary production, William of Worcester's Itinerary contrasts very unfavorably with later writings on the same subject. Dean Alford, or Elihu Burritt's works certainly show a decided progress on the travel writing of the fifteenth century ; and, so even does Leland, who if dry and concise, is still fairly lucid, and tells us a good deal worth knowing. Had William Bottoner dreamt of the value his book would have in future ages, he probably would have told us much more, but he was perhaps the first of English tourists who wrote their tours, so he had no experience to guide him, and thus the Itinerary, written in somewhat canine Latin, is very confused, and provokingly meagre.

After a short description of the Scilly Isles (from hearsay, for he never visited them), and other matters, he describes S. Michael's Mount more at length. He says it was formerly called the "*Hore-rok in the wodd*," and there was there wood with meadow and arable land between the Mount and Scilly (?) and there were 140 churches submerged (!) between that Mount and Scilly. S. Michael's Mount was in those days, he says, six miles from the sea. Of this legend we speak elsewhere. He gives some curious quotation from the Mount's records. He tells us then the Church of S. Michael's Mount is 30 *steppys* (paces) in length, 12 in breadth, and the new chapel 20 by 10 *steppys.* The Isle of S. Michael's Mount is about one mile in circuit, and is about an arrow's shot distant from *terra firma.*

"Mðuntes Bay," we are informed in English, in a special *memorandum,* " lyeth froe le setre yn the est party to the poynte of Mousehole yn the west partye : and the chef rode of the bay for see men that comyth thes way ys the Gooveslake cum a yense neekly." So even William of Worcester saw that Gwavas Lake was the best part of Mount's Bay for sheltering small vessels.

Such is the jejeune account of the first English traveller who gave an account of his journey to these parts to the literary world. It is very meagre, and the aggravating part is that it nearly all relates to matters in which there could be no change during these four centuries. The towns could not have gone away from each other. Even the distances are not accurate, and must have been gained mostly from hearsay from the monks and pilgrims at S. Michael's Mount, or perchance from Robert Bracey. However, the attempt was honest to inform his readers of what the places in Cornwall were, and William of Worcester was far more truthful than many a modern book-maker.

Besides William's, there is also the Itinerary, or rather as it is styled the " Viagium " of Thomas Clerk, of Ware, who rode from Ware (A.D. 1476) to S. Michael's Mount, in 10 days, and back again in 10 days. This, however, is a mere list of names.

But we have to introduce a third visitor to our readers.

It is an August day, 1496. The air is blowing warm over West Penwith. Strange rumours of discontent have been floating through West Cornwall. The new Tudor king does not quite please the people. Perhaps they remember prosperity under the Yorkish dynasty. Cornishmen do not generally

M

like sudden changes, and that change at Bosworth field, whereby Henry Tudor, Earl of Richmond, becomes King of England, and the old Yorkist dynasty disappears, is not altogether to public taste. Some say King Richard III., for so many years Sheriff of Cornwall (as we have seen), has made the way clear for the Lancastrian party by exterminating the royal race, but there are many people who are not so sure of that.

Taxation has oppressed the Cornish people. The little love they had felt for "Henry Tydder" as he is called, grows less still, when they feel the weight of his taxes. There has been a rebellion at Bodmin, felt more or less throughout the county. Flammock, an attorney, and Joseph the farrier, have roused the Cornishmen against the king. Sixteen thousand have taken arms against Henry VII. The Cornish army has marched through Salisbury and Winchester, into Kent, and has encamped at Blackheath. The Cornish bowmen fought nobly at Deptford Strand, but the artillery overwhelmed them. Two thousand were slain, fifteen hundred taken prisoners. Flammock and Joseph were hung. " Order reigned in Cornwall."

Four ships appear in the offing, coming from the north-west. They draw nearer to the Land's End. They are war ships it is evident. Landing is effected by the soldiers; they march over the moors. The town of S. Ives makes no resistance. It is taken in the name of King Richard IV., the supposed representative of the royal house of York.

By a bold stroke the *fortalitium* of S. Michael's Mount is taken for the monks, who secretly favor the Yorkist interest, and the Lady Katherine is left there as in a fortress of comparative safety. Her husband with his retainers and Cornish friends marches on Bodmin, to be there proclaimed King Richard IV.; thence he marches towards Taunton—and to death.

Meanwhile Lady Katherine was staying at the Mount.*

Had Perkin succeeded, she would have been in safety, as the fortress was strong, and the Cornish people friendly. But he had not succeeded, and S. Michael's Mount was hardly a fortress to defy the King of England. Lord

---

* Can the Cornish legend of the Queen seen at Burnuhall be any tradition of Lady Katherine, who would be of course called the Queen of England by her retainers? She was young and very pretty. See Mr. Botterill's "Traditions and Hearthside Stories of West Cornwall," pp. 67–73.

Daubeny was sent to the Mount with his forces to summon it to surrender, in the name of King Henry VII. Resistance would have been useless. Lady Katherine was surrendered as a prisoner. She was brought to the king; with much blushing and many tears she was ushered into the royal presence. Either her beauty or policy moved Henry; he pardoned her, nay more, received her at court, where she was called the "White Rose." She does not seem (now her life and liberty were safe) to have greatly lamented her fate of not being Queen of England; and in the end, after Perkin's execution, consoled herself by marrying Sir Matthew Cradock, a respectable Welsh knight.

The religious history of the Mount is far less interesting. The first event of importance after the constitution of the priory, is the visit of Bishop Grandisson in 1336, of which we spoke elsewhere. The income of the priory was then £100, a large sum in those days.

Prior Hardy, in 1356, got into trouble; he was arrested for treason, and indicted at Launceston for sending money to the king's enemies, and harbouring two Frenchmen (spies?). He was, however, acquitted.

William Lambert was probably the last prior. In his days (*temp.* Henry V.) the priory was annexed to Sion House. King's College, Cambridge, claimed it for a time, but gave way in the end, and Sion House held the Mount till Henry VIII's time.

About 1427, a stone quay was built by William Morton, chaplain of the Mount. The tolls were licensed by Henry VI.

A list of the priors will be found in the appendix.

CHAPTER V.

STATE OF SOCIETY AND CORNISH ARCHITECTURE DURING THE MIDDLE AGES.

"Cara, gorthya, ha ouna Dew,
An Mateyrn, ha'n lahez en guz pleu
Ouna Dêw, par tey Mateyrn
Ha cara goz contrevogion."— *Cornish Motto*—GWAVAS.

Love, worship, and fear God,
The King and the Laws, in your parish ;
Fear God, honour the King ;
And love your neighbour.

T is extremely difficult to realize the state of society among the
poor in the olden time. Contemporary poems, pictures, and
antiquities, are almost our sole guide. In West Cornwall all these
fail us, or nearly so. The real mediæval dramas (except " Beunans
Meriasek," itself of the epoch of the Wars of the Roses, if not later) refer to
exalted and sacred, and not to local subjects. We have no Cornish Chaucer,
no Troubadours, to instruct us as to men and manners in the olden time ;
until William of Worcester we have no literary tourist to describe what he
saw in West Cornwall, and even William is meagre in the extreme in his
statements ; the native antiquities of this period are almost confined to the
carvings in the churches, either of wood or stone, and those are mostly of
either the fifteenth or sixteenth centuries; tradition even gives up dating itself
anterior to Edward IV, and in most cases to Henry VIII, and we are left to
guess if a droll be of the early Christian Cornu-British, or the old Heathen
Danmonian, or of the mediæval epoch. Perhaps it is most honest and frank,
therefore, to own that of the social and internal condition of the Cornwall of

Richard, king of the Romans, or even of Edward the Black Prince, the first Duke of Cornwall, we know extremely little.

Perchance the remarks of M. Victor Hugo about the Breton of the eighteenth century, may not be altogether unsuited to the realization of the state of the miners and fishermen of West Penwith in the olden time, when Cornwall's treasures all but gave a Cornish Earl to the Empire of the West. Brittany is in many things like Cornwall, only more mediæval, more old world less civilized, less enlightened, less truly free. The enlightened rule of England has helped the Cornishman to development and civilization, while the Breton remains much as he was in those days. M. Victor Hugo's description may, therefore, *cum grano*, be perhaps accepted as of the ancient Cornu-Briton.

"This grave, strange, savage man, with eagle glance and flowing hair—his ideas bounded by his thatched roof, his hedge and his ditch, able to distinguish the sound of each village bell of the neighbourhood, using water only to drink—speaking a dead language, forcing his thoughts to dwell in a tomb— devoted to the altar, but also to the lofty mysterious tomb standing in the midst of the moor, a labourer in the plain, a fisher on the coast, a poacher in the thicket, loving his king, his lords, his priest, pensive, often immoveable for hours on the great sea shore, a melancholy listener to the sea."

Such may have been the "old men" of the Cornish miner's drolls of the past, the mediæval peasant of old Cornwall. But as we draw nearer to the fifteenth and sixteenth centuries, we need not altogether lean on untrustworthy analogies. Carew has most graphically described the Cornishman of the Tudor period, and it may be from the contrasts he draws between his own age and that which went before it, we may roughly conjecture the state of the county in the latter part of the era of the struggle between the houses of York and Lancaster. The condition of the labouring classes in the generation preceding his own times, *i.e.* the early part of the sixteenth, or it may be at the end of the fifteenth century, Carew thus concisely and withal touchingly sums up. They had "little bread corn; their drink water, or at best but whey (our Good Templar friends would not grumble at that), for the richest farmers brewed not above twice a year, and then, God wotte, what liquor (?), their meat whitsul as they call it, namely milk, sour milk, cheese, curds, butter, and such like as came from the cow and ewe; their apparel, coarse in matter, ill shapen in manner; their legs and feet naked and bare, to which sundry old folk had so accustomed their youth that they could hardly abide to wear any shoes, complaining how it kept them over hot. Their horses shod only before, and for all furniture a pad and a halter." The country girls, Carew further says rode astride, even in his times, as the English ladies indeed are said generally to have done till Richard II's queen brought over the foreign fashion of a side saddle. Their cottages were very poor, "walls of earth, low thatched roofs, few partitions, no planchings or glass windows, and scarcely any chimneys, *(sic)* other than a hole in the wall to let out the smoke, their beds straw and a blanket; as for sheets, so much linen cloth had not yet stepped over the narrow channel between them and Brittany. To conclude, a mazer and a pan or two comprised all their substance."[*]

All this reads sadly, but probably it represents the state of the peasantry, not only of Cornwall, but of most parts of England, of France, and Germany, in fact of Europe generally during the middle ages, and tens of millions of our European neighbours are no better off in this civilized nineteenth century. Many a peasant of Russia, Austria, or Italy, would no doubt gladly exchange with the state of Cornish mediæval "tinners."[†]

Travelling was uncommon, and therefore little provided for. The special grievance of strangers however, appears to have been the bad (*i.e.* probably weak home-brewed) beer, and such a defect at least encouraged sobriety. About food, we hear less complaints. Norden, however, says "the ordinary provisions in these places are very mean."

The mediæval Cornish could not, therefore, have been a drunken people, for the best of all reasons. They could get no strong drink.

The mediæval mode of building private houses of the upper classes in West Cornwall, was to "lay the stones with mortar of lime and sand, to make the

---

[*] Carew, p. 183.

[†] "At the beginning of the fifteenth century, as in the fourteenth, the houses of the peasantry were hovels of poverty and filth, and the villages were mere clusters of mud built huts, covered with reeds and straw. The furniture of a mediæval cottage was miserably scanty, a cupboard, a bench, and a few wooden platters and utensils for cooking 'constituted all.'" "Domestic Architecture in England," from Ric. II to Hen. VIII. Part I, p. 21.—Oxford 1859, See Account of Russian peasants in Wallace's Russia.

walls thick, their windows arched and little, and their lights inwards to the court" (in the old French *hôtel* mode), to set hearths in the midst of the rooms for chimneys, which vented the smoke at the lover in the top, to cover their planchings with earth, to frame the rooms not to exceed two stories, and the roofs to rise in length above proportion, and to be packed thick with timber, seeking there-through only strength and warmness.* As for glass and plaster in private houses, Carew says in his time they were "of late years introduction." Such were the residences of the wealthier yeoman and gentry in the middle ages.

So much for the poor, now a few words on the upper classes.

Of the higher nobility, West Penwith has never been rich, nor is it now. Feudalism does not appear ever to have found a congenial soil in West Cornwall. The tendency of the Celtic people was against it, their occupation as miners and fishers taught them a spirit of independence. When his fellow peasant of the midland counties was groaning in predial servitude, but little superior to the Russian serf, his West Cornish brother was probably to all intents a free man, paying indeed dues and rents to the Earl or his feudatories, but to all practical purposes as free a man as any of the peasantry of Europe. If then Cornish history offers us few of the pageants of the age of chivalry, those spectacles of proud barons, and terrible castles, and gaudy tournaments, neither does it present us the other side of the picture, the dark cruelties, the ceaseless warfare, the brutal tyrannies of old feudalism. In its poverty of incident, Cornish history points probably to comparative peace, contentment, and liberty. Even the rebellions of a later time point rather to foreign than intestine war.

Probably, it was to the interest of the Earls of Cornwall that there should be no powerful barons in the far west, to divide allegiance, and possibly to defy their power. They wished to have but one great and potent noble in the county, and that to be themselves. So nobility never has been common in the far west. Neither the Earl nor his subjects cared to carry out feudalism in its full extent, as it existed in other parts of Europe. This was fortunate for Cornwall. If we compare the history of Cornwall with that of Brittany,

* Carew, p. 142.

we must see how lucky it was for the Cornish not to be given over to a set of petty tyrants, even though those tyrants were not half as wicked, or cruel as the French historians and novelists of the present day delight to describe them.

Two noble families, however, for a time flourished in West Penwith. The Tyes of Alverton (or Madron, and S. Paul) and the Brays of S. Just. The former family had their chief residence at Castle Horneck (the Iron Castle), probably the nearest approach to a feudal fastness in Penwith. The prosperity of the family was short lived. The title of Baron Tyes became extinct in 1332.

Another family of West Penwith has had a history the direct opposite to the Tyes; mere gentry during the middle ages, they were ennobled when feudalism had practically died out in England, and when their power could no longer be of danger. I refer to the Boscawens of Burian, the family of Lord Falmouth.

In the time of King John the Boscawens held the manor of Boscawen Rose, in Burian, whence they derived their name, and thus they come into prominence about the time of Richard, King of the Romans. In 1334, John Boscawen married Joan, daughter and heiress of John de Tregothnan, whence the Tregothnan estates passed into the family, an estate now familiar to tourists, from Lord Falmouth's superb park and, one may say, palace, the finest nobleman's residence in West Cornwall. During the wars of the Roses they acquired by marriage the Tregarrick and Trevilla estates. Since then their records are a narrative of progress in wealth and importance.

The family was not ennobled till the eighteenth century. Hugh, the first Viscount Falmouth, died in 1735. The present Lord Falmouth owns some estates in Sennen and Buryan.

The Godolphin's of Breage and S. Hilary, have shone in diplomacy and war. There is a quaint legend about the name ; How John Knava, a Cornishman, was in favour with Henry VII. The monarch, however, did not like his name (a Cornish one, by the bye, not identical with the English meaning). He said so honest a man ought not to be called a Knave. So he changed his name with royal approval to Godolcan or Godolphin.

The present representative of the Godolphin's (on the female side, the male being extinct) is the Duke of Leeds.

Two of the chief families of the mediæval gentry still residing in Penwith, are the Saint Aubyn's and Borlase's. There are abundant materials for their history amply sufficient for an interesting work for each family. I feel it would be unjust to them to try to condense their records into a few paragraphs.*

One can hardly express the difficulty of this subject better than in Carew's words, who refused to publish his list of the Cornish aristocracy, "because the publishing thereof might perhaps be so accompanied with divers wrongs to my much reverend friends the heralds, by thrusting my sickle into their harvest; to a great many my countrymen, whom my want of information should be forced to over unmentioned; and to the truth itself, where my report (relying upon other men's credits) might through their error entitle me, the publisher (though not the author) of falsehood; I rather thought fit to omit it."

From individuals, let us then proceed to generalities.

Of the condition of the Cornish gentry in his times, the Elizabethan age, which therefore stands at the conclusion of the age of chivalry, Carew gives us a graphic description. It may, perhaps, be accepted *cum grano* for an earlier period. "The most Cornish gentlemen can better vaunt," he says "of their pedigree than their livelihood, for that they derive from great antiquity whereas this declineth to the mean." Poor, but proud, they seem somewhat to have been like the Spanish hidalgos of a later epoch. Military service, law, and merchandise were more or less denied to them as professions, and so they lived on their estates. Still we learn that though in actual wealth poor, they were better off than many who owned far more money in other countries. "The cheapness of their provisions, and their casualties of tin and fines (which two latter ordinarily treble the certain revenue of their rents), enable them with their few scores to equal the expenses of those eastern dwellers, who reckon by the hundreds." These poor gentry of high birth,

---

* There is reason to hope we may soon see a history of one at least of these families in the press from a member of it. The subject is well worthy much study, as a charming book might well be written.

N

Carew thinks more numerous in Cornwall than in any county of England. Did the cheapness of provisions and opportunity of living quietly without keeping up great appearances have anything to do with their number?

The proverb, so common still in Devon, "that all Cornish gentlemen are cousins," appears to date from the middle ages, and Carew laments that it "endeth in an injurious consequence that the King hath there no cousins," meaning that the Cornish families did not have a chance of intermarrying with royalty—a serious evil in mediæval times, as cutting off their chances of high privileges and promotion. Their hospitality appears to have been almost proverbial likewise. Carew sums up their merits capitally. "They keep liberal, but not costly builded or furnished houses; give kind entertainment to strangers, make even at the year's end with the profits of their living; are reverenced and beloved of their neighbours; live void of factions amongst themselves (at least such as break out into any dangerous excess), and delight not in bravery of apparel;" but then he cannot resist a remark on the Cornish ladies of the period, who "would be very loth to come behind the fashion, in new fangledness of the manner, if not in costliness of the matter, which perhaps might overempty their husbands purses." Now-a-days, there is hardly a mining village in the county where "the fashions" are not regularly studied, and where some fashion magazine is not taken in. How the Cornish ladies did manage about knowing the London and Paris fashions in the Yorkist or Tudor epochs, I regret I cannot inform my fair readers. I suppose the hawkers and packmen of the period managed it somehow. Norden, speaks more severely of the gentry, especially of their "voluptuous life," which he says brought many to ruin.

There seems to have been plenty of what is now called "society" in those days—indeed as much as anyone could wish. The formation of a "party" among the old Cornish gentry is thus quaintly told by Carew. "They converse familiarly together, and often visit one another. A gentleman and his wife will ride to make merry with his next neighbour; and after a day or twain, those two couples go to a third, in which progress they increase like snow balls, till through their burdensome weight they break down." Perchance after all, these old Cornish gentry were not so much to be pitied as their descendants may suppose, even though they had not our modern luxuries. Even, as far as the age went, they were not badly off, for the most part, says Norden, "for household and table furniture and kind entertainment may challenge equal commendation with most parts of the kingdom." So, relatively speaking, things were under Queen Bess much as under Queen Victoria. The civilization of the period came down to the manor houses of old Cornwall. What with friendly visiting, *guares*, churchales or feasten days, peace and plenty, in days when the midland counties were so often devastated by civil war with all its horrors, the Cornish gentry may have led happy, if unambitious lives. Such were the people who figure in the old family genealogies of West Penwith.

* * * * * *

To form a just and fair estimate of Cornish Art and Cornish Literature during the middle ages, we should consider the immense difficulties which surrounded the developement of either. There has perhaps been no people in Europe whose artistic efforts have been so unjustly and harshly depreciated as the old Cornish. People, even educated people of the county, have been so apt to regard the Cornishman of the middle ages as a sort of semi-savage, that the beauties and the originality of the mediæval works at their very doors have been quite looked over.

When we consider the difficulties that surrounded them, I cannot but express my own opinion, that the efforts of mediæval Cornishmen, both in literature and art, are highly creditable to their genius and natural ability, and such as their descendants might be proud of. Of literature, I speak elsewhere. Of art, one point with regard to West Penwith is worth noticing, that of the buildings in West Penwith having any architectural pretentions, except S. John's Hall, Penzance Market, the Parish Churches of Newlyn, Hals Town, and Pendeen, and a few dwelling houses, nearly all the edifices having architectural pretences are the work of Cornishmen of the middle ages, or of the early Tudor period. The seventeenth and eighteenth centuries did actually nothing for art in the district.

Certainly, compared with the great works of the middle ages in the cities or centres of civilization of England, France, Belgium, or Germany, what we have to show is poor. A traveller, fresh from our great cathedrals, or Belgium, from Normandy, or the Rhine land, would not be rapturous about Cornish architecture. Still a true and honest critic must notice many marks of artistic genius, of originality and adaptation of material, and suitableness to the natural scenery in the Cornish mediæval buildings, and the men who did such work under such difficulties might have done far greater things, had the means been offered them. Almost isolated from the rest of the civilized world by remoteness, and by difference of nationality, with the hardest of stones (one usually rejected by architects) to work on, with stinted means, and remote from any great city, the Cornish Architects deserve all credit for the work they have done.

There are two points to be considered in our Cornish buildings. (1). The difficulty of working in granite. (2).—The exposure to the effects of great storms.

As to the first, it may be said that granite has been unduly depreciated by architects. The problem of the effective use of granite in ornamental architecture may as yet be unsolved, but it does not follow that it is insoluble. Granite of itself is a majestic, and in some senses a beautiful stone. For a religious purpose, no rock is more fitted to symbolize the eternal and unchangeable than this. Of all materials good granite is the least liable to change by time. Its aspect is grave and dignified. The neutral tints of granite are capable of being the back-ground of almost any ornamentation. Nothing looks tawdry and gaudy on such a back-ground as this. Still, its hardness necessarily implies treatment in masses to produce the effect of majesty, rather than of grace and lightness. Perhaps S. John's Hall, Penzance, is one of the most effective facades of granite in the Palladian style we can find, and it was not at all a costly edifice, only £14,403.[*] It may be that granite is better fitted for this style than the Gothic. However, for all that, we have some fine mediæval work in granite in the Land's End district. S. Burian, Madron, Gulval, have each their beauties, and considering their moderate size, much dignity and gravity of aspect.

---

[*] The cost, I learn, was :—Council's portion, £5,069 17s. 2d. ; Public Buildings Co., £6,333 7s. 9d. Geological Society's portion, £3,000.—£14,403.

The lowness of the roofs of the Cornish Churches is probably a result of the exposure to violent gales. Their architects had too much prudence to rear lofty roofs. Perhaps, the legend of Towednack may explain this. Often "the powers of the air" kept Cornish edifices low, unless, like S. Paul and Burian towers, they were very carefully built. If the roofs were low and wanted lightness and grace, they still may have been for this reason more suitable for colouring. A low roof shows ornaments and colour better than a lofty one. When coloured they may have been very handsome, without it they look heavy and depressed. Sennen Church may be cited as an instance. The ancient fresco at the east end is possibly a remnant of what once was common in Cornish Churches, the ornamentation of the walls with designs. Carnmenellis (in Kirrier) is one of the few modern churches so adorned. The recent restorations of the sanctuaries of Lelant and S. Erth show the striking effects of a brilliant colour on a low roof.

As anyone acquainted with the subject will notice, most of the Penwith churches are of the later pointed style, reared probably in that revival of prosperity to which Carew adverts, *i.e.* about the epoch of the wars of the Roses. Burian church, it is needless now to say, is not "still disposed nearly as Athelstan left it," as Whitaker supposed. Possibly there is not a vestige in the present building of the Athelstan edifice, the ancient arch in the sanctuary even being of Norman work. Most of the church is probably of the fifteenth century. The transept of S. Levan is early English, and the font transitional, but most of the church is much later. S. Paul is of course post-mediæval, *i.e.* after the burning in Elizabeth's reign. The date of Sennen is given 1441-43 (?); Sancreed seems to be of rather later date. S. Just belongs to the same epoch, nothing now remaining of the church which Bishop Grandisson consecrated in 1336.* So this district is poorer in early mediæval work than very many in England. Our antiquities rather are of the Ancient British or Romano-British age, than of the days of the Crusades. The fonts may be ancient, the edifices themselves are of the latter end of the middle ages, the generation after Geoffrey Chaucer lived and wrote.

---

* The interest expressed at the Archæological Congress of 1876 shows how valuable our Penwith churches are from an architectural and archæological point of view.

Our rood screens must have been very rich, and were an important point in the low roofed churches. The famed screen at Burian, with its rich carving, once glorious in colour, the disused screen of Sancreed (now in the vestry) are fine examples of old Cornish screens, in olden times the most prominent points in our churches, and probably not destroyed till the ravages of Shrubsall and the Puritans.

Our secular mediæval architecture was probably far behind the ecclesiastical, and so we need not regret its passing away. Carew's account of the old Cornish manor house we refer to elsewhere. No such manor however exists now, most of Trewoofe, as it now stands, being post-mediæval, and Pendeen House being a manor of the time of Charles II.

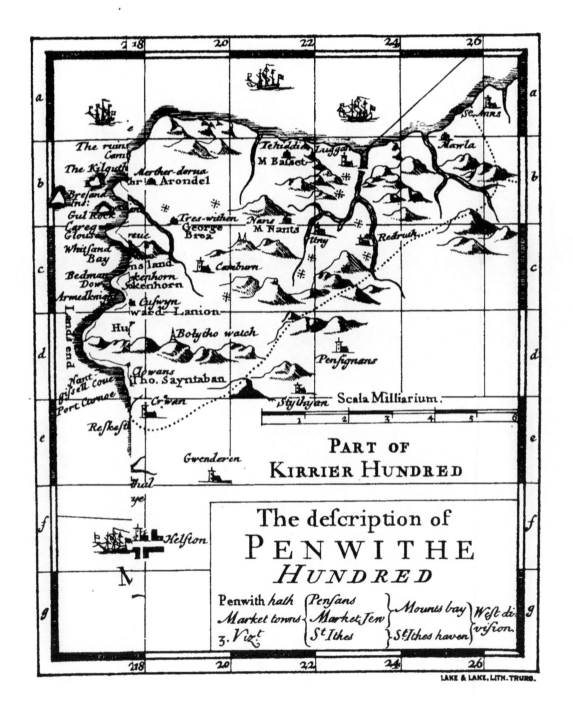

PART OF
KIRRIER HUNDRED

Scala Milliarium.

The description of

PENWITHE
HUNDRED

Penwith *hath*
Market *towns*
3. *Viz:*

{ Pensans
{ Market *Jew*
{ St *Ithes*

{ Mounts *bay*
{ St *Ithes haven*

West *di-*
vision.

PART IV.—THE SIXTEENTH AND SEVENTEENTH CENTURIES.

CHAPTER I.

THE REFORMATION PERIOD.

> " Yma parys tus arvov
> Thagis gortheby oma
> Dugh pan vynnogh
> Soudrys dehesugh detha."
>
> *Beunans Meriasek, 3531-6.*
>
> Ready are armed men to answer you here come
> When ye will.   Soldiers ! strike at them !
> " Hov serrys pana aray
> Leferugh thym w'out nay
> Pyv a ros dywhy lescyans."
>
> *Beunans Meriasek, 3461.*
>
> How Sirs ! what an array
> Tell ye me without nay
> Who hath given you license.

THE beginning of the reign of Henry VIII is remarkable for two reasons :—The first is the Royal grant of king Henry VIII. It is addressed to " Our Styward, Receyvour, Auditor, Reves and Bayliffs of our towne of Pensans (*sic*) within our countye of Cornwall, and to our Admyrall and Hauenar, and to alle other our officers and other liegemen within our said countye," and bestowed on the tenants of the " said towne of Pensans " the profits of " the ankerage, kylage, and busselage " of ships as long as they kept the quay in repair.

This is the first notice of Penzance, as a town, by an English sovereign. It marks an important era in its municipal history, indeed it is the beginning of it.   Its date is 1512.

The second event occurred soon after.   A French fleet is seen in the Bay. The fortress of the Mount is too strong to be attempted, but Marazion lies defenceless. Near it the Frenchmen land. The Cornish after slight resistance flee. The town is held by the French soldiers for a few days, and then is set on fire by them. The French fleet make off toward the Lizard.

But the reign of Henry VIII is illustrious in our history for graver reasons than the grant to " Pensans " or even the French raid on Marazion. The Tudor epoch—the English Renaissance epoch—was an age of a great change in many things, but in none greater than in religion. It was the era of the Reformation.

The memory of Catherine of Arragon is closely connected with the West country, *i.e.* with Plymouth, if not with Penzance. There the ill-fated Queen landed on English soil. Two events are important as illustrating the state of things at this time. The one is " Wolsey's Inquisition into the value of the benefices," the other is Leland's visit.

The enquiry into the value of benefices of Penwith, both at the Reformation period and at the period of the great Taxation in 1294, though useful as a branch of parochial history, is one that would not be of great value in a general sketch like this, is exceedingly dry to the ordinary reader, and moreover is easily accessible in all its details in Lake's " Parochial History of the County of Cornwall," where every particular of importance may be found. Suffice it to say that the value of the benefices, counting in the purchasing power of money, was generally less than now, that most of them seem to have been under the patronage of great religious corporations, *e.g.* the Deans Chapter of Exeter, the Prior of S. Germans or S. Michael's Mount, and that most of the Vicars appear to have been Cornishmen.

But we have a still more valuable and fairly authentic record of the state of things in the reign of Henry VIII in West Penwith in the narrative of John Leland, King Henry's antiquary, who was sent over the realm to report on the curiosities of England.

Let us begin with the east. The passage to Lelant was over " a great strond and then over Hayle river." " The toune of Lannant is praty. The Church thereof is S. Unine." S. Erth Bridge of three arches, he says, was made 200 years before, *i.e.* in the fourteenth century. Before then there was a ferry.

S. Ives is two miles from Lelant, on a peninsula extended into the sea of Severn as a cape. The peninsula is a mile round. Most of the houses were pressed on by the sands then. But the calamity seems to have been a recent one, *i.e.* since the accession of Henry VIII. In Leland's time most of the town was on the south side of the peninsula " towards another hill for defence from the sands." It would seem from this that old S. Ives was built more on the Isthmus, and towards the " Battery." There was a Blockhouse (for defence of the town) and a fair pier on the east of the peninsula, but the pier was choked with sand. He then gives the story of S. Ive and S. Elwyn landing here. On Pendinas Point there then stood S. Nicholas chapel and a pharos or rude lighthouse for ships. S. Ives was then well supplied with water from the neighbouring hills.

Marazion, Leland twice describes. His account rather differs from local tradition of the past riches and prosperity of Market Jew, but these may refer to the age before the burning. His account is that he found " a poor chapel in the midst of a poor town, and a little chapel (now Chapel Rock) in the sand near the town towards the Mount." In another place, however, he calls it a " great long town." S. Hilary was the parish church then, a mile off. Near Marazion, or Marhasdeythyon as he calls it, were the marshes which he denominates a lake.

Of S. Michael's Mount we have a fairly circumstantial account, but marking little change from now. On the S.S.W. side there was some pasturage and a rabbit warren. On the N.N.E. as now there was a garden with houses and shops for fishermen, and the usual ascent was from the north. On the outer ward was a court strongly walled, on the south side of which was the S. Michael's, on the east the Lady Chapel. The captains' and priests' lodgings were on the south side to the west of S. Michael's Chapel.

If the account of Marazion and S. Ives would to some extent suit the present day, that of Penzance would be unjust. The fact is Penzance must have changed much. Leland says it was a " myle from Mowsehole (*sic.*)." Oh, Mr. Leland, a very long mile ! " Standing fast by Mount's Bay (or Mont Bay as he spelt it) is the westest town of all Cornwall." Penzance harbour was thought unsafe in those days, for there was " no succour for boats or ships."

O

We learn the curious statement—" There is a chapel in the said town as is in Newlyn, for their parish churches are more than a mile off." This is the one reference to old Newlyn chapel—the predecessor of our S. Peter's Church. The S. Clare and S. Raphael or S. Anthony chapels of Penzance are not referred to. Perhaps they were ruinous. I have no doubt that St. Mary's on the site of S. Mary's Church is what Leland refers to.

Newlyn would seem then to have relatively been a more important place than now, though only " a poor fischar towne " (*sic*). Leland refers to it many times, as if it had been his head quarters in the Land's End district. Perhaps he lodged here at some ancient tavern, long since forgotten, or with some hospitable Newlyn man. He mentions the Quay for ships and boats, and the " little succour of land water "—the Newlyn river ; but he makes a gross slip of the pen in saying that a little island (no doubt S. Clement's island is what he means) with a chapel on it was within an arrow shot of the pier. It would be a longbow that would shoot there. I imagine his Mousehole and Newlyn notes must have got confused somehow. Mousehole he calls a pretty fishing village in the west of Mount's Bay, lying hard by the shore, and hath no safeguard for ships but a forced pier.

From S. Just to Newlyn eastward, we learn the country then, as now, " was hilly and fertile of grass, with tin works both wet and dry, without haven or creek, saving that in divers places there remain capstans, like engines, wherewith they draw their boats on dry land, and fish only in fair weather." Two or three similar capstans may still be seen. Treryn Castle also caught Leland's attention, but his description is not very graphic to modern readers. In S. Burian, as we said, he only found not above 8 dwelling houses. There was a dean and a few prebendaries " who almost be never there." In another place he summarizes the history of S. Burian, an *ex voto* offering, as he says, of King " Ethelstane." S. Just would seem then to be far humbler than now, for there was nothing but a parish church and some scattered houses.

As now, the main occupation of the people beside agriculture were mining and fishing. The subject of ancient Cornish mining has been well treated by Mr. Worth, and to his book on the subject I refer the reader. The usual miners' daily wages in Norden's time was 8d, or £5 or £6 per annum, " and in all this to find themselves all necessaries."* So Cornish mining (even giving allowance for the change in value of money), was no better paid then than now. The overseers were called " captaynes" then, as now, as both Norden and Carew remind us.

The curing of Pilchards is described by both Carew and Norden as already one of the great industries of the coast. It seems during the middle age the pilchards were mostly smoked and dried, hence the term Fumados. The system of " bulking" both Norden and Carew refer to as a (then) new invention. " After they have been ripped out of the bulk, reffed upon sticks (this is now discontinued), and washed, they pack then orderly in hogsheads made purposely leaky, which afterwards they press on with great weights, to the end that the train oil may soak from them into the vessel placed in the ground to receive it." The seine, the tuck net, shrimping net were all known ; but it would seem as if, from Carew, the lobster or crab-pot and trawling were not used in Cornwall even in the reign of Elizabeth.

The aspect of the country, excepting of course the absence of the larger mines and the sparsity of population, would probably be much then as now. Norden, indeed, asserts that Cornwall under King John "*tota fuit foresta ;*" but he may have meant only in the legal sense not actually. In the Elizabethan age, however, " the greatest want that the country hath is wood and timber. The west part of the country, as Penwith . . . are in a manner bereft of this benefit." There seem to have been no parks in Penwith, and probably not even such grounds as we have. There seem to have been no coppices even west of Godolphin or Crowan. The warmth of the climate was noticed then, (even in ages long anterior to meteorological observations), and Norden tries to explain it by a theory that the " sea's saltness sendeth warm evaporations, which cherish the earth as with a continual sweet dew." A graceful way of describing the climate of Penzance. N.B.—They did not know about the Gulf stream in those days.

The S. Keverne plot of 1538, though the locality of it was not actually in the Land's End district, was so close to its borders and so much affected the whole of Cornwall, that it cannot be passed over in silence, curious " romance

---

* The calculation is Norden's not mine. I suppose they had many holidays then.

of history " as it is. To understand it we must glance a moment at the state of England at the time. Henry VIII by his divorce of Queen Catherine of Arragon, and declaration of the independence of the Church of England from the Papacy, had excited against himself great irritation both in England from the old Roman Catholic gentry and country people who wished to go on in their fathers' ways, and also on the continent among the great foreign powers, the chief of which then was the Emperor of the West and King of Spain Charles V. Little more than a year before, *i.e.* in the autumn of 1536 there had been a very serious rebellion in Yorkshire and Lincolnshire. This was suppressed, but a good deal of discontent remained in the country, fomented to some extent by foreigners.

Now, one of the chiefs of the nobility of the West of England was Henry Courtenay, Marquis of Exeter, the grand-son of King Edward IV (being son of Edward's youngest daughter Catherine and William Courtenay Earl of Devon, a descendant of the Latin Emperors of the East), and so from a Yorkist point of view, a near heir of the crown of England. As one of the chief of the western nobility, he had very great influence in Devon and Cornwall. The idea seems to have struck his friends whether he should not be set forward as heir-apparent or even claimant to the Crown of England. Three classes of interests were in his favour :—

(1.) The Yorkists, who would wish to see a grandson of Edward IV, who had no Lancastrian blood in him, King of England.

(2.) The Romanists, who wanted to get rid of Henry VIII.

(3.) The Cornish and Devonshire men, who would be but too proud to put a West country nobleman, one of themselves, with their interests and feelings and prejudices, upon the throne of England.

But more than this, the Emperor Charles V would have been glad, without doubt, to see another king than Henry VIII in England, and neither money nor men would have been wanting from Spain to help on the enterprise.

The plot progressed. Whispers of revenge for Flammock's defeat sounded in the Cornish villages. "The Cornishmen should no longer be oppressed by gentlemen in London, or the North country, they would have a king of their own—nay, more, they would give all England a king, a West countryman like themselves."* And supposing the Cornish and Devonshire men were not equal to the troops of the rest of England (and on only a part of these could the King rely), was there not the Emperor (that mysterious potentate), and was not Spain but a few days' sail?

Nor was this notion of the possibility of foreign intervention altogether a dream. Mount's Bay only the year before had sounded with the strife of war. England was not yet the mistress of the seas, nor could the Channel Fleet always keep foreigners from the coast. On an August afternoon in 1837 the inhabitants of Penzance saw even in their bay a naval battle. Four French men of war were driven in by the English fleet. The battle lasted till night. During the darkness three of the French ships escaped, but one was lost. At an earlier date we have seen that the foreign fleets had been more lucky, and Marazion suffered for their success. At a later date, as we shall see, the Spaniards did come and land here in earnest, though not in great force. So it was no dream to think of a foreign intervention, and for this foreign intervention the Yorkists, especially Reginald Pole, were plotting.

Two Cornishmen, however, bravely saved England from her great peril. One of them was a poor working painter, the other Sir William Godolphin of Breage. One day the painter came to Sir William to say that he had been hired by a man of S. Kevern to make a banner with a strange device. The painter, a loyal and cautious man, had asked what the banner was for. The S. Kevern man replied that he had been at Southampton, and there, when selling his fish in the town, someone had asked him "why the Cornishmen had not risen against the king when the Yorkshiremen rose." He said that now he found that the Cornishmen wanted to rise, and were "sworn on the book" to do so, and the banner was needed to be carried around the parishes to raise the people. Sir William acted as prudently and firmly as his descendant Sir Francis did, 60 years after. He did not at once make arrests. He sent to London, immediately, a private messenger to inform the government, and he collected forces quietly in case the storm should burst. "If there be stirring among them," wrote Sir William, "I will rid as many as be about the banner,

* The effect of Henry Courtenay's plot on the popular mind is still manifest by the tradition at Tiverton mentioned by Mrs. Whitcombe. See "Bygone Days" in Devonshire and Cornwall, p. 117.

or else I and a great many will die for it." The government in London was roused by the message. Courtenay's servants were led to betray him. Becket and Wroth, two of the King's confidential attendants, were sent down into Cornwall. Bit by bit the plot was unravelled, and Henry Courtenay was beheaded as a traitor on Tower Hill, instead of (as he and his friends had hoped) being crowned King of England. Most Cornishmen now will be glad things turned out as they did. Had the S. Kevern plot succeeded, had Devon and Cornwall risen for Henry Courtenay, and the Emperor landed an army in Mount's Bay, England would probably not have been so free as she is. However, it very nearly happened that Cornishmen gave a king and a dynasty to England.

The strong hand of Henry VIII had suppressed the rebellion, but it was scotched, not crushed. The great despot passed away, and his young son Edward VI succeeded him. The Reformation made more than ever progress under the regency. The old service books were abolished, the new prayer book, *i.e.* that which we call Edward's First Book, ordered to be issued, but the Cornish were not prepared for sudden changes. It is curious that in the county where the Reformation was ultimately most entirely accepted, it was at first the most resisted.

Matters soon came to a crisis. As Body, the King's Commissioner for destroying images, was performing his iconoclastic work at Bodmin (Norden says at Helston, and so does Hals) Church, Mr. Kilter, of St. Keverne, with some comrades, took the law into their own hands and slew him. Kilter was arrested, sent to London (the government did not dare to trust a Cornish jury), tried at Westminster, and deservedly executed. The Cornish, however, were not quieted. They were jealous of the acts of the government "up in London," and its interference with their religious opinions.

The mining districts were in a ferment. Many rough acts were committed in the name of religion. The justices of the peace did their best. Several offenders were arrested and punished; but the ferment increased. The Cornish people did not like to be dictated to in their religious affairs (perhaps they do not like it now, only in another way). The miners and fishermen looked for a leader. At length they found one, a Cornish gentleman of old family, wealth, and influence,—no bad soldier, either—Sir Humphrey Arundell, the Governor of S. Michael's Mount. At a signal from him, Cornwall burst into insurrection.

S. Ives rises with the rest. John Payne, the Mayor, is made Captain. Arundell assumes the position of General of the Cornish Army. He leaves the Mount to take command of his rude host of miners, fishermen, and countrymen. The gentry of Penwith are alarmed for their goods and lives. Socialism has been spreading in the mining districts. The miners do not like lawyers, and they declare they will put them down. They are angry with the magistrates, who have been of late rather hard on them, and they declare they will put them down also. The county magistrates and the county gentry begin to think that discretion is the better part of valour. Arundell has deserted the Mount, why not seize on that fortress and secure their families and goods? They effect their end by a rapid stroke. S. Michael's Mount is taken.

But Arundell is not to be despoiled of his fortress. He sends a division of his growing army, cavalry and infantry, to regain the Mount. They watch till the tide goes down, and then march across to the island—now a peninsula. The lower part is stormed with little trouble. Trusses of hay are brought over and carried by the besiegers in front of them. Under these rude but effective shields they storm the heights. The bullets strike in vain. The summit is gained. As anyone of the defenders appear on the battlements, a shower of arrows meet them. The alarm of the ladies, and the failure of provisions quench the courage of the country squires and their servants. They surrender at discretion, and are too glad to escape with their lives from the hands of Arundell's rude army.

The army at Bodmin, meanwhile, has swollen to 6,000 men. Boyer, the Mayor of Bodmin, joins them. Arundell takes the command. He marches towards the Tamar. Job Militon, Lord of Pengersic, in vain attempts to oppose them. There is something romantic in the enthusiasm of that little Cornish army going on a crusade against the established government of England. In the centre of the host, a kind of ark (possibly in memory of the Israelites in the wilderness) of religious emblems is carried in a cart. The miners, and fishers, and yeomen, are divided into companies under separate commanders. Firm in resolution they advance. One is reminded of the revolt of the Bretons in *La Vendée*, though one cannot sympathize so much with the cause. "*C'est magnifique, mais ce n'est pas la guerre,*" as was said of our Balaklava charge. They advance on Trematon Castle (the venerable keep near Saltash, conspicuous from the Cornish Railway), where some of the gentry of East Cornwall have fled for refuge. Sir Richard Grenville holds the castle. The Cornish miners besiege it, but wanting cannon can do but little. But there is treason within. The retainers of the Granville's will not fight against their countrymen, and they escape by night to Arundell's camp. Sir Richard is induced by this new danger to go out for a parley with the rebels. The miners break faith, they cut off his retreat, and he is made a prisoner. The castle surrenders, and "stripped from their apparel to their very smocks," those who are within are allowed to escape with their lives only. Trematon Castle is sacked.

The Cornish host then crosses the Tamar. The men of Devon are not unfriendly with them. They have their own grievances against the government, and some of them also are in arms. The Cornishmen, meanwhile, press forward. Dartmoor is no hindrance to them. It is summer weather and the roads are in fair state. On July 2, they see before them the Norman towers of Exeter Cathedral, and the country around the Exe full of their armed allies—the men of Devon. The city is summoned to surrender. Blackhall, the Mayor, refuses. The gates are barricaded, the citizens rise in arms for the king.

Had Arundell pressed forward to London, there could be nothing to resist him. The Protector Somerset knew the danger. He ordered the bridge of Staines to be broken. But success at S. Michael's Mount and at Trematon had turned Arundell's head. He has cannon and 20,000 brave men. Why dishearten the half disciplined army by leaving Exeter behind them? The siege is not badly conducted. The water pipes are cut; the artillery open fire on the city; the miners (skilled at that sort of work) dig under the city walls; a correspondence is opened with the disaffected in the city. Still Mayor Blackhall persists. For 6 weeks the city is besieged; those six weeks saved England.

Lord Russell, meanwhile, was gathering the royal forces. Alarmed at Arundell's successes, he had retired to Sherbourne, but the news of re-inforcements led him to return to Honiton (a little town well-known to western travellers on the S.W.R.). There he halted to wait for Lord Grey. On July 27 news was brought that the Cornishmen were advancing upon him. A council of war was held, and a battle decided on.

The troops advance to Fennington Bridge. The Carews' storm the bridge, and the Cornishmen retreat. The royal troops, scattered for plunder, are attacked by the reserves of the Cornish army, with great loss. Russell drives back the Cornish, but retreats hastily to Honiton. This ended the first battle between the royal army and the Cornish.

On Saturday, August 3, Russell's army marches towards Exeter. There is a skirmish at S. Mary Clyst (near Topsham) that evening, in which the Devonshire ploughmen fight like heroes. The news of the skirmish draws the Cornish army to the spot; as night closes in 6,000 insurgents are on the hills. On Sunday, August 4, is fought the memorable battle of S. Mary Clyst. The foreign mercenaries of the King (Edward VI) are taken in an ambuscade by Sir Thomas Pomeroy (a descendant of Sir Henry Pomeroy, of S. Michael's Mount), and a panic ensues. In the *melée* the king's cannon and ammunition waggons are taken by the insurgents. The royal army, however, rallies on the heath. Again the battle rages in the village. The houses are set on fire, the insurgents give way, and many are drowned in the Exe. On Monday, the battle is renewed, and Lord Grey, a tried warrior, confesses "such was the valour and stoutness of the men that he never in all the wars he had been in did know the like." Again, however, the insurgents were defeated with great loss. On Tuesday, the siege of Exeter was raised, and the Cornish were retreating towards Dartmoor.

On Friday, August 15, 1549, was fought the last great battle between the Cornish and the English. It was near the village of Sampford Courtney. The Cornishmen with their Devonshire allies were strongly entrenched (again the miners were useful for these works). Lord Russell orders a heavy cannonade, and then the mercenaries and royal troops advance to storm the position. But Sir Humphrey Arundell is a ready strategist. With a body

P

of Cornishmen he gets behind the storming party and attacks them.   A panic siezes the king's troops.   Lord Grey is compelled to face Arundell.   Herbert, who is left in command of the party to attack the camp, rallies his soldiers and presses forwards.   He succeeds in routing the insurgents.   Arundell is then attacked by superior forces, when Herbert's troops return and the Cornish at length give way, and Arundell flees to Launceston, his soldiers getting across the Tamar as best they can.

One body made their way to Somersetshire, but were overwhelmed.   Martial law was proclaimed in Devon and Cornwall.   Sir Anthony Kingston makes his name notorious by his cruelties as provost marshal.

The Mayors of Bodmin and of S. Ives were hanged, and the county terrorized.   This ends the last rebellion of Cornwall against a king of England.

The disastrous reign of Mary I, strange to say, is almost a blank in our records, except in relation to the borough of S. Ives, and to Lord Bray of S. Just.   She seems, however, to have disgusted her Cornish as much as her other subjects, for on Elizabeth's accession they assented to the Reformation without a murmur.

CHAPTER II.

PENWITH UNDER QUEEN ELIZABETH.

"Swift to east and swift to west the ghastly war flames spread,
  High on St. Michael's Mount it shone : it shone on Beachy Head.
Far on the deep the Spaniard saw along each southern shire,
Cape beyond cape, in endless range, those twinkling points of fire.
The fisher left his skiff to rock on Tamar's glittering waves :
The rugged miners poured to war from Mendips sunless caves ;
O'er Longleats towers, o'er Cranbourne's oaks, the fiery herald flew :
He roused the shepherd of Stonehenge, the rangers of Beaulieu."
Lord Macaulay.

BOUT the Elizabethan period a certain halo of romance lingers, which makes it one of the most interesting ages of English History. The noble national struggle against foreign despotism, spiritual and political, culminating in the defeat of the Armada ; the heroic daring of our great west countrymen, Drake, Hawkins, Gilbert, Raleigh ; the brilliant literary geniuses of the epoch, Shakespeare, Spenser, Bacon, Hooker, all confer on the Elizabethan age a claim to our especial interest. In what state was Cornwall in the days while Shakespeare was writing his world famed dramas ; while Drake was circumnavigating the world ; while Bacon was thinking out his inductive philosophy ? The answer is not hard to find. Among the minor geniuses of that active intellectual age, was a shrewd and clever Cornish landowner, at once a lawyer, diplomist, militia officer, and naturalist,* Richard Carew, of Antony, in East Cornwall, who in 1602, published a capital "Survey of Cornwall," and dedicated it to Sir Walter Raleigh, then Lieutenant General of Cornwall. To this we may add the valuable work of Norden, written a little before, but also full of useful information on the county and the people.

---

* Carew, it seems, was the first Cornishman who thought of a marine aquarium. He carried out his scheme at Antony. v, p. 248-53. It is to be hoped Penzance will soon imitate his plan with all the improvements of our modern science.

The first impression one receives from reading Carew's work is its graphic accuracy of the main features of Cornish life in the present day, and how strongly conservative the people must be to have changed so little since the Elizabethan period. Of course the great mining operations of our day were then unknown; the railway was not dreamt of till more than two centuries later; Penzance was a mere fishing village, and tourists for pleasure in the Land's End District were extremely few; visitors for health, none at all. And yet much that Carew says is still true, or at least partially true. Whether, had most of our other counties produced a native historian of the Elizabethan epoch, his statement would have read in 1877 as like a modern guide book, as is Carew's "Survey," one cannot say—certainly of Lancashire, Staffordshire, or Middlesex the account would have read very differently compared to modern facts: as it is, with Leland and Carew as his guide books, a traveller might almost to this day "do Cornwall."

The population of Cornwall during the Tudor period appears to have increased rapidly, although Carew states, and his statement has a peculiar interest now-a-days, arguments were brought forward by persons who held that Cornwall had once been far more populous than in the sixteenth century. To these arguments he thus replies :—"I suppose that those waste grounds were inhabited and manured when the Saxons and Danes continual invasions drove them to abandon the sea coast, save in such towns as were able to muster, upon a sudden occasion, a sufficient number for their own defence; the residue retired into the heart of the land, where, upon a longer warning, they might sooner assemble from all sides to make head, and the enemy in so far a march and retreat should adventure a greater hazard to be distressed by the way...Touching the decayed inland towns, they are counter vailed with a surplusage of increase of those on the coast ;" *i.e.* the population was more inland and less on the coast in the middle ages, *e.g.* at Burian than Penzance.

The condition of the working classes had certainly improved during the century, although Carew laments the immigration of numerous poor Irish who increased the number of the vagrant and pauper class. His description of this grievance is very quaint. "Ireland prescribeth to be the nursery which sendeth over yearly whole shiploads of these crooked slips, and the dishabited towns afford them rooting, so upon the matter the whole county maketh a contribution to pay those lords their rent." The Cornish peasant, however, he describes as industrious and prosperous. "He can maintain himself and his family in a competent decency to their calling, and findeth money to bestow weekly at the markets for his provisions of necessity and pleasure." Shoes and stockings appear from his statement to have now become general, and the hardy or economical habits of the Scotch and Irish peasant of going bare legged were already discarded. The houses also of all classes were improved. In one point however, Carew reproves his countrymen of the working classes, for their "fostering a fresh memory of their expulsion long ago by the English, they second the same with a bitter repining of their fellowship...Amongst themselves they agree well, and company lovingly together; to their gentlemen they carry a very dutiful regard, as inured in their obeisance from their ancestors, and holding them as Roytelets because they know no greater." Norden also says they "retain a concealed envy against the English, whom they affect with a desire of revenge for their fathers' sake, by whom their fathers received the repulse."

The towns people "conceive themselves an estranged society from the upland dwellers, and carry, I will not say a malice, but an emulation against them." The chief business was done at weekly markets, and Carew wonders why they did not speculate more in foreign traffic, wholesale dealings, or ship building.

House building seems to have improved in the Tudor period. Instead of the low houses with thick walls and small arched windows, they now built high, "their walls thin, lay them with earthen mortar, raise them to three or four stories, mould their lights large and outward, and their roofs square and slight, coveting chiefly prospect and pleasing." (Surely this refers to the dwellings of the upper classes). The houses of cottagers were still, and indeed until the beginning of our own XIXth century, cob walls and thatched roofs.

The roads appear to have been much better in West than East Cornwall; strangers observed "that the Cornish miles are much longer than those about London; if at least the weariness of their bodies (after so painful a journey) blemish not the conjecture of their minds." Unless however, the Cornish roads actually fell off during the seventeenth century, they must have been what we should call very bad, for traditions and written statements of the eighteenth century represent them as such. Probably they were usually mere bridle paths.

Provisions were generally cheap, and this formed an inducement to persons of small means to settle in Cornwall. . As yet, and for two centuries after, communications were not good enough to enable the London market to much affect Cornish prices. As to the sin of drunkeness, it would seem that (except perchance in the last generation) the Cornish were generally a sober people. In the sixteenth and earlier centuries they must have been so by the strongest of all reasons—necessity. Little liquor seems to have been imported, and the home-brewed beer was very weak, a matter of which travellers greatly complained.

Such was Cornwall under Elizabeth. Perhaps Carew may be accused of giving too *couleur-de-rose* an account, but extraneous evidence (apart from his own respectability) shows it was pretty accurate. Let those who think the "old men" of the Cornwall of Elizabeth's days were "heathens and savages," just compare it with Lord Macaulay's account of two other Celtic populations of the British dominions, the Irish and the Gaelic Highlanders of a hundred years later,[*] and the French account of Brittany two hundred years later (in 1793), and see whether the Cornish might not then claim to have been the most civilized Celtic people in the world?

*　　　*　　　*　　　*　　　*

The Armada is the central point of Elizabethan History, especially in the "west country." It takes much the same position in the annals of modern England as the Persian invasion by Xerxes does in classic Greek records—a chivalric age of noble resistance of a brave free little nation, against the hordes of a mighty tyrant. In the peril of that epoch, and in the events which immediately preceded and succeeded it, West countrymen took a leading share, Drake, Raleigh, Hawkins, Gilbert, but to Devon mainly the palm belongs, and around Plymouth gathers the halo of the Armada days.

---

[*] Macaulay, vol. III, p. 172....p. 300....This account, however, has been denounced as exaggerated.

Still, Cornwall had a share. Raleigh was then " General of Cornwall." The blow might have fallen on West Penwith, in 1588 as it did in 1595. It was the nearest point to Spain, and might have been first struck (as indeed in the end it alone was really smitten) by " the Dons." Those must have been anxious days for Cornish homes. They no longer wished for the Spaniards to come, as their fathers or grandfathers did in the days of Henry Courtenay, or of Humphrey Arundell. They knew them too well now. The stories of the brutalities of Alva in the Netherlands, the horrors of the Inquisition, and of Spanish cruelty in America roused the people and opened their minds to facts. Well was it for Cornwall that Henry Courtenay had died on the scaffold, that the king's troops had routed Arundell's Cornish army at S. Mary Clyst. The dictation of " the gentlemen in London " might be hard to bear, but the brutality of Spanish hidalgos would be far worse.

At length the expectancy of years came to a point. On July 19, the news arrived that the Armada had been seen off the Cornish coast. Perhaps already the intelligence had got wind that Mount's Bay was the rendezvous selected by Medina Sidonia in case of the scattering of his fleet. That night was such as England never knew before nor since. Tradition hints that S. Michael's Mount gave the signal of the beacon fires. From height to height the blaze spread in lurid glare over the hills of England. It illumined the Cornish Moors and swept over the Dartmoor Tors on to London. The Spaniards had come, the Armada had arrived. Nor was it a false alarm. As the sun shone forth on Saturday, July 20th, far away to the south on the blue sea " the floating Babel " of the Spanish fleet was visible, its white sails rising as a mighty city on the waters.

A Cornish fishing boat scuds out towards that armament. The roar of cannon booms over the waters. The white puffs of smoke float over the blue sea. One or two men-of-war give chase. The boat is better handled. She runs before the wind and escapes. Again the cannon sound. A signal is given from the Admiral's ship ; the fleet shortens sails ; boats are rowing towards the San Martin. Medina Sidonia is holding a council of war ; that council is now no secret. They resolve on going to Margate Roads. The Armada sweeps on towards Rame Head and Plymouth.

The rest belongs to English, not Cornish history. The story of the battle outside Plymouth Sound, the fireships off Calais, the storms in the North Sea, the wrecks on the Irish Coast, ought to be known by every Englishman. The ruin of the " Invincible Armada " is a landmark in history.

> " Where are those Spaniards
> That make so great a boast O,
> They shall eat the grey goose feather,
> And we will eat the roast O."
> *The Helston " Furry Song."*

The Spaniards did however come to Penzance and Newlyn in earnest. It was a misty July morning in 1595, that four foreign ships were seen approaching Mousehole. The little town lay in tranquil repose, suspecting no danger, unarmed and defenceless. Some boats are sent off from the foreign ships. They make for Point Spaniard, a retired little point under the cliff to the west of the town, close to the fatal Merlin Rock of which the prophecy had been written :—

> " Ewra tey a war meane Merlyn
> Ara Lesky Pawle, Penzanz, La Newlyn."
> " There shall stand on the rock of Merlyn,
> Those who shall burn Paul, Penzance, and Newlyn."

Two hundred Spanish soldiers are here landed, armed with pikes and muskets, who send forth skirmishers to occupy and ravage the scattered farmsteads of Paul as far as the Churchtown. The main body advance on Mousehole. The fishermen are unprepared to meet in battle the trained troops of Alva and Parma. They flee in terror. The brave Squire Jenkin Keigwin alone makes a stand for his mansion, and is killed by the enemy. The town is set on fire. Mousehole, except the granite mansion of the Keigwins (now an Inn, the Keigwin Arms), is reduced to ruins. The Church of St. Paul fares no better. It is burnt likewise, and two pillars of the chancel alone mark what once it was.

Sir Francis Godolphin that morning, July 23, had been going to Penzance. He had seen the fire and smoke from the hills, and met the Mousehole fugitives at Penzance Green. Sir Francis sent messengers at once to Sir Francis Drake and Sir John Hawkins, to Plymouth, for help. He gathered together the fugitives, about 100 men, with 30 or 40 firearms, and those mostly unserviceable. The Cornishmen, however, clamoured to be led on against their foes, to stop them from further ravages.

The Spaniards re-embark and move their four gallies into Mount's Bay, anchoring just off Newlyn. Again they land their troops there. They ascend the hill at the back of the little fishing town and form in order of battle, now 400 strong, sending out skirmishers to the top of the hill. Seeing only Sir Francis Godolphin's little band, they advance towards Penzance. Sir Francis seeing their move, retires to the town (from Street-an-Nowan?). As soon as the little band of Cornishmen enter the Green, the artillery from the galleys open fire. The cannonade is not so serious as alarming. One constable only is unhorsed, but the untrained Cornishmen are much shaken by it. "Some, says Carew, fell flat to the ground, and others ran away."

Sir Francis would not, it is manifest, have much chance with such warriors against the 400 trained soldiers whom Don Diego de Brochero was bringing against him. Still he calls on them to make a stand at Penzance. This order in the panic is forgotten. "He found at the market place but only two resolute shot, and some ten or twelve others that followed him, most of them his own servants; the rest surprised with fear fled, whom neither with his persuasions, nor threatening with his rapier drawn he could recall."

The Spaniards enter Penzance in three parts; Sir Francis sees his position hopeless. The houses behind him are set on fire and soon Penzance is a mass of flames as well as Newlyn. Having made the three smiling little towns a desolation, the Spanish troops re-embark ou their gallies.

As evening approaches, the Cornish troops rallying under Sir Francis with help from other parts, encamp on Marazion Green to defend the Mount and the road to the interior.

Next day, July 24th, the Spaniards make a reconnaissance on the west side of the bay, but seeing the Cornishmen resolute, they re-embark, and the Cornish fire from the land proving galling to them, they move their ships further off from the shore.*

On the third day (July 25, 1595), the long desired help from Plymouth arrives. Sir Nicholas Clifford and Sir Henry Harris are in command of the troops while the English fleet is making for the Lizard; but they come too

---

* A relic probably of this cannonade is still to be found in Mr. Curnow's garden at Newlyn, where a large cannon ball was recently dug up. There is another Spanish cannon ball at Mousehole.

late. The wind veers from S.E. to N.W.; the Spaniards take advantage of it and make off before the brave English commanders can punish them for their audacity.

Thus ended the only important landing of the Spaniards as enemies on British soil. There may have been two or three small forays of a few sailors beside them. It was greatly exaggerated at the time in England and gave rise to a pretty thorough re-organization of the military forces in Cornwall, which Carew describes. On Spain it had a greater effect, for it was among the incentive causes which led to the burning of Cadiz, and the other bold expeditions of the British fleet at the end of Elizabeth's reign.

A curious record of the Spanish landing is to be found in the S. Paul register. The record of the burning of the parish church, and the entry of burial of three men killed by the enemy is there recorded; an entry which reads strange in the records of an English parish church.

The reign of Elizabeth is not without claims of interest from other grounds in Penzance records. At the death of the Earl of Rutland, who had received it from Edward VI about 1550, the manor of Alverton reverted in 1563 to the Crown. Queen Elizabeth granted the tithes of Madron, Penzance, and St. Clare, in 1574, to Peter Coryton and William Hogben. These great tithes had formerly belonged to the Knights of S. John. The manor of Alverton was granted to the Whitmore family, from which it passed by marriage to the Daniells.

In 1578 the plague visited Penzance, and its ravages seem to have been, considering the small population, serious. So the reign of Elizabeth was not uneventful here.

THE CHARTERS OF THE BOROUGHS.

"Ouna Dêw, par tey Mateyrn
Ha cara gox contrevogion."
Cornish Proverb.—GWAVAS.
Fear God, honour the King.
And love your neighbour.

PENZANCE, after this great catastrophe, appears to have soon risen from its ashes. Instead of a calamity it proved in the end a benefit to the town. Its chief rival Mousehole was removed, and though that town was also being rebuilt, yet now the race was fair between them, and the prestige and advantages of the past could not weigh any more. The central position of Penzance probably settled the matter. Its market was of value to the neighbourhood; its quay, which could not be burnt, proved useful to the fishermen and small traders. So Penzance prospered.

Whether it was for pity at the little town of the far West being burnt, or whether Penzance really had grown to deserve the position of a borough town is now hardly clear, all we know is the fact that on May 9, 1614, His Majesty King James I decided that Penzance should be one of the boroughs of England.

The Charter of Penzance, the palladium of the rights of our borough, exists in a safe closet in S. John's Hall. It is a formidable roll of parchment, beautifully engrossed in black letter, with the great seal attached to it.

The preamble sets forth in Latin in the name of Jacobus Angliæ Scoticæ et Franciæ Rex,

"That our vill of Penzance is an ancient vill and port both populous" (I do not suppose it had over 1000 inhabitants then) "and of great force and strength" (O advisers of the "second Solomon" what are the fortifications you are referring to?) "to resist the enemies that shall there invade, and to defend the country there adjoining......and is also a vill that exercised merchandise from time wherein the memory of men existeth not " (*i.e.* probably the reign of Edward III) "and also having much commerce in and upon the high sea by means of the port of the same vill, and whereas the inhabitants of the same vill in times past have been manifoldly burthened and are daily heavily burthened with expense in fortification and defence of the vill aforesaid " (from this it would seem fortifications were planned which were never thoroughly carried out) "and of the fort of the same, and in the maintenance, reparation, and support of divers sea fosses, banks, ways, and of a certain pier or key " (the predecessor of our present) "formerly built, erected, and constructed ; and all other necessary charges in the same vill and the precincts of the same, and especially in the taking and appre- hending of pirates and marine felons and robbers upon the high sea " (there were plenty such around the Bay, as we shall see)......"and very lately in the new erection and re-edifying the vill aforesaid, which was by the invasion of the Spaniards " (*i.e.* in 1595) "invidiously and in a hostile manner demolished and burnt to the injury of the inhabitants."* &c., &c., &c.

Seven fairs were allowed to the town, the chief of which being (the sole survivor) Corpus Christi fair.

The charter vested the government of the new borough in a mayor, recorder, eight aldermen, and 12 common councillors. The first mayor was Mr. Maddern, whose tomb is to be seen in Madron church. The 8 discreet men selected for aldermen were Messrs. Clies, Game, Dunkyn, Polkinghorne, Lympayne, Yonge, Madern (jun.), and Luke. Their 12 assistants were Luer, Sampson, Roche, Tompkyn, Davye, Bennet, Teynney, Penbease, Game, Trott, Pen- quite, and Hooper. Not a few of these names are still well-known in Penzance.

The corporation of Penzance seems to have shown energy from the begin- ning. They did not "let the grass grow under their feet." One of their first acts was to buy from the lord of Alverton manor, Richard Daniell, his rights over the tolls of the pier and market, which henceforth were vested in the corporation. A site for a market house was also purchased of him, *i.e.* "one three corner plott of waste land, lying in the said towne and village of Pen- zance and bounded on every part thereof with the king's highway." On this site the "old" market house, of which we give an illustration, was erected and shops built around it ; more picturesque, perhaps, but far less commodious than those we now see. There Clies, afterwards mayor, built several houses. His tomb and epitaph is to be seen (as well as Maddern's) in Madron churchyard.

The oldest market charter of West Penwith was probably that of Marazion, granted as we have seen by Richard King of the Romans, who was so liberal in his acts towards the small Cornish towns, and to whom therefore the county is substantially indebted for initiating much of their civic life. As a matter

---

* I use the official translation.

of fact Richard appears to have been sincerely attached to his Cornish domains, and to have done his best to develop Cornish commercial and civic interests.

The borough charter of Marazion, however, is of Elizabeth's reign. Like Penzance charter, it is a ponderous parchment, but with the portrait of Elizabeth in its initial letter instead of James I. The date is 1595, the very year of the Spanish raid, and of the burning of Penzance, Newlyn, and Mousehole. The great seal of Elizabeth appended to it, was formerly much injured, but has been put in good condition by the present Mayor. The Documents of Marazion during the seventeenth century are much fuller than those of Penzance, and there are fair materials extant of a complete history of Marazion from the Armada epoch, the records apparently having not been injured during the Commonwealth; and some of the borough documents refer to an epoch little remembered in English history, *i.e.* the period when Richard Cromwell was Lord Protector of the Commonwealth. A complete census of the adult inhabitants was made in 1660 at the Restoration, probably for assessment purposes, and is still extant.

The mode of spelling the name of the town is especially interesting, in relation to the researches of Prof. Max Müller, in his *Chips of a German Workshop.* The inscription on the borough mace of Elizabeth's time is Margasiewe. In the Commonwealth the town is officially called Margazion, but in the time of Charles II seems to revert to Marghazion and also Marhazion. In 1726 it is spelt Marazion.

S. Ives returned members to parliament in 1558, in the last year of Mary I's not very popular reign. The chief borough officer was called Portreeve. The borough was formally incorporated by Charles I. Sir Francis Basset, of Tehidy, was the recorder, who presented a corporation cup. S. Ives, as we shall see, did not shew lively gratitude to Charles I for his charter.

The charter of Charles I was forfeited in 1685, but next year James II granted a new one to S. Ives, vesting the government of the town in a mayor, recorder, town clerk, ten aldermen, and 12 common councilmen. This corporation in modern times has been reduced to a mayor, four aldermen, and 12 councillors.

S. Ives used to send two members to parliament, but by the Reform Bill of 1832 it was reduced to one, and the inhabitants of Towednack and Lelant shared with the burgesses the privileges of election.

It is perhaps noteworthy that neither Mousehole nor Lelant ever attained the position of chartered towns, though they had markets. Lelant appears to have sent members to parliament, and begged off, tradition says, from poverty. Even still it cannot be regarded as disfranchised, for the Lelant voters share with the burghers of the more fortunate daughter town of S. Ives in returning members to parliament. It seems Lelant has a custom-house. As time went on by the shifting of the sands it ceased to be of importance, and its trade was transferred to Hayle.

Chapter IV.

THE CIVIL WARS UNDER CHARLES I.

"And well for thee, saying in my dark hour,
 When all the purport of my throne hath fail'd ;
 That quick or dead thou holdest me for king.
 King am I, whatsoever be their cry ;
 And one last act of knighthood shalt thou see
 Yet ere I pass.
                                    Tennyson.
 En Hav perkou Gwâv
 In Summer remember winter.
                            The Gwâvas motto.

HERE were two Cornishmen who were leading agents in the ruin of Charles I by their extreme lines of action, John Eliot and William Noye. Of the former this is not the place to speak, as he was an East Cornwall landowner who had little to do with Penwith or Penzance. William Noye, on the other hand, was one of ourselves. It is needless to say much of him, for it is to be hoped that a biography of him may shortly enrich our historical literature, but we cannot be quite silent about one of the most eminent lawyers of the far West, the most famed of Burian men.

Here in 1577 was born William Noye. As he attains man's estate the young Cornishman goes to Exeter College, Oxford, the great college for Westcountry-men, and then becomes a student of law in Lincoln's Inn. A hard dry cynical man of wily but intellectual face (as the portraits handed down to us represent him), he devoted himself to severe legal study, and soon became eminent as a lawyer and a writer. Local interest and his known abilities combined to point him out as a fitting M.P. for the borough of S. Ives, and afterwards of the borough of Mitchell, near Truro. He soon shone in the house, taking the strong Radical side, and became one of the leading repre-sentatives of the democratic party in the West of England.

King Charles I noted his ability and acumen, and in his council was advised, if possible, to win Noye over to the Court side. "Every man has his price," is the theory of some statesmen. Untrue though this is of many persons, it was not so of Noye. He had his price, or at least circumstances led people at the time to think so. He accepted the offer of the attorney generalship from Charles, and then with the zeal of a new convert turned against his old associates. The stroke of policy of the king appeared at first a good one, the event, however, proved it otherwise. Noye went too far. He urged on the king, it is said, the ship-money, and the results of that ship-money all know. He ferreted out old statutes, and planned new exactions. The royal prerogative he stretched to the utmost. In fact he worked to make England a despotism. Whether in all this he really was sincere for the king or not one does not know. Perhaps he secretly was working for his own party by driving them to extremes. Perhaps he thought reconciliation between the parties impossible and strong measures needed. At any rate he managed to enrich himself.

He became a great favourite with the king, and one day when King Charles dined with him, Ben Jonson, the poet, who watched them from the opposite house, sent the witty epigram :—

> When the world was drowned
> No deer was found
> Because there was no park ;
> And here I sitt
> Without ere a bitt
> Cause Noyah hath all in his Arke.

King Charles took the hint, and entering into the spirit of the joke, sent over some venison with the amended verses—

> When the world was drowned
> There deer was found,
> Although there was no park ;
> I send thee a bitt
> To quicken thy witt,
> Which comes from Noya's Arke.

An anagram was made of William Noye's name, "I moyle in law." He prosecuted for King Charles I the members of the House of Commons in 1628, *i.e.* Eliot, Coryton, and others, so was pretty generally disliked by the Puritans. Noye died before the great catastrophe came which he had done so much by his violence to prepare for; at the age of 57 he passed away at Tunbridge Wells, in 1634. Archbishop Laud's eulogium of him was not quite deserved—"I have lost a dear friend of him, and the Church the greatest she had of his condition since she needed any such."

As West Penwith leads nowhere (save to the wide Atlantic), it has fortunately, as we have seen, never been a scene of large military operations. No general in his senses would seek a pitched battle in a *cûl de sac*, where retreat is out of the question. So in both the Wars of the Roses and the Civil Wars of Charles I, this region was rather avoided than otherwise by the generals on both sides. The Cornish campaign of Charles I, so interesting a feature in the general history of the county, was almost confined to east and central Cornwall, and hardly touched the western division—not to say Penwith. No doubt, however, deep anxiety existed in these regions. The Civil Wars must ever have been present to the mind of the people. Not merely the anxious news from other parts must have fully occupied the village politicians, but the constant drilling and arming even in remote hamlets, the presence of Hopton's cavalry, the unwonted sight of the "pomp and panoply of glorious war" must have struck both young and old. Above all, the constant anxiety for friends on campaign in other counties.

Cornwall, generally, was very loyal to Church and King in those troublous times. S. Ives may have been an exception, but Penzance was not. The loyalty of the county called forth the memorable letter once fixed in all the parish churches of West Penwith, but now usually removed. It may, however, be still seen and read in S. Erth and S. Leven and Lelant churches.

C.R. (="Carolus Rex")   To the Inhabitants of Cornwall.

"We are so highly sensible of the merit of our county of Cornwall, of their zeal for the defence of our person, and the just rights of our crown, in a time when we could contribute so little to our own defence, or to their assistance; in a time when not only no reward appeared, but great and probable dangers were threatened to obedience and loyalty: of their great and eminent courage and patience in their indefatigable prosecution of their great work against so potent an enemy, backed with so strong, rich, and populous cities, and so plentifully furnished and supplied with men, arms, money, ammunition and provisions of all kinds; and of the wonderful success with which it pleased Almighty God (though with the loss of some most eminent persons who shall never be forgotten by us to reward their loyalty and patience) by many strange victories over their and our enemies in despight (*sic*) of all human probability and all imaginable disadvantages; that as we can not be forgetful of so great desert, so we cannot but desire to publish it to all the world, and perpetuate to all time the memory of their merits, and of our acceptance of the same; and to that end, we do hereby render our royal thanks to that our county, in the most public and lasting manner we can devise, commanding copies

B

hereof to be printed and published, and one of them to be read in every church and chapel therein, and to be kept for ever as a record of the same, that as long as the history of these times and of this nation shall continue, the memory of how much that county has merited from us and our crown, may be derived with it to posterity."

Given at our Camp at Sudeley Castle, the 10th day of September, 1643.

There are some episodes in the Civil Wars which are not without interest as especially characteristic of the period and the place.

I. In 1644 some of the S. Ives men, with their neighbours of Lelant and Towednack, resolved on rebelling against the king and taking the side of the parliament. The rest of West Penwith, like Cornwall generally, was loyal; but S. Ives appears to have been, as in 1549, the local headquarters of the revolutionary party. Perhaps the heavy taxation they underwent in the early part of the war, and their position by the sea shore, causing frequent intercourse with strangers, were the causes of their rather un-Cornish line of action.

Charles was alarmed at this rebellion of the far west, and sent Sir Richard Grenville into Penwith with some infantry and cavalry to suppress the revolt. The S. Ives men were encamped on Longstone Downs, a mile and a half from the town.

They only numbered 200, variously and rudely armed. At the sight of Sir Richard's troops, their courage evaporated, and holding the Falstaffian maxim that "the better part of valour is discretion," they "made a strategical movement to the rear" as euphoniously it is called, but with such agility over the rough country that the king's cavalry could not catch them, and only a few were killed.

The troops then marched on S. Ives and entered the town in triumph. Sir Richard billeted himself on the mayor, and fined him £500 for suffering this rebellion. The mayor could not or would not pay. He was committed to Launceston gaol. After 3 months, Prince Charles ordered his release.

But vengeance did not stop here. Philips, a constable of Zennor, was hanged for treason; Arundell, the leader of the rebellion (these Arundells had much to do with Cornish revolts in the olden time) was proclaimed a traitor, and sentenced to death. He escaped to Bridgewater, and served under Fairfax. Two S. Ives men were caught and hanged, the one at Helston, and the other at Truro.

This was not the end, however, of the military troubles of S. Ives in 1644. General Goring marched on the town, but the people stopped the roads with barrels of sand, and kept a threatening watch, so the general thought it wiser to retire.

II. The conduct of Penzance was very different. When Lord Goring's and Lord Hopton's troops were driven by Fairfax into the far west in 1646, they were most hospitably received by the Penzance people. The cavalier officers were welcomed by the local gentry, and the humbler troopers found a hearty Cornish welcome from the people generally. The Penzance people loved their king and the brave soldiers who were fighting for him, and they showed it by their acts. Perhaps they had many sons and brothers in the other corps of the Royal army.

The reports of Penzance liberality reached the ears of Fairfax, and with a brutal disregard for the laws of war, the unarmed and unfortified little town was doomed to a two day's sack, as though it had been a fortress taken after siege or by storm. The parliamentary troopers entered the town, and taking due precautions against a surprise from the enraged Cornishmen, proceeded to the work of plunder and devastation. What military violence is we, happily in England, have well nigh forgotten. The scenes of the Franco-Prussian war perhaps give only an imperfect idea of the roughness of the soldiery of the seventeenth century.

The town was thoroughly plundered, and it would seem as if, even then, there were wealthy persons in Penzance, for one trooper, Edward Best (a Cornish parliamentary soldier), got as his share "five gallons (it sounds quaint that measuring money by the gallon) of English coin, silver and gold, and pieces of eight." (Query :—Surely Best must have been an officer, Penzance never could have been rich enough to afford such a share of spoil to an ordinary trooper?) Among the other plunderers Hals preserves, doubtless for the admiration of the Penzance people, the names of Littlecott, Keen, and Lockyer of Roche.

It is hard for us now to realize the local misery caused by such military violence. Families in comfort or comparative affluence reduced in a day to poverty and want, cherished heirlooms wrested from their rightful owners, who had wished to leave them to their children's children, bright happy homes covered with misery and gloom. Penzance thus suffered in one century two cruel wrongs—the one its burning by the Spaniards, and from which it seems in a generation to have struggled into new life ; the other now comes, its brutal sack by the Roundheads. If anywhere a peace advocate ought to be listened to, it is here. Few unfortified towns have suffered from war, in days gone bye, more than Penzance.

This was the first sack of the town. Penzance did not suffer meekly. In June, 1648, Penzance rose against the Puritans. Alexander Daniels relates how " ye Lord preserved my life at ye Penzance rout fro' a bloody souldier that heaved up his musket to knock me o' the head." The regalia of the borough were then taken away and borne in derisive procession through Penryn. A description of this procession is given by a contemporary and eye witness. (1) Three soldiers bearing up on the points of their swords carried upright three silver balls used in hurling. (2) 3 soldiers wearing alderman's gowns. (3) Troops bearing favours and ribbons stolen from Penzance, and firing their muskets at intervals. (4) Forty prisoners. (5) Horses bearing the pillage of Penzance household stuffs, beds, &c. The procession marched up S. Thomas Street, Penryn, to the upper end of the town. The unfortunate prisoners were afterwards shut up in the Market-place of Penryn.

It seems that in this sack the records of the borough must have been destroyed. Such was civil war to Penzance.

III. St. Michael's Mount had been occupied by the king's troops at the commencement of the war, on account of its military importance. William Cecil, Earl of Salisbury, its owner, having deserted the king, the care of the island fortress was committed to Sir Francis Basset, with orders to provide it with ammunition and provisions. In February, 1643, it was visited by Prince Maurice.

It did not, however, prove of much use to the Royal cause. Colonel Hammond, the parliamentary commander, laid siege, and after some resistance, it surrendered. At the restoration, the Basset family, who had been much impoverished by the civil wars, sold it to the S. Aubyns, who ever since have possessed it.

Chapter V.

WEST PENWITH DURING THE COMMONWEALTH.

Kenz ol Tra Tonkin
Ouna Deil Matern yn.
The Tonkin Motto (Pryce).
Above all things, Tonkin,
Fear God in the king.

N January 30, 1649, a great storm, with thunder and lightning (unusual in winter), is said to have raged over West Penwith. A ship bound for France, in S. Ives Bay, with king Charles I's wardrobe on board, broke from her moorings, and was wrecked on Godrevy Island (near where the lighthouse now stands.) Of 60 persons on board only two were saved. A few days later the news arrived from London how on that day a king of England had died on the scaffold. Cornishmen dwelt much on the coincidence.

In 1653 S. Ives beheld a very different scene. The militia of the town, 100 strong, are called out under the command of Major Peter Ceely. They march through the streets in warlike array, to the admiration of their fellow townsmen. Every soldier wears two yards of ribbon (what a vanity for Puritan times !) one white and the other blue. They form into line. A document is read to them. Oliver Cromwell is proclaimed Lord Protector of the Realm, by the will of the Commons of England, or rather by the power of the sword. The S. Ives militiamen present their muskets for a *feu-de-joie* and fire three volleys. S. Ives has got the best of it after all for a time. The monarchy is suspended. The commonwealth takes its place.

Mr. Peter Ceely appears to have been a lucky man by sea as well as land. Next year, his privateer (for he fits out a ship for the Protector at his own cost), makes a good haul for S. Ives. Not pilchards, by the bye, nor mackerel, but larger fish come to Mr. Ceely's net. Five French barques are taken, and sold as prizes. He now becomes not merely a Major on shore, but a Vice-Admiral at sea. Not merely French barques, but English merchantmen suit his net. The cargoes of two ships wrecked in Monnt's Bay are entrusted to his care. How much their owners received out of the salvage is not stated. A rich Dutch ship in 1659 was also wrecked at Whitsand Bay, and the silver and more valuable of the wrecked cargo (*i.e.* which the wreckers did not appropriate to their own private use) were entrusted to the Admiral.

Major or Admiral Ceely (which is the correct title?) was pretty energetic out of S. Ives as well as in it. His commission from " Oliver, Lord Protector of the Commonwealth of England, Scotland, and Ireland " is still extant, and is given at length by Mr. Buller in his history of S. Just.* The orders given by Ceely to Captain Arundell, in 1659, have also been published, and certainly do not speak much for that gallant officer's spelling, even allowing for the eccentricities of the period.

A levy was raised of the S. Just men for Arundell's company. The Borlases did not join it, as Dr. Borlase was proud to say in after years. One of them, Nicholas Borlase, of Treludra, has a place in the local history of those troublous times. He was a cavalry Colonel under Charles I. There was a jocular saying that once Colonel Borlase routed a large detachment of the parliamentarians by running away. The fact was that being much pressed, he made a running fight, and prudently, to cover his retreat, set the woods on fire. The parliamentarians alarmed, thought it was the camp fires of the King's army, and fled with precipitation, leaving to the Colonel and his cavaliers their baggage. The parliamentarian authorities, when the fortunes of Charles I became hopeless, did not forget the Colonel's stratagem. Most of his property was confiscated, and his family reduced almost to starvation, when by ready wit he saved a part. One Sunday he went into Oliver Cromwell's seat, at meeting, as if by mistake. On seeing the Protector, he got out. " No,' said Cromwell, " cousin Borlase, I am glad to see you here," and kept him during the sermon. Seeing through the ruse, Oliver promised him a part of

---

* " Statistical Account of the parish of S. Just-in-Penwith," by Rev. J. Buller, p. 73, 74.

his property. Another story is told that Nicholas Borlase asked Oliver Cromwell to sign a recommendation for him, while the Protector was walking in S. James Park. Oliver said he had no pen or ink. " Please your Highness I have both," said Colonel Borlase. " But I have no desk," said Oliver. " Write on my back," said the Colonel. Oliver signed the recommendation, admitting perchance the ready wit of this brave and able Cornishman.

Other cavaliers were less fortunate. We read how Levelis hid several of them from the parliamentary troops in the Fogou or artificial cave at Trewoof —a most uncomfortable place, one would say, for a gentleman's residence.

The borough records of Penzance begin at 1655, probably as Mr. Millet conjectures, in consequence of the first book of the record having " been destroyed during the pillage of the town." A remonstrance to Oliver Cromwell is one of the earliest acts recorded in this book. The town had to be terrorized. Major Peter Ceely sent Captain Arundell's squadron to the town of Penzance, and quartered them there. Penzance men were seized by the press gang, and driven to serve on the Commonwealth's ships. The ruin of some of the antiquities of the neighbourhood, *e.g.* Madron Chapel was another wrong, a sentimental one, but deeply felt and long remembered, for Cornishmen have rarely or never been iconoclasts. Here much of the ruin is attributed to Peter Ceely, as Shrubsall is credited with the work of destruction in Kerrier. The people did not like it, and it is unjust to charge them or their descendants with the ruin of our ancient remains. Vandalism never became common among us till the nineteenth century. The old Cornish loved their past and its precious relics, little though they might anticipate the priceless value of these remains to the Archæologists of the future. However, taken all in all, the destruction of antiquities in Cornwall by the Puritans was not to be compared with the ruin in other counties. Hence it is that in the far west we can better realize what old England really was—whether the England of the middle ages, or the Britain of the Roman or ancient age—than in most parts of our country.

CHAPTER VI.

THE RESTORATION AND THE REVOLUTION.

"I made them lay their hands in mine and swear
To reverence the king, as if he were
Their conscience, ond their conscience as their king,
To break the heathen and uphold the Christ.
Tennyson.

OTHING could have been more generally acceptable in West Penwith than the Restoration as indeed it was throughout England. The Cornish gentry had suffered much for their loyalty, and the miners and fishermen preferred to be ruled by a king to either a despotism of a parliament in which they could scarcely expect to be fairly represented, or a tyranny of a soldiery whom they regarded almost as foreigners. If Penzance had suffered from the vengeance of Fairfax, it might now hope for favour from Charles II.

To express their loyalty the corporation seem to have enjoyed themselves after the good old English fashion, by having a grand dinner, for we find an entry "Coronation expenses at Mr. Veale's—wine and beer, £14 10s." Well, they greeted the return of the merry Monarch in his own merry way. I hope none of them were the worse for it.

But they had not merely to drink the health of royalty, for royalty was soon to be among them. Queen Catherine of Braganza's ship put into Gwavas lake, and gave the loyal Penzance and Newlyn folk a chance of seeing the Queen, and of having a fête in her honor.

Charles II was not ungrateful to Penzance. On August 18, 1663, he granted their charter as a coinage town. The preamble states " Whereas we have been informed that the greater part of the Tynne (still Tynne not Tin) now and for some years past gained with our said Stannary of Penwith and Kirrier, is and hath been so gayned in places within the said stannary very far and remote from Helston afore said . . . . We, taking the said premises into our princely consideration, doe by these presents for us, our heir and successors, nominate and appoint our towne of Pensance to be from henceforth for ever one of the Coynage townes within the said stannery." The Coinage charter was brought to Penzance by Lord Godolphin's porter.

When the charter was got the next thing to do was to build a Coinage Hall. With praiseworthy energy the corporation set about it." " Penzance men are about to build a Coinage Hall upon your wastrell of the street below their Market House," wrote Alexander Daniell to Larrigan, to his son Richard, in 1664. They did build it, and the Coinages were done there till 1816 (with a short interval under James II).

The loyalty of the corporation comes out curiously in some of their minutes. On the anniversary of the execution of King Charles I, there seems to have been a solemn drinking to his memory, while bonfires were lighted on " Oak Apple Day" (May 29), the festival of the Restoration of Charles II. At the 'same time to keep their own dignity, in 1669, two new maces were procured for the borough. The old ones had been stolen it seems by the soldiers of Fairfax. The peace with Holland, in 1674, gave cause for further festivities.

But the Penzance men did not only think of these things. Devoted to the Crown, they thought of the Church also. Mr. John Tremenheere gave a small endowment for the minister of S. Mary's. The building was now to be consecrated. It would seem that in those days in old S. Mary's, the men and women sat separately, the women in the central part. The accommodation would not seem excessive, or the appropriated sittings were only a small part of the whole, for there were only some 200 seats—114 to women, and 86 to men, besides the corporation pews, &c.

The consecration of old S. Mary's must have been a great event for the quiet little borough. It was dedicated as " a Chapel of Ease to the Vicarial Church of Madron." Not a very beautiful edifice by the bye, but its quaint and (not ungraceful) spire, inold pictures of Penzance, forms a feature in the landscape.

S

The reign of king James II did not open very auspiciously in our borough records. It is indeed with a rejoicing, but one of a dubious character ; the storm of war in its worst form, Civil war, had burst over England. Monmouth had raised the West. Penwith and Penzance happily had escaped his emmissaries. They were let alone. But the story of Sedgmoor must have disturbed many a Penzance person's rest. The borough, however, was very loyal, and showed its loyalty to King James by a demonstration, rejoicing at Monmouth's being routed. Their loyalty was not well repaid by the King. Like other boroughs, the Penzance charters were called in question, and more than a year's revenue was expended in defending their rights.

James II issued a proclamation forbidding Englishmen "from listing *(sic.)* under foreign Princes"—a hit at William of Orange (afterwards William III). This was proclaimed in Penzance. On the birth of "the old Pretender," the son of James II by Queen Mary d' Este, the loyal little borough again had a fête. Guns were fired, bells rung, and merry-making general, though, by the bye, they could not have cared so very deeply about it, as only a few months later we have again a fête for the coronation of that same little boy's brother-in-law and adversary, Prince William of Orange, *alias* King William III. Perhaps the Penzance people were ready for any occasion for a holiday, and did not care or know very much about politics. They must have been rather "out of the world" in those days. The news of Prince James Francis Edward's (the Pretender's) birth took five days to come down from London, although the government must have had reasons for dispatch. Till well on in Charles II's reign the ordinary post stopped at Marazion, whence it went to London only once a week. An ordinary letter took (to judge by Alexander Daniel's letters) some 8 days coming from London, and as we have seen a government dispatch took 5 days. We complain of the post now, but what should we say of the good old days !

It is a singular coincidence that both in the earlier stages of what used to be called "the Great Rebellion" which ruined Charles I, and in the "Revolution" which drove out his son James II, Cornishmen took a leading share. Whether we suppose this merely accidental, or attribute it to Cornishmen being more quick in reading the signs of the times than other Englishmen, I cannot decide. The fact remains that if Noye and Eliot (as we have seen) ruined Charles I, the Trelawneys had a leading share in bringing his expulsion on James II.

Dr. Jonathan Trelawney was hardly a West Cornishman. He was born at Pelynt in 1650. But Penwith claimed him as her own. In 1692, when the toils of the Revolution were over, Penzance corporation publicly entertained the two Cornish liberators, the Bishop and the General, at a public feast.

The story of the seven Bishops ought to be well known to every educated Englishman. It was an important crisis in our national history. Jonathan Trelawney, then Bishop of Bristol, was one of the seven. When ushered into the King's presence, after he had read the paper, James II said " I tell you this is a standard of rebellion." "Rebellion !" exclaimed Trelawney, "for God's sake, Sir, do not say so hard a thing of us. No Trelawney can be a rebel. Remember that my family has fought for the crown. Remember how I served your majesty when Monmouth was in the West." But James II was resolved to go in his course. He would not stand the opposition of the seven prelates. They were sent to the Tower, tried, and as " every schoolboy " knows, acquitted. Cornwall was deeply moved at the insult to their county. It was not only a Bishop and a learned doctor, it was a leading Cornishman who was imprisoned. " One and all " they resented the wrong to the county. There is one Cornishman who is especially angry, not only at the wrong to not merely his county and his Church, but his family. Colonel Trelawney commands a Tangier regiment for James. He feels, but is silent, biding his time.

Neither he nor his countrymen had long to wait. On a wet November day that same year, 1688, the rumour spread like wild fire through Cornwall that William Prince of Orange had landed at Brixham, with an army which the excitement of the Devonshire people exaggerated in size. Then, in that week of excitement comes the story of the fall of Exeter, the preparations of King James, the wavering at Plymouth. Lord Bath with his Cornish regiment secures that fortress. William does not call on the Cornish miners to rise. He trusts in his regular troops, and what he knows of the disaffection of the English army. James collects his forces at Salisbury. William advanced eastward from

Devon, the whole of the west practically being his, for the Plymouth garrison has given in, and the Cornish remember their wrong. Colonel Trelawney with Kirke holds Warminster for James. At a critical moment Colonel Trelawney goes over to William. Churchill and other generals do the same. James has lost the Crown of England. A few weeks later he is a fugitive at S. Germains, and William III is king.

In July, 1690, the Cornish had a new alarm, a threat of the same danger in that same fatal month, which a century before had laid Penzance in ashes. Tourville, with the great fleet which Louis XIV had collected, menaced our southern shores. Cornwall " one and all " rose at the rumour. Ten thousand miners (it is said) signed or rather put their marks (for they could not write) to an address to queen Mary II, during the absence of William III on his famous Irish campaign, declaring they were ready to serve her Majesty against every enemy. They were brought to the test. One July night the warning beacons were blazing on the hills. The miners crowded into the towns. It was no false alarm. Wearied dust-covered couriers rode over the country. The French had landed. Teignmouth, in Devon, had been taken and been burnt. De Tourville's troops were on Devonshire soil. The Cornishmen marched on to the Tamar. But it was not needed. The Devonshire men and the garrison of Plymouth had made such a determined show of resistence that De Tourville thought it wiser to make off, and England was spared an invasion.* The Cornish men went home quietly to their mines and fishing boats.

The history of Penzance in the latter part of the reign of William III does not appear to have been very eventful. We have records of fêtes at the Peace of Ryswick, and other entertainments on divers occasions, but not much of general interest.

It is difficult to realize in this our nineteenth century, when piracy is well nigh relegated to the China Seas, and even there is being pretty efficiently stamped out by European navies, how large a number of the events of West Penwith in past ages are connected with piratical expeditions. Whether the Cornish people ever did anything in the buccaneering line themselves it is

---

* For description of this landing see Lord Macauley's History, Vol. III, p. 649-55.

not for me to say ; on that topic, though speech be " silvern," silence may be golden, but most assuredly those wicked " foreign " pirates often must have sadly shaken the nerves of the old ladies of the Land's End district.

As these pirate stories, though fairly authenticated, are not particularly edifying or instructive, we shall merely select four as illustrations of the " good old times :"—

I. In 1634, *i.e.* in Charles I. reign, there were many Turkish (or Algerine ?) pirates on the Cornish seas. Some S. Ives fishermen met two derelict vessels. Their crews had been murdered or enslaved, but many casks of rum (the Moslems were forbidden by their Koran the use of spiritous liquors) were found on board. The fishermen took them into S. Ives and gave them up to Sir John Arundell, who restored one ship with its rum to the fishermen, and sent the other to Padstow. What the fishermen did with the rum history does not declare. I suppose they drank some, and sold the rest to the " licensed victuallers of the period."

II. Next year, a Turkish pirate of 12 guns and a crew of ninety men, cruising along the Cornish coast, captured three vessels of Fowey and Looe. The sailors were kept on board to be sold as slaves, the ships were turned adrift. The brave Cornishmen conspired against the Turks. Watching a favorable moment, one of them struck down the Moslem captain, and threw him, while stunned, overboard. The pirates, surprised, were overcome and driven below. The Cornishmen seeing the breeze favourable, sailed for S. Ives, though the Turks continued to fire up from the hold. The vice-admiral of S. Ives secured the ship, and the pirates were kept for some time prisoners in the town. This story has probably given rise to some of the Cornish pirate legends.

III. A French privateer (a little better than a pirate, but not much according to our modern notions) in 1705, chased two ships (one Dutch, the other English) into S. Ives bay. The castle fired on the enemy. The Frenchman replied, and, moreover, fired into the town. A young woman, walking the streets, was mortally wounded. The French ship escaped.

IV. On the night of September 29, 1760, the inhabitants of Penzance and Newlyn were disturbed by the firing of cannon in the bay. Great commotion ensued. We were then at war with France, and there had been many fears expressed of predatory excursions. The alarm sounded in the streets. The Penzance volunteer company were called to arms, and marched out in the direction of Newlyn, to what was then the Western Green. A large ship was seen in the darkness close to Newlyn, evidently stranded. On board were crowds of strange-looking, fierce-bearded dark men, with turbans on their heads. Alarm increased at this sight. It was not the French, it was worse, the Turks had come to plunder and murder. The terror was intense, but shortly appeared to be mutual. If the Cornishmen were afraid of being murdered, the Algerines were as much afraid of being drowned, and that fear was the more reasonable, for their ship was fast becoming a total wreck. As the real state of things began to be perceived, the courage of the volunteers increased, and they partly led partly drove the ship-wrecked Turks into a building on the Western Green (near Alexandra Road), where they were put under strict guard. The authorities communicated with the general at Plymouth, who sent down some troops to Penzance. A new alarm then arose. "Might they not bring into Penzance the plague." A sanitary cordon was formed, but the one fear proved as needless as the other. On the whole, the poor fellows were kindly treated, and were at length sent to Algiers by a man-of-war. The ship was an Algerine corsair of 24 guns. The captain had supposed himself near Cadiz. The nautical examinations of the period could not have been very severe, it would seem.

As one reads these pirate stories one is reminded of some characteristic Cornish verses :—

> " Kymero 'wyth guz lavarack powz :
> Guz ogan, ha guz aur ;
> Ma ladran moz, en termen noz,
> Reb vor Loundrez Tur."
>
> *John Boson of Newlyn.*
>
> "Take care of your heavy breeches ;
> Your silver and your gold ;
> Thieves do go in the night time,
> By the way of London Tower."

PART V.—MODERN TIMES.

CHAPTER I.

PENZANCE IN THE LAST CENTURY, AND SIR HUMPHRY DAVY.

Doktour brays kekefrys
Yv gelwy fiour an bysmas
Sur in clergy.
The great Doctor likewise that is called the " Flower of the world " in learning.
Beunans Meriasek, 1380-3.

ITH the seventeenth century the romantic side of our Penwith history, may be said to end. The Cornish drolls seem to own it, for the vague date 200 years ago points to the Stuarts and not to the Georges. The legends of Squire Lovel, of Tregeagle, and many other mythic characters of the Cornish droll, all point back to times before the Hanovarian succession was talked of. That event seems to have had a benumbing and soberizing effect on Cornish imagination.

And so also with the real history. The sudden raid of the Spaniards, the cannonade on the Green, the burning of old Penzance, its rising from its ashes, its loyalty to Charles I, its sack by Fairfax, its enthusiastic loyalty at the restoration, the whispered alarms of French invasion, the pirates in Mount's Bay, all give even its real history a certain quaint tinge of poetry. My readers must expect little more of this, or if there is a poetry, it is of another type, The poetry, if it can be said to exist, gathers round the triumphs of science, the progress of commerce, and the moving of religious enthusiasm.

The age of the mythic Lovel and Tregeagle, of the real Noye and Trelawney, has passed, we are coming to the era of Keigwin, Tonkin, Lluyd, and Gwavas, and then of Dr. Borlase and of Wesley; later on still, of Davy and Barrington. The poetry of mere imagination is passing, the poetry of antiquarianism, of philosophy, of religious enthusiasm, is taking its place.

The reign of Queen Anne was not very eventful in our borough history. Mr. Carveth appears "by force and violence," as is said in the borough records, to have retained the mayoralty for three years.   The charter was endangered. A petition of the aldermen to Queen Anne received attention, and the charter was restored, but it cost the borough nearly £200. A commission was issued. A new mayor, William Tonkin, was elected. The story of this little *coup d' etat* is obscure.   The borough records state that "John Carveth stood in mayor *(sic)*" unlawfully, and so "the said town forfeited their charter."   Four blank pages occur in the borough records, and the accounts of 1702 do not seem to have been passed till 1708.   The reign of the usurper was an interregnum. How ever John Carveth managed to make himself dictator of the little town is not quite clear.   He seems to have had a little body-guard of pseudo constables, who afterwards were tried at Bodmin.

The old custom of keeping up the anniversary of the restoration, May 29th, at public expense, appears to have continued, but on a smaller scale.   Nor was the town without a fête at proclaiming the peace of Utrecht.

The Hanoverian succession is ushered in by a very curious entry in the borough accounts: "To cash given the Mob at the King's coronation £1 5s." Perhaps this might imply that some of the Penzance people did not see any reason to cheer at George I's coronation unless they were paid for it.   King George's birthday was also kept up gaily with bonfires, and at public expense. There is something in all this reminding one of a French prefect in Napoleonic days.

The corporation, at the same time that they were so jealous about king George's dignity being realized by the populace, were not forgetful of their own.   The mayor was granted, in 1721, a liberal allowance of £40 for "Serjeants' cloaks, hats, and other expenses inseparable from the mayoralty," while two years later a public grant was made for lining the mayrish's (spelling bees were not yet a Penzance institution—kind reader—I suppose "Mayoress" is here meant) seat with blue shalloon.

Early in George II's reign the borough made a decided step in progress in getting their post three times a week—a wonderful advance on the old once a

week system, when the post stopped at Marazion.   S. Mary's chapel was enlarged in 1728, by a chancel at the east end—a not very beautiful nor costly
erection, but an improvement as things went.

After many years of quiet, Penzance was disturbed by riots in 1728.
Soldiers were billeted in the town.   The room over the Coinage Hall was
given up to them.   The borough records at this point have quite a martial
aspect.   Purchases of powder, shot, and bullets, appointing guards, procla-
mations against the "riotous" tinners, disbursements of various kinds to the
soldiers.   The troops were placed at Market-jew Street to guard the approach
from Marazion.

About this time some distinguished visitors seem to have come to Mount's
Bay, not for health nor to see the Land's End, but on business matters, for we
read in 1730 that the town was honored by a mysterious visitor, "Prince
Chesroan Abu Gemblat Hassar Abaisci, of Mount Libanus in Syria.   In 1736,
another distinguished visitor, the Prince of Canaase, came to Penzance.

Among the curious entries in the borough accounts, at this time, are three
which strikingly exhibit the change which less than a century and a half has
made in our manners and ideas.

I.   "Pasco Biscay was paid for carrying cenders *(sic)* under the Aldermen's
and Assistant seats."   At first sight this might appear to imply that these
honourable members of the corporation sat over a dust heap, or a coal-hole.
This would not be accurate.   It seems the foreign custom then existed at
Penzance of using chafing dishes under the seats in cold weather, good stoves
had not yet been invented.

II.   Thomas Pidwell, in 1738, sold to the borough that rather singular and
ungallant instrument "a woman's bridle."   This is a striking relic of the "good
old times," when inveterate scolding was punished as an offence against
society.   A capital picture and amusing description of it is given by Mr.
Millet.   I believe it is no longer a part of the Corporation property.

Those must have been trying days for ladies who used their tongues "not
wisely but too well" in our good borough.

III.   In the same year a new Maypole was ordered.   What became of the
said Maypole? I cannot either inform my readers.   We have not yet, how-

T

ever, given up May customs—they were kept up as vigorously in 1877 as ever, only with all love for archæology, I question whether the good old British custom of making May morn disagreeable—I must not say hideous—with May day horns, is a custom more honored in the breach than the observance, though some enthusiastic Oxonians often say it reminds them of Alma Mater, for in Oxford the same old custom prevails.

The state of society at this time, or a little later, in the town of Penzance, is thus described by Sir Humphry Davy's brother. "The roads which traversed the country were rather bridle paths than carriage roads; carriages were almost unknown, and even carts were very little used . . . There was only one cart in the town of Penzance, and if a carriage occasionally appeared in the streets it attracted universal attention. Pack horses were then in general use for conveying merchandise, and the prevailing manner of travelling was on horseback. At that period the luxuries of furniture and living, now enjoyed by people of the middle class, were confined almost entirely to the great and wealthy; and in the same town (Penzance) where the population was about 2000 persons, there was only one carpet; the floors of the rooms were sprinkled over with sea sand, and there was not a single silver fork (!). The only newspaper which then circulated in the West of England was the Sherbourne Mercury, and it was carried through the county not by the post, but by a man on horseback specially employed in distributing it." In 1761, the turnpike road did not go beyond Falmouth. An attempt was made to extend it to Penzance and the Land's End, but on account of the opposition here, it was only carried to Marazion. The carriage roads to Morvah and to S. Just were made in 1763.

The condition of the country districts it is not easy to discern. There were strange stories of smuggling, wrecking, and piracy, which still linger in local traditions, of which Messrs. Hunt and Botterill's works give us some inkling. Society was rougher than now, but its faults, I think, have been greatly exaggerated, and perhaps its honest virtues often forgotten. The aged people with whom I often conversed, who professed to recollect in their childhood the state of things at the end of the last century.—I refer to persons of between eighty or ninety years of age, who retain their mental faculties—certainly give on dark account of days gone bye. Indeed, not a few lament how things have changed, how much less kindliness, and heartiness, and "homeliness" (I use the word in its Cornish sense) there was then than now ; how much more respect for parents and for old people, much more neighbourliness to fellow creatures in distress, much less pride and false pretence than now. The account they gave of the old Cornwall of the period of the great French Revolution is not unlike, in substance, Carew and Norden's description of the still older Cornwall of the Elizabethan age ; and I think the character and manners of the old folk who describe it, often tallies with the description of the society in which their youth was formed.

We may have gained something, but I think we have lost something also. If our school boards, institutes, and cheap literature could teach our youth to combine the rugged virtues of the past with the civilization of the present, it would be well. But the task is a hard one, it may be an impossible one. Let us instead of dreaming of that Utopia, consider the history of one of the greatest of the great men of Penwith—a man of the eighteenth century, but who did much to form the civilization of the nineteenth.

How many romances there are of real life which are never known except when connected with the biography of eminent persons ! One such, connected with Penzance, I must lay before my readers. Few novelists have imagined a more striking plot than this real Penzance romance, as authenticated by Dr. Paris, by Davy, and by others.

There is a house in Penzance that is stricken with deadly fever. In it the father and mother of the family are both attacked. In both the disease grows more and more alarming. The father, at length, succumbs. The awful news is revealed to the dying mother. She shrinks, even in death agony, from the thought of leaving her three girls orphans in a cold hard world. They have been wealthy and well connected, but reverse of fortune has impoverished them. Her daughters may want. The doctor is touched at the dying mother's anxiety : he promises to do his best for the orphans. All is over. Mr. Tonkin takes the three little girls to his home and adopts them as his children. The second of them is called Grace Millett—a sweet, gentle, sensible girl, who when she grows up is wooed and won by a young wood carver of Penzance (born of the Ludgvan family of Davys) by name Robert Davy, and after their marriage at S. Mary's, they live together in Market Jew Street. Their eldest son is born December 17, 1778, and is baptized (at S. Mary's Chapel) by the name of Humphry.

Some ninety years ago, if one had been walking by Penzance pier, a little boy might have been seen, a rather uncouth looking little fellow, very fond of play and not very fond of work, but deeply devoted to piscatorial pursuits. He has a theory of his own about how to catch grey mullet, and is very strong on the subject. He delights in composing pantomimes and tournaments, and in making "thunder powder and fireworks." The boys like him, but his master thinks the ferule ought to be often used, and Master Humphry Davy has frequently to experience in his own person the chastening effects of the rod. He is incorrigible, however. He will go on with his fishing rods, and fireworks, and pantomimes just the same.

At length, in 1793, when 15 years of age, he is sent to Dr. Cardew, at Truro, a rather celebrated schoolmaster at that time. He, however, makes but little progress, nor gives much satisfaction. Dr. Cardew writes, " I could not discern the faculties by which he was afterwards so much distinguished ; I discovered, indeed, his taste for poetry, which I did not omit to encourage." As a poet, however, Davy never was, and perhaps never could be really celebrated. Of his scientific acumen, his master never appears to have had an inkling. How difficult is the study of human character !

In 1794 Robert Davy died, and next year Master Humphry was apprenticed to Mr. John H. Borlase, a surgeon and apothecary of Penzance. When studying with him, his attention was first drawn seriously to chemistry, by his wish to procure superior pigments for his paintings (he seems to have dabbled in nearly everything). He was now always making experiments in the garret of the kind guardian of his mother (long an orphan, now widowed also). One day a grand explosion took place, which put in jeopardy not only all the glass bottles, but the Doctor himself. " This boy Humphry is incorrigible ! He will blow us all up in the air."

The career of Davy as a medical student at Penzance would not be of interest to the general public. A desultory life of long walks, poetical effusions, chemical experiments, and varied reading, appears to have interfered much with his medical studies. Still, he made progress in his knowledge of natural science. Some scientific men who, for health or for purposes of examining the geological formation of Cornwall, visited Penzance, took an interest in the young scientific enthusiast. Among these was Dr. Beddoes, of Bristol, whom Davy conducted over the interesting parts of the Land's End district. The Doctor was struck by the young man's ability, and when he started his Pneumatic Institution at Bristol (a failure by the bye, but a very useful one to science), he offered the situation of assistant to young Davy, then nineteen. Dr. Tonkin, who wished Davy to be a surgeon in his native town, was very angry, but it was useless. Humphry would go. He started from Penzance on October 2, 1798, and his route was gladdened by the cheerful omen of meeting the mail coach from London adorned with laurels and ribbons, bringing the joyful news of Nelson's victory of the Nile. Little did his fellow passengers think that that handsome young Penzance man was going to win, in another sphere, a victory as brilliant as Nelson's !

The rest belongs rather to the history of science than of Penzance. That young Cornishman had before him a career, in rapidity and brilliancy, almost unequalled in scientific annals. In four years, without money, friends, or interest, he springs into an European reputation. It is rapidly but not easily won. At Bristol he almost dies a "martyr of science." Full of young enthusiasm, he daringly enters into nature's inmost secrets, breathing gases never before inhaled by mortal man (and very rarely likely to be breathed again). He was almost poisoned by them, and was forced to revisit his native Penzance to recruit an apparently injured constitution. He was then offered a lectureship of the Royal Institution in London, in January, 1801. Here his passionate enthusiasm breathed freshness and poetry into the cold domains of scientific research. His rude eloquence carried his audience with him. Even the fashionable world crowded to hear the young enthusiastic professor of only 23 summers. The Duchess of Gordon and other leaders of fashion invited him to their soirées. But greater triumphs awaited the young Cornishman. On October 19, 1807 (a date to be ever remembered in the annals of chemistry as marking a new epoch), he, first of the human race, was permitted rapturously to gaze on the new metal Potassium. Those few glittering globules revolutionized chemistry.   Shortly after he first separated Sodium.   Then, with the researches of other chemists, the various new metals followed.   He soon afterwards was made LL.D. of Dublin, and in 1812 was knighted at Carlton House.   A few days after he married a rich heiress, who henceforth shared with Dame Nature his affections.   His life was closed in a foreign land, and the government of Geneva honored the Penzance chemist with a funeral at the national expense.   He died May 28th, 1829.

Towards the end of the century, the literary movement, in which Penzance has so shone, and taking such a high position among the secondary towns of England, may be said to have begun.   Davy's birth, in 1778, may be said to have occured just about the commencement of that literary and scientific movement, in which he was the chief ornament.   The ladies seem to have preceded the gentlemen in this matter.   The Penzance Ladies' Book Club was established in 1770, the Gentlemen's Book Club a few years after.   The Gentlemen's News Room was established at the end of the century, in the exciting era of the French Revolution.

In other matters also, Penzance took rather a forward position in the progress of the age.   The West Penwith Agricultural Society was established as long ago as 1798.

For a town of three thousand inhabitants, in a remote corner of England, this was not bad. If we compare it with what was done, and even still, is being done in towns of that size in other parts of England, we may not be ashamed of the literary movement of Penzance a hundred years ago.

CHAPTER II.

THE DECLINE OF THE CORNISH LANGUAGE.

"Elo why clapier Kernuack."
Cornish phrase (Pryce).
Can you speak Cornish ?

THE extinction of an European language is not a common phenom-
enon in modern history, and therefore is an event of general as
well as special interest.   Each stage of the decay acquires an
importance extraneous to the intrinsic weight of the event itself.
Language has a marvellous vitality. If we consider the subject, we see few languages of modern Europe have actually died out, and what we call death is often
merely a dialectic modification. Provençal, in some sense, may be called
dead ; but the French which has superseded it, is only a sister dialect of the
same Romance family.   Cornish, on the other hand, is of an utterly distinct
branch of Aryan speech from English.   Of the expiring languages of
Europe, none are actually dead.   Wendish still lingers even in Germany,
Lithuanian has not been quite stamped out by Russian. The Celtic sisters
of the Cornish have a marvellous vitality.   A century ago they were already
in appearance dying, but none of them is yet quite dead. Perhaps they are
in less real danger now than then, for should they linger out another generation, it is not impossible that the growing enthusiasm about philological
subjects may transfer them from the merely vernacular into the literary stage,
and from the sign of the ignorance of the peasant into the accomplishment of
the literary or patriotic enthusiast.   The tendency of civilization is not only
centralizing, it does sometimes encourage nationality.   Men do not like to be
lost in the crowd, and so the knowledge of what the rest of mankind do not
know, is a thing to be attained.   In another generation, it is possible that there

may be as many Manx and Gaelic scholars as now there are peasants who use Manx and Gaelic for their ordinary tongue.

The old Cornish was less fortunate than its Celtic sisters. Its period of decay preceded, by a century or more, our modern philological enthusiasm. In the days of its decadence it was looked on as a mere barbarous tongue of little commercial use, and no scientific interest, which had better, as a sort of linguistic vermin, be stamped out. Till the present century no Cornish book was given to the press. No manual of the language had been published until it was just expiring, indeed, in the vernacular, as a mode of conversation, it was already dead. Lhuyd's work marks the transition of the Cornish from the vernacular of peasants and miners, to the dead language of the Celtic scholar. Let us trace the language in its former stage, in the latter we have spoken elsewhere.

The battle of Sampford Courtenay was the death knell of the old Cornish. The cannon of Russell's army sounded its funeral salute. One of the grievances of the Cornishmen had been " we will not receive the new service.... And so we, the Cornishmen (whereof certain of us understand no English), utterly refuse this new English."

Henceforth, *i.e.*, after the reaction of Mary I was over, the English was used in the Church service, though for sometime the sermon in certain parishes and the words of administration in the Holy Communion were in Cornish. The last Cornish sermon was probably preached at Landewednack in 1678, the Cornish words of administration were retained in the reign of Charles I, at Feock (and probably other parishes), till 1640. It does not seem, however, that the old Cornish died without a struggle. During the reigns of Elizabeth and James I. there appears to have been a definite effort made by a few of the Cornish gentry to preserve and restore the language. Of this effort Jordan's " Creacon " in 1611, is supposed to be a relic. The *guares* were still acted, though in a purgated form. Whether this effort would have been attended with any success had the county not been disturbed by the Civil Wars, it is difficult to say. As it is, probably the extinction of the old Cornish was due almost as much to those wars as to the Reformation. By the latter English was introduced into every church, by the former into every home.

The military occupation of Cornwall by the contending armies (in Penwith by Goring and Hopton's troops, and then by those of Fairfax's) the moving of Cornishmen to other parts of England, the cessation of the miracle plays, all must have forced Cornishmen to speak in English. But Penwith was one of the last strongholds. Norden, writing about 1584, says " In the weste parte of " the countrye, as in the hundreds of Penwith and Kerrier *(sic.)* the Cornishe " is moste in use amongste the inhabitantes, and yet (which is to be marveyled) " though the husband and wife, parents and children, master and servants, doe " mutually communicate in their native language, yet there is none of them in " manner but is able to convers with a stranger in the English tongue, unless it " be some obscure people, that seldom confer with the better sorte." Carew, a little later, says "that most" *i.e.* taking East and West together (N.B. Carew was an east Cornishman) "can speak no word but Cornish, but very few are ignorant of the English, though they sometimes affect to be." Scawen, how- ever, in the days of Charles II, said that some old people still spoke Cornish only. In 1650, *i.e.* during the Commonwealth, Cornish was still the common language of the fisherwomen of S. Paul and the tinners of S. Just. Mr. Ray, the naturalist, who visited Cornwall in 1662, reported " Mr. Dicken Gwyn was considered as the only person who could then write in the Cornish language ; and who lived in one of the most western parishes called S. Just, *where there were few* but could speak English ; while few of the children could speak Cornish, so that the language would soon be lost." Norden and Carew, a cen- tury before, had both prophesied the same catastrophe. The epoch of venacular extinction nearly coincides, as we said, with literary revival. Sir Francis North, afterwards Lord Keeper, when holding assizes at Launceston, in 1678, expressed regret at the decay of the old Cornish. The poor, indeed, could sometimes speak Cornish, but " they were laughed at by the rich, who understood it not, which is their own fault in not endeavouring after it." Soon after this the first efforts were made, for literary and scientific purposes, to save the relics of the expiring language. John Keigwin was the last educated man able to speak Cornish, and the first to translate his country's literary relics. Edward Lhuyd, the keeper of the Ashmolean Museum, a zealous Celtic scholar, utilized his labours.

U

As we have said, S. Paul and S. Just were the two last strongholds of the Cornish language.   The reason is manifest, both were remote from the West of England, and yet in them a tolerably large population was concentrated. The fishing industry of S. Paul and the mines of S. Just kept together the last speakers of the language, probably a generation or two after the Sancreed and Sennen people had been forced to learn English.   At length the S. Just speakers of Cornish died away, and the young people only talked English. S. Paul alone remained.   Here even it would seem the country people were forced to learn English, and got to use it commonly.   Kimmiel and Lamorna people found Cornish of little good.   It at last narrowed to Newlyn and Mousehole, where a few old people, it may be enthusiasts for the "good old times," still chattered in their old Celtic tongue, by the fireside, or in the fishing-boat.   Perchance the enthusiasm of John Keigwin for his native tongue inspired a few of the people of Mousehole to keep up their dying language, when it had been silenced elsewhere.

The fame of John Keigwin is about *nil.* out of the county, and not very great in it, in fact, nine Cornishmen out of ten never heard of his name, and yet to none of her sons, in a literary sense, is Cornwall more indebted than to this almost forgotten writer.   Without him, the old Cornish language—the language that is, in all probability, of the southern and western tribes of the ancient Britons—would have been hopelessly lost.   Until his time, no interest was taken in the dying "barbarous" tongue.

But philology was not yet awakened—perhaps some may affirm it hardly existed—till a generation after Mr. Keigwin's death, when the discoveries of Bopp, Grimm, and Sir William Jones revolutionized our notions of language.

There is a something touching and noble in the life and work of this man, living in an obscure fishing village, far off from libraries, unencouraged by applause or even the conviction that he was winning for himself renown, gathering together the dying embers of his native expiring language, and employing his acquaintance with it in the translation of the chief native epic, and in the assistance of literary enquirers.   None of the ordinary inducements to a study were there.   No fame awaited him in this life, and he must have known it; no pecuniary reward, for few of his contemporaries cared for his book or his labours, no sympathy even among his neighbours—poor fishermen and small farmers who could have had little conception of the greatness and importance of his work. It was by pure love of knowledge and patriotic attachment to old Cornish, that John Keigwin was spurred to his valuable labours.

Martin, the grandson of Jenkin Keigwin (who, as we have stated, was killed in the attack on Mousehole, in 1595) was born in that same year as his native town was burnt, and his grandfather was killed. He (Martin) married twice. By his second wife (a Penrose) he had John, in 1641. It seems both father and son were greatly attached to the old Cornish language. John had a good classical education, for Dr. Borlase speaks of him as "a gentleman well versed in the learned languages, as well as his own," but at what school he was taught is uncertain. In 1666, he married, and afterwards had five children.

His edition of Mount Calvary was published in 1682, with a translation and preface in English. In the latter he confesses "The design was (so much as in him lay) to cause English men (as well as he could) to understand the Cornish tongue, which is now altogether obsolete and almost obliterate, and without keeping himself to (you may say) disorder in ye English, ye Cornish words would not be readily apprehended; hopeing yt ye disorder of ye English will be rectifyed by some learned person," and frankly owns himself to be "a Cornishman meanly instructed in popular English, much less artificial." When we remember that Keigwin lived a generation after Shakespeare's death, and was almost contemporary with Swift and Addison, we must see that his English is that of a foreigner "meanly instructed in popular English." We have, perhaps, in his composition a sample of the style of a literary West Cornish gentleman of the seventeenth century.

It is said the translation was advised by Lord Francis North—who attended Bodmin Assizes, in 1678, and there met Keigwin—and by Bishop Trelawney.

In one person at last Mr. Keigwin found an appreciating disciple, and a valuable assistant. In 1700 Lhuyd came into Cornwall, and gathered together the materials for his invaluable work on "Cornish and its congeners."

In the early part of the XVIII century, Keigwin carried on a correspondence in Cornish with Tonkin and Gwavas. However, although they knew something of the language, both Lhuyd and Borlase witness that Keigwin was the best master of it.   The former says he was "without any comparison, the most skilful judge of our age of the Cornish language."   Dr. Borlase writes that had it not been for Keigwin and Lhuyd, the Cornish tongue "had wholly perished."

Keigwin died about 1710, soon after Lhuyd.   With him, perhaps more correctly than with Dolly Pentreath, Cornish may be said to have died, for his acquaintance with it was probably of a far more complete and accurate character.

At last the Cornish-speaking people were reduced to two, William Bodener and Dolly Pentreath.   *Place aux dames.*   We will talk of the lady first, especially as like not a few of her townswomen, she proved quite capable of sounding her own trumpet.

This singular woman appears (according to Mr. Halliwell), to have been born in 1714, *i.e.* shortly after Keigwin's death, though from Daines Barrington's statement one would suppose she had been born in the seventeenth century, in the reign of James II.   She seems to have been an intelligent woman, of good memory, and having been brought up among people who spoke Cornish freely, she remembered it when others forgot it entirely from want of use.   It was probably then (at the beginning of the eighteenth century) used in Mousehole and Newlyn much as Welsh is in many towns of South Wales now, as a sort of linguistic luxury, for private use in families, while English was the language of business and all public affairs.   As time went on, old Cornish became (as I rather suspect Welsh is becoming in parts of Monmouthshire) looked on as a sort of joke, a kind of slang, and then when Wesley's preaching produced an effect, at length was thought something wrong, naughty words, with a sort of mysterious, naughty meaning, which may have given rise to the notion that Dolly Pentreath used to swear in Cornish.   The story of Dolly's interview with Daines Barrington is curious, and is related again and again in provincial histories.   Peter Pindar puts it comically :—

> "Hail Mousehole! birth place of old Doll Pentreath,
> The last who jabbered Cornish— so says Daines,
> Who bat-like haunted ruins, lane and heath,
> With Will o' Wisp to brighten up his brains."

It seems that Dorothy (a still far commoner name here than in most parts of England) used occasionally her knowledge of Cornish to eke out her humble means, and to excite respect and fear among her neighbours.   A rebuke in Cornish must have sounded especially awful. Many strange stories are told of this last talker of Cornish. She died in December, 1777, and with 1778 it may be said that the Cornish language expired as a vernacular though in the early part of the present century there must have been many who remembered (as still a very few of our old folk do) sentences as well as words of the old language. But many years ago there were some who could still say the Lord's Prayer in Cornish. Still, in round numbers, one may say that Cornish has been a dead language for just one hundred years, and its centenary is due in 1878.

William Bodener's fame is not so great as Dolly's, and yet his pretensions to being the last who could speak Cornish are, perhaps, the better of the two. At any rate, his was not a mere jabber, but real Cornish, treasured still in the British Museum, and republished in "Specimens of Cornish Provincial Dialect," and elsewhere. He wrote this in July, 3, 1776 :—

BODENER'S LETTER.

Bluth uee Eue try Egence a pemp. Theatra vee deen Boadjack an pascas. Me rig deskey Cornoack termen me vee mawe. Me vee demore gen cara vee a pemp dean moy en cock. Me rig scant lower clowes Edenger sowsnrch cowes en cock, rag sythen ware bar. No rig a vee biscath gweller lever Cornoack. Me deskey Cornoack mous da more gen tees coath. Na ges moye vel pager pe pemp endreau nye, ell classia Cornoack leben pòble coath pager eyance blouth. Cornoach ewe all ne cea ves yen poble younk.

"My age is three-score and five. I am a poor fisherman. I learnt Cornish when I was a boy. I have been to sea with my father and five other men in the boat, and have not heard one word of English spoke in the boat for a week together. I never saw a Cornish book. I learned Cornish going to sea with old men. There is not more than four or five in our town can talk Cornish now—old people four-score years old. Cornish is all forgot with young people." And yet to this day in Newlyn (and I believe in Mousehole also) I have found two or three persons who can count to twenty in old Cornish; while many of the local words *e.g.*, bucca, crillas, bal, cheel, véan, are Celtic, not English.* The Cornish accent is not Teutonic, but Celtic. In few countries is purer English spoken by the poor than here (for the past generations learnt English from the parson, squire, or travelling merchant), as every visitor notices, but the accent is still foreign.

* For the existing vestiges of Cornish, I would refer the reader to Rev. G. Harvey's Mullyon, Mr. H. Jenner's paper on the subject read before the Philological Society, and my own article on it in the *Revue Celtique*, of 1877.

JOHN WESLEY.

Nefre me ny fanna cur
Marnes a vn ena sur.
Du roy thym y lel revlya.
Beunans Meriasek, 2845-8.

" Never do I wish a cure,
Unless of one soul sure,
God grant it loyally I may rule."

N Wednesday morning, August 31, 1743, there might be seen in S. Ives market-place a middle-aged clergyman, in cassock and bands, going with a party towards S. Ives Church. A crowd was gathered to receive him, and with many jeers and scoffs not exactly suiting the occasion.

As he draws near them the crowd jestingly raise a loud huzza, and a little ditty is to be heard in S. Ives just then, with which the strange parson has been serenaded during the night.

" Charles Wesley is come to town,
To try if he can pull the churches down."

That middle-aged parson is John Wesley—the man whose name is a watchword in Cornwall, and who is to utterly revolutionize Cornish society.

John Wesley the father of the chief religious revival of the eighteenth century, was one of the greatest evangelists the Church of England has produced since the days of Boniface of Devon. In John Wesley we see one of the noblest of the clergy of the last century—a mighty preacher of righteousness, and one, who though not himself a Cornishman, produced more effect on the religious and even social life of the county than any Cornishman that ever lived. The reverence with which he is remembered among a large portion of the Cornish people to this day realizes in our nineteenth century the superstitious reverence of many an old Brito-Celtic Saint, of a S. Piran, or a S. Levan, or a S. Neot during the middle ages. The real man and his real history is, in scarcely a century, lost in the halo of the panegyrics of his enthusiastic followers. Hea Moor Rock, the rock on which he stood, enclosed in a chapel, shows how his Penzance disciples felt towards his memory.

"Wesley" says Mr. Taine, that skilful French critic of English society and literature, "was a scholar or Oxford student . . . . . At Oxford he fasted and wearied himself until he spat blood and almost died; at sea, when he departed for America, he only ate bread, and slept on deck; he lived the life of an apostle, giving away all that he earned, travelling and preaching all the year and every year, till the age of 88; it has been reckoned that he gave away £30,000, travelled about a hundred thousand miles, and preached forty-thousand sermons. What could such a man have done in France in the XVIII century? Here he was listened to and followed. At his death he had eighty thousand disciples, now he has a million."*

The religious bearings of Wesley's work in Cornwall or out of it, I cannot speak of here. My object is to give an impartial judgment on the events of Cornwall's past, and the work of Wesley is too much a present force to belong to the past. I shall therefore confine myself to a little "cameo" from the history of his early work here as he himself relates it, leaving to others the description of the history of his entire "mission" in Cornwall, which, indeed, properly treated (even without much extraneous or explanatory matter), might easily fill a volume larger than this. Indeed, such a book, if fairly written, would be a most valuable addition to county and religious history, whether the work of an admirer, or of a critic of the great evangelist of the XVIIIth century.

On Friday, September 2nd, 1743, Wesley goes from S. Ives westward to Morvah, and here, amidst that glorious north-coast scenery, he seizes on the appropriate text "The land of Zebulon and the land of Nephthalim by the way of the sea :—the people which sat in darkness saw great light; and to them which sat in the region and shadow of death light is sprung up." Some

---

* Taine's "History of English Literature," Laine's Translation, vol. 2, p. 5, 8, 59.

may say it was a prophetic text. There were sad deeds done on that coast on stormy winter evenings. Awful legends still linger of the deeds of the wreckers, and yet worse of wreckers' death beds, and there may have been some few who had had a share in those black deeds amidst that congregation of which John Wesley said " I did not find one who was convinced of sin." The stranger had not yet found out the right chord. Wesley owns he spoke in vain.

On Tuesday he tries again, " but still I could find no way into the hearts of the hearers, although they were earnest to hear what they understood not." Next day he tries Zennor, and finds (so characteristic of any strange work among the Cornish country people) " much good will in them, but no life." On Saturday, the 10th, he preached at S. Just at the Cross to a thousand people. Here and at Sennen, for the first time, he seems in Cornwall to have made an impression. " Why will ye die, O house of Israel !" cries the preacher. " The people trembled, and were still," he says, The fire is lighted at last. For good or evil, Wesleyanism becomes a fact and a power in the county. Some may say John Wesley only persuaded the people to " alter their sins," others that he converted them to righteousness. It is not for the historian to enter into theological questions. All he can say is the *vis inertia* is broken, the new force is in action, Methodism, henceforth, is felt a power in the county. Strange that close to the *Plân-an-guare*, the great kindling place of religious enthusiasm in the far West of Cornwall during the middle ages, the fire of the eighteenth century should be rekindled. There seems a poetic justice, a providential unity in the fact.

At 6, he preached at Sennen. On Sunday morning after sermon, he went to the Land's End, which he thus describes : " It was an awful sight ! But how will these melt away when God ariseth to judgment ! The sea between does indeed, boil like a pot. One would think the deep to be hoary. But though they swell, yet can they not prevail. He hath set their bounds which they cannot pass."

On Tuesday he went to the Scilly Isles, in the boat of the Mayor of St. Ives.

At Morvah, and at Zennor, the same success followed as at S. Just and at S. Ives., where already some progress had been made. The Cornish were "one and all" then as now. Success, however, called down the hatred of the world.

An illustration of the sort of stories told of Wesley, and used by his enemies to irritate the public opinion against him, is narrated by himself thus :—" I assure you Mr. W. is a Papist (said Miss Gr—), and so am I ; he converted me. You know how I used to pray to Saints and to the Virgin Mary, it was Mr. W. taught me when I was in the Bands. And I saw him rock the cradle on Christmas Eve. You know I scorn to tell a lie.*" Such was the wretched little tattle that the enemy used to hamper the work of this great man. He was spoken of as a Papist, a Jesuit, a French spy, an emissary of the King of Spain, an agent of the Pretender.

On the evening of Friday, September 16, 1743, as John Wesley was preaching in S. Ives, "the mob of the town burst into the room and created much disturbance ; roaring and striking those that stood in their way, as though Legion himself possessed them. I would fain have persuaded our people to stand still ; but the zeal of some and the fear of others, had no ears ; so that finding the uproar increase (says Wesley) I went into the midst, and brought the head of the mob up with me to the desk. I received but one blow on the side of the head ; after which we reasoned the case, till he grew milder and milder, and at length undertook to quiet his companions."

Next day (in spite of the *one blow*, and the irritation of the S. Ives mob) Wesley preached again at S. Just and at the Land's End, and on Sunday four times : at S. Just, at Morvah, at Zennor, and closing the evening at S. Ives.

Still, troubles were not over. On Monday he was told that "the rabble had designed to make their general assault in the evening. But one of the aldermen came at the request of the mayor, and stayed with us the whole time of the service."

Next day Wesley left the Land's End district, making his way back by way of Gwennap, Launceston, Exeter, and Taunton to Bristol, then one of the headquarters of the revival.

Wesley's next visit to West Cornwall was in April, 1744. He reached S. Ives on the 3rd, and was "saluted, as usual, with a huzza and a few stones or

---

* Wesley's Journal in Wesley's Works, I. 392.

V

pieces of dirt." The western district was somewhat disturbed by the assertion that Mr. Wesley had been seen with the Pretender. Still, John Wesley went on preaching boldly, and with some success at Morvah, S. Just, Triggivary Downs, Gulval, and Zennor. On Monday, April 9, he preached 2 miles from Penzance, and near Gulval. The clergyman of S. Ives publicly denounced the followers of Wesley as " enemies of the Church, Jacobites, Papists." The effect of this sermon was not satisfactory. A riot arose in the town, and the mayor had to read the Riot Act. On the 14th, Wesley concluded his second visit.

The third visit was more eventful and interesting as illustrating the state of things a hundred years ago in the far west. Wesley did not commence his work at S. Ives, but had to go to Marazion on a somewhat different errand. The county magistrates had thought fit to impress some Methodists as "proper persons to serve His Majesty in the land service." The justices kept Wesley waiting till 9 o'clock, and then he was told that Maxfield, the preacher, had been sent away for a soldier. Maxfield was not the only man arrested. After Wesley's sermon at S. Just, Greenfield, a miner, was arrested by a warrant from Dr. Borlase. At S. Ives, on the next Sunday, while Wesley was preach-ing, it seems, the riot act was read. On the Tuesday, John Wesley himself was arrested (but in a very polite manner), and on Wednesday brought to Dr. Borlase. The latter seems to have been afraid of any decided action, and would not see Wesley, so the warrant being executed, the preacher was set free. He was not safe, however ; the same afternoon at Gwennap, he was arrested again. He was seized by his cassock. (John Wesley was ritualist enough to wear a cassock in the streets). " I take you to serve His Majesty." Wesley's calmness, however, rather took his adversary aback, and he was re-leased a second time. Next day were the famous Falmouth riots, when Wesley was actually in danger of his life, and after he had escaped from these was again in great danger of arrest at Tolcarn, in (what is now) Carnmenellis parish, a warrant having been issued against him by the Helston magistrates. The charge was that he had been " a long time in France and Spain, and was now sent by the Pretender, and that these societies are to join him." An old College friend, Mr. Collins, of Redruth, however, saved him then. At the same spot (Tolcarn in Carnmenellis) a more cowardly mode of attack was employed a few days after. As he was standing on a high wall preaching, some men, getting behind, threw him down. He fortunately lighted on his feet.

Thus hunted on the mainland, Wesley retired to the Land's End district. Here he was again in danger. At S. Just he was once more arrested, on the plea that he had promised not to preach for a month there, but was set free in half-an-hour. At Trevonan, in Morvah, next day, during the sermon, the constable came to read the proclamation against riots. "We will do as you require," said Wesley, "we will disperse within an hour"; and so he finished his sermon, and boldly preached at Zennor and Gulval as well.

Such was religious persecution in the last century. It is strange men should have thought they could advance God's truth by beating people and sending them to prison. But one might fill a volume with the story of Wesley's adventures in West Cornwall.* I must ask my readers to be satisfied with these little Cameos, and proceed.

Thre is one curious point in this little episode of Wesley's, and of Penwith history. The two men were brought into contact as opponents, who have had more to form the history of Penzance since, than any of the men of the eighteenth century—I mean John Wesley and the learned Dr. Borlase. As the religious movement in Penwith has ever since been at least materially affected by the former and his followers, so the intellectual movement which has done so much to give Penzance a high position in the history of modern civilization, may be said to dawn with the latter. The name of Borlase will be ever honored where Cornish antiquarianism is valued, and where the educated men of Cornwall go. He was the real father of the school of modern Cornish antiquaries, and the founder of the literary tastes of the far west.

---

* Wesley's description of a sermon at Newlyn, in 1747, is as follows :--"I rode to Newlyn, a little town on the South Sea, about a mile from Penzance. At five I walked to a rising ground near the sea shore, where was a smooth white sand to stand on. An immense multitude of people was gathered together, but their voice was as the roaring of the sea. I began to speak, and the noise died away: but before I had ended my prayer, some poor wretches of Penzance began cursing and swearing, and thrusting the people off the bank. In two minutes I was thrown into the midst of them ; when one of Newlyn, a bitter opposer till then, turned about and swore ' None shall meddle with the man ; I will lose my life first.' Many others were of his mind. So I walked a hundred yards forward, and finished my sermon without any interruption."

Born at Pendeen House—a fine old mansion of the Restoration epoch, in 1698, a scion of that Borlase family of which I have already spoken as among our most noted mediæval families of the far West, he had his school education at Plymouth, and went thence to Exeter College, Oxford. His account of society there, in 1715, is extremely interesting, as showing how Jacobite notions were shaking England at the time of the Pretender's invasion. Soon after leaving Oxford he was ordained, and, at an early age, by favour of the Duke of Bolton, was instituted Rector of Ludgvan. Here, in 1719, he formed a social and literary club of the neighbouring gentry, and Gwavas wrote a little poem in old Cornish (perhaps the last composition of the dying language) to inaugurate the occasion. It seems strange, however, that swan-like song in a dying language should inaugurate the literary movement, which should mark Penzance for such an honorable position among the little country towns of England. Within a few years from this, the Godly Club of Sacramentarians was founded by Charles Wesley, at Oxford, destined to have an even yet greater influence on the modern history of the people of Penwith.

But I must leave both Wesley and Borlase, though with regret. A book as large as this might be filled with records of their doings in and for Cornwall. I trust such may be written. I leave, as I said, a mere Cameo in their history.*

---

* For a modern statement on Dr. Borlase, see Mr. W. C. Borlase's able article in the Quarterly of 1875, for details of Wesley in Penwith, see his Journal.

Chapter IV.

PENZANCE IN THE NINETEENTH CENTURY.

"Cornwall no more the barbarous wreckers hails
The stranded ship, and plies his robber trade ;
But honesty, and kindness walk thy vales,
And art and science these bright homes have made.
Proud, loyal are thy sons, and many a name
Sheds on thy cairn-crowned hills the light of fame ;
Davy and Opie, stars unfading, shine,
And while they flash their lustre, heighten thine."
Michell.

ONTEMPORARY history is notoriously the most difficult branch of historical work, so difficult indeed that many hold, and I somewhat agree with them, that it ought not to be attempted. It is well nigh impossible for us to take a comprehensive view of events of which we are spectators, or of which the spectators still live, and to speak of scenes the actors of which are yet among us. History is, after all, the annals of the dead, not of the living. As, thanks to the longevity of our Penwith people, there are some scores of persons whose memories still go back to the close of the last century and the commencement of this, one might, on that theory, consider our task completed, as at the end of the eighteenth century history is ceasing to become the records of the dead, and one of which living eye-witnesses can speak ; yet, especially for strangers, and as the real prosperity of Penzance dates from the early part of this XIX century, perhaps a few words, a brief hasty statement of a few leading outlines of our recent progress may not be out of place. A book larger than this might be easily filled with mere detailed and accurate statements of the events of our century, but a very short sketch of the chief of them will, no doubt, be all that is at present desirable.

In 1801, Penzance had only 3382 inhabitants, according to the census. It was, therefore, only one third of its present size, and in population no greater than Newlyn or St. Just parish are now. The aspect of the town must have been very different to its present. Old St. Mary's, with its quaint low spire, still stood an unpretending, and if the pictures of it be correct, a rather unbeautiful building of no particular style at all, but a poor specimen of the Stuart epoch. A reminder of it still remains in the pictures which were engraved at the periods of its supercession by the new S. Mary's Church.*

The head of Market-jew street must have looked very different in the beginning of the century to what it does now. Mr. Botterill thus describes it : "Who that remembers the picturesque and interesting old market house with the

---

* Morvah Church was rebuilt in 1828. Some verses of a hymn, by Rev. C. V. Le Grice, sung at the opening, are worth quoting as by a local man on a local subject.

> " Again we hear the Sabbath bell
>   A welcome joyful sound ;
> O'er rock and moor and down the dell
>   Its cheering peals resound.
>
> Come, come again they seem to say
>   To God's own house repair ;
> Come with a heart of faith to pray,
>   And Christ will meet you there.
>
> Tho' floods of water beat around
>   On ever shifting sands ;
> A rock is the foundation ground
>   On which our Temple stands.
>
> The winds may roar, the tempest frown,
>   Each breast from fear is free :
> The worshipper looks calmly down
>   Upon the troubled sea.
>
> So 'mid the storms of human life
>   The Christian is secure,
> And far above the fretful strife
>   His path serene and sure.
>
> Tho' built by man our Temple gate
>   The way by which it leads
> To one " not made with hands " is straight
>   If faith for mercy pleads.   .
>
> For mercy, while 'tis called to day
>   To plead we'll hasten near
> . Ere the same bell, that bids to pray,
>   Shall greet our coming bier."

corresponding buildings surrounding or near it, such as the house in which Sir Humphry Davy was born, the cosy nook under the balcony of the Star Inn, where often of an evening he held his youthful comrades spell bound by the wonderful stories that his poetical imagination inspired, can help regretting their removal and loss. The picturesque scene is gone, never to be restored, which was formed by the projecting balcony with its rustic pillars and case-mented light, combined with the high gables, mullioned and labled window, with the penthouse-like projections of the old Market house." Such are the words of one who knew and loved old Penzance. I cannot agree, however, with his strictures on the present Market house. That edifice may be less pictur-esque than the old one it superseded, but it has its good points and has a certain originality and power in it. At least it gives Penzance, as viewed in the distance, a distinct look from that of any other English watering place. As the winter visitor enjoys the soft air blowing over the Gulf stream, he may almost fancy himself by the blue Mediteranean as he looks on the dome of the *prefecture*—I beg pardon—the Market house and Post Office of Penzance.

There were two eras of building energy in the century, the one that of William IV. in which S. Mary's (1832-5) and our Market house (1837) were erected; the other—the last twelve years in which S. John's Hall, (erected in 1867-8 for £14,000), the Queen's Hotel, and (if one may look beyond the borough borders) our own little church of S. Peters were erected. The two epochs are clearly and characteristically marked in the two styles of archi-tecture. During the latter epoch, since 1866, more has probably been done for the restoration of our rural parish churches of Penwith than in any similar period since the days of Henry VII.

In the commerce of the town the opening of the railway, of course, marks an era. The fish trade has been immensely enlarged by it, and the facilities offered to tourists increased. Cornwall has now been opened up and it is to be hoped that the G.W.R. now will still further increase our prosperity. Good-railway accommodation is the first need of Penzance.

Those who visit Penzance and complain of its arrangement (as perhaps they may if fresh from Brighton, Cheltenham, Torquay, or Bournemouth), ought to remember that it was not orignally laid out for a watering place, and that Penzance architects and their employers have had immense difficulties to contend against. The arrangement of the town would appear to sanction the theory that it really has been the result of an amalgamation of contiguous villages. Its markets and its quay were the sources of the wealth of its earlier days. In fact it was originally built for use rather than beauty. Later efforts have tended to diminish these defects, but more might still be done. That it ever should become a show place was probably what its earlier mayors, merchants, and master builders never expected, and they only considered the exigencies of their times. Nature has, however, done wonders for it, and a little more aid from Art might make Penzance one of our most beautiful towns. "See Naples and die" says the proverb, and yet Mount's Bay is considered more like the Bay of Naples than any part of Great Britain. The Bay never tires the eye. It is constantly changing, and the lover of nature may still find new beauties though having walked its shores a hundred times.

The period of the Franco-Pussian war, in 1870-1, brought thousands to Penzance who otherwise would have gone to France. It is to be hoped that our town will not now need such external aids to make its merits realized. It combines many advantages not easily to be found elsewhere. A very mild climate (the mildest to be obtained in Great Britain, or indeed anywhere in the world, north of 50° of latitude), a picturesque scenery, charming historical reminiscences of which we have striven to show a few plentiful and curious antiquities, and above all, what an Englishman ought especially to value, the comforts and security of old England. There is just enough of strange and and unusual to refresh the mind with some, at least, of the interest of foreign travel, and yet at every turn, in every place, the invalid or tourist must feel, though in a corner of England, he is still on British soil and is not an exile in a foreign land.

The real present and future position of Penzance among English towns, probably more depends on its recognition as a watering place than a seaport or mart for fishing and mining industry. To realize the position we should remember that the latitude of Penzance is the latitude of Omsk and Labrador ; and that while regions in our latitude of 50 degrees north are enchained for months with rigid frost, sometimes the very mercury freezing in the thermometers, and the spirits in the bottles, during a whole winter we may not have a frost for 24 hours, our hills may never for 12 hours be white with snow ; the dracaena, the aloe, the mesembryanthemum flourish all the year round in the open air.

> " Mild blows the zephyr o'er the ocean dark.
> The zephyr wafting the grey twilight clouds
> Across the waves, to drink the solar rays
> And blush with purple. . . By the orient gleam
> Whitening the foam of the blue waves that breaks
> Around his granite feet, but dimly seen
> Majestic Michael rises. He whose brow
> Is crowned with castles, and whose rocky sides
> Are clad with dusky ivy."
>
> *Sir H. Davy* (v. *Paris's Life of Davy, p. 36.*)

Why is this ? Even 300 years ago the question was asked our forefathers. Norden puts the reply rather poetically. "The Seas saltness sendeth warm evaporation which cherish the earth as with a continual sweet dew, which yield to the earth's increase quick maturity, and prevents the bitterness of the nipping frost, which cannot long continue violent, nor the most continuing fall of the thickening snow make a dangerous deepness to remain long."

The first person, it is said, who was ordered to winter in Penzance for his health, was Mr. John Price,[*] a descendant of a Mr. Price who, in the expedition of Venables and Penn, had a share in the conquest of Jamaica during the Commonwealth, and obtained a large grant of land, on which his family, the Prices, settled. Early in the last century young Mr. Price was sent to England for education. He had occasion to consult the then celebrated Dr. Frank Nicholls, afterwards physician of King George II, and even then a medical man of great promise. Dr. Nicholls was a very eminent writer and practitioner, whose nine communications to the Philosophical transactions and learned physiological works, placed him almost at the head of the profession. Now Dr. Nicholls' eldest brother resided at Trereife, and the idea seems to have struck Dr. Nicholls that perhaps the mild air of Penzance might suit his West Indian patient. At any rate it was tried. Mr. Price came down, settled with the Badcocks of Penzance (Mrs. Badcock was a daughter of the famous John Keigwin), was cured, and married Margery, their daughter. Sir Rose Price was a grandson of this couple.

---

[*] My authority for this statement is Davies Gilbert.

W

Perhaps there is no watering place in Western Europe for which nature has done so much as for Penzance. A wonderfully equable climate, considering its northern latitude, a bay in miniature resembling the world-famed Bay of Naples, a scenery varied within a few miles from the wildest to the most tame, from the most desolate to the most fertile; a region rich in natural curiosities, including in a day's drive two of the chief promontories of England, the westernmost and southernmost points of Great Britain; all these combine natural attractions which few if any other watering places in Europe, not to say England, can rival. Still, if nature has done so much, art has, as yet, done little; and both invalid and tourist expect art to aid nature in a watering place. The difficulties of Penzance, however, are obvious. Its remoteness from London, or indeed any great city; the condition of its railway communication; the absence of really large capital for public improvements, crush, or at least hinder, the position of the town. The queen of watering places, Brighton, is little more than an hour from London; Penzance is twelve hours. Nice and Mentone offer the advantages and excitement of foreign travel.

In the early part of this century, during the Napoleon wars, it was a good deal used, and as evidence of its mild climate has accumulated (especially since Sir James Clarke declared so strongly for it) the number of invalids coming to winter here has steadily increased. If its merits were better known, and distance from London practically abridged by improved railway accommodation, no doubt the number of visitors for health would be greatly increased.

EMINENT PENZANCE MEN.

Few towns of England of its size have produced so many celebrated men as Penzance. This is the more remarkable considering that until the beginning of the present century it was a very small place, and moreover, that its remoteness from London and great cities would appear to be likely to cramp intellectual energy. Whether the scene of nature in her grandest and most various aspects may have a compensating power, is not for us to say, all that is certain is the result. Penzance holds a certain position in the history of modern civilization to which its size would not by any means entitle it.

Sir Humphry Davy alone would confer celebrity on his birth-place, for we are only beginning to realise the immense importance of his discoveries on human progress. Of him, however, we speak elsewhere. Lesser lights, however, have shone in the western-most town of England.

Not a few men of Penzance, it may be said, are among us whose names will be remembered in ages to come as honest workers in the field of literature, but of them we must not speak but leave their fame for posterity to estimate. A few words on some of the worthy deceased townsmen who have adorned the literary movement of this nineteenth century may not be out of place.

After Sir Humphrey Davey we should mention (on account of similarity of studies) Mr. Richard Quiller Couch, the naturalist, who, though not born in the town, may in some sense be claimed by it as one who spent there the most important portion of his life. He was the son of another eminent Cornish naturalist, Jonathan Couch. Brought up to the medical profession, he studied at Guy's Hospital and obtained a silver medal for skill in ophthalmic surgery. Among Mr. Couch's earliest independent lines of research were :—(1) The development of the fog. (2) The metamorphoses of Diapod Crustaceans. (3) Nests of fishes. One of his earlier papers, communicated to the Penzance Natural History Society, was noticed by a French Naturalist and translated into French. Thence it was translated back into English, the Literary world in London seeming thus to ignore the scientific labours of the naturalist of the far West. Days have changed since then, let us hope. Mr. Couch also catalogued the Zoophytes and Corallines of the Cornish coast. Among Mr. Couch's works are very many which illustrate his labours for science.

Mr. Henry Boase and his eldest son Dr. Henry S. Boase both acquired fame in natural science. They both laboured mainly in the same department, geology. The geological portions of Davies Gilbert's works, and of the new Parochial History of Cornwall, are by Dr. Boase, and show much industry and ability. Mr. Boase, sen., long resided in London, but ultimately returned to Penzance, and as a magistrate and member of the corporation did much for the town.

Rev. John James Carne was an able antiquary in Cornish subjects. Mr. Joseph Carne his uncle, like the Boase's, devoted himself to geology. The labours of both of them were very valuable.

One of the best known and most influential of the clergy of Penwith during this century was not even a Cornishman except by adoption. I refer to the eloquent vicar of Pendeen, the far-famed Robert Aitken, a name which will be remembered for ages to come among us as that of one of the most gifted preachers and powerful evangelists of the Church of England. His church and parsonage of Pendeen, a monument in stone to his genius and energy, deserves a pilgrimage from every visitor.

Among the scientific men to whom Penzance and Cornwall are especially indebted we should place the name of Dr. Paris, the founder, in 1814, of the Geological Society, and author of the history of Mount's Bay. After a long residence here, Dr. Paris removed to a more lucrative field of labour, and in London became a medical practitioner of some eminence. Much of the scientific movements in Penzance, at the early part of this century, is due to him and to the Boase family.

Another person to whom Penzance owed a great deal of its rise in the end of the last and in the beginning of this century, was Mr. Thomas Giddy, who came to Penzance in 1774, and was so much respected by the corporation that they paid him the extraordinary compliment of electing him ten times to be their chief magistrate, as mayor of Penzance. He removed the Coinage Hall from its old position near the Market-place down to the Quay. Mr. Giddy died July 26th, 1825, aged 84. His partner in life, to whom he had been married above 60 years, survived him.*

But it is in another and far different sphere that Penzance has attained fame. Admiral Pellew here received the first rudiments of education. He was a brave kind hearted boy. Many are the local stories told of his juvenile exploits. Few dreamt that that rash boy should be conquerer of Algiers, the founder of the noble family of Exmouth. Rare indeed may be the great warriors of Penwith, for the excellence of our western men has been in peace rather than war, but among these Lord Exmouth stands pre-eminent.

---

* Vide Davies Gilbert, vol. III. p. 96.

Among many other Penzance men whose names added lustre to their native place in the early part of this century, or the end of the last, I may mention Mr. John Tonkin the protector and friend of Sir Humphry Davy, the Principal of East India College; Rev. J. H. Batten, D.D., third wrangler at Cambridge and fellow of his college; Dr. S. Luke, a medical man of some celebrity, who practised at Falmouth, Exeter, and London, and died in 1829. Mr. Vibert the architect of the Market-house, whose ancestors for generations appear in Penzance records. His son was the devoted incumbent of St. Peter's, Newlyn, to whom the parish is indebted for the fabric of its pretty little church, and moreover, the foundations of the good devoted spiritual work on which we are striving to build. The Rev. John Pope Vibert's memory, however, is too well enshrined in the affections of his parishioners and friends for my praises to be able to add to the esteem in which he is held. His courage, zeal, self-denial, and single heartedness set him forth as one of the noblest and best of the sons of Penzance.

CHAPTER VI.

THOUGHTS ON THE PRESENT AND FUTURE.

"Ha'n Dew enhella vedn ry,
Peth yu gwella ol rag why."

And God, supreme, will do for you—
What He thinks best is good for you.

NE of the main reasons of the importance of the study of the history of the past is the understanding of the present and, it may be, the forecasting of the future. We have dwelt on Penwith as it was in the days gone bye, as far as our dim and vague records can teach us to read the past, as it was when the Phœnician and Greek traders came to Mount's Bay in the galleys to buy tin for the ancient world; as it was when the old Danmonii bent before the legions of Imperial Rome; as it was in the days of the native Cornish kings, and of the early Christian hermits from Ireland, Brittany, and Wales, whose names still linger in our parishes; as it was when the Saxon and the "red haired Dane" came as conquerors; as it was when the knights of William of Normandy were founding the old Cornish families of the upper classes; as it was when Richard, Earl of Cornwall was crowned by Archbishop Conrad at Aachen, King of the Romans, Cæsar of the West; as it was when the era of the wars of the Roses opens to us the dawn of modern civilization, in the era of the Renaissance; as it was under Henry VIII and Elizabeth, the great era of the Tudors; as it was in the civil wars, when Cornwall stood so bravely by King Charles I, and at the Revolution, when twenty thousand Cornishmen did seek vengeance on the persecutor of Trelawny; as it was in the days when the preaching of John Wesley sounded on the moorlands; as it was when Humphry Davy won his fame. Scene by scene the shadowy drama of the half-forgotten past has been enacted before us, and the "old men" of the miners' tales have become a living fact; again they have spoken to us even in their own words and their quaint Celtic language; we have seen them at the Plan-an-guâre, at the stream-work, and on the battle field. "And what is the good of all this?" asks the utilitarian, "will it raise the price of tin or mackerel?" Let "the old men" answer in their quaint Cornish :—*Kemer, uith na rey gara an vôr goth rag an vor noueth.*" "Take care not to yield to leave an old way for a new way." The tried old way is the safer, and history points to and explains the old ways of the past, and the experience we may derive from them.

One of the lessons to be learnt from such experience is that West Penwith has had its share, and for a remote region a very important share, in the development of European civilization. From the days when Tyrian traders came to Ictis for tin, to when Sir Humphry Davy saw the potassium globules glistening under his battery, the Land's End district has been, if not a leading, yet a not unimportant factor in the history of human progress. There is no reason then why Cornishmen should not be proud of their ancestors, and strive to make the present and future emulate the past in the solid glory of adding to the happiness of the greatest possible number of the human race.

This leads to another point. It may be that the future field for the energy of the Cornish miner lies not in Cornubia, but in distant regions of the earth. How much the Cornish miner has done and is doing as a pioneer of civilization it is hard to estimate. In California, in the Australian bush, in the cold regions of the copper mines of the Lake district of America, beneath the burning sun of Queensland, the Cornish miner is preceding the agriculturist and even the shepherd in winning to civilization, and industry, the wildernesses of the earth. Metals are costly and rare; they are worth going far to seek for, even though they may be mostly found in desolate regions. So the miner has to push forward into lands which the herdsman and the squatter consider as yet too remote for their purpose; he stands in the extreme van of the ever-advancing army of the human subduers of nature's solitude. After him come the more settled phalanx of reclaimers of the virgin soil, of traders and artizans. In future ages great and prosperous states and cities may rise in regions where the Cornish miner with pick and shovel first broke the virgin soiL   The story of Ballarat and San Francisco is not utterly unconnected with the history of CornwalL

Perhaps, in days to come, when settled in his new home, without a vestige of the past around him earlier than the second half of the nineteenth century, the Cornishman may look back on the land of Cromlechs and Menhirs, of quaint old Celtic crosses, and granite mediæval churches, of strange memories and legends of the "old men," and their quaint dead language and curious old world ways, and tell his children that it is not Australia or America which is their real fatherland, but that rock-bound promontory, close by famed Ictis, glorious with a hundred memories of the past.

One thing at least they may be proud of.   The triumphs of the "old men" were not so much on the bloodstained field of battle as in patient industry, science, and commerce.   Penwith, as we have seen, does not appear ever to have been a land of slavery, of the oppressors and the oppressed, but of free men patiently trying, in a remote region, to work honestly and soberly, and do their duty in the state of life in which it had pleased God to place them.   The glory of mediæval pageant and tournament, of battle and siege, does not so much belong to Cornish history as the establishment of fairs and markets, the building of piers and churches.   The very antiquities, save the few rude, it may be pre-historic hill-forts, are not gloomy castles of robber barons, lofty walls of fortified cities, or memorials of battle fields, but chieftains' tombs and mine-works, crosses and chapelries.   After all these monuments imply "peace and goodwill towards men," and "glory to God," the two great principles of the gospeL   The turretted walls of Chester or York, the peel-towers and castles of Northumbria, the fastnesses of Breton nobles, and the picturesque castles of the robber barons of the Rhine may be a great deal prettier than any secular antiquity Penwith has to show, but they do not speak so much for the happiness of the people in the "good old times."   The Cornishmen of the past thousand years can neither be honestly described, as some hasty thinkers suppose, as "mere heathens," or "savages," but people who certainly lived quite up to the average of civilization in the other Celtic populations of Europe, it may be a good deal above it.

There is one striking point in Cornish history, *i.e.*, the unity of the national character, and its unchangeableness. As we have seen, the opinion of Diodorus and Mr. Mortimer Collins of the Cornish is about the same; the same kindliness and courtesy to strangers, the same inoffensiveness, the same industry struck the Phœnician and Roman traders to Mount's Bay as now the modern tourist. Except in the Tudor period the Cornish appear eminently unwarlike. The wars we have had to record were forced on them. Henry de la Pomeroy and John de Vere, Athelstan and Fairfax were not Cornishmen, and only forced Cornishmen to fight *nolens volens*. The warlike spirit evidenced in the Tudor period may partly be attributed to Cornish conservatism, partly, perhaps, to a hatred of Tudor despotism. Throughout we notice the same woof running in the cloth. The bards of old become the modern droll tellers, the myths of giants and fairies, of mermaids and witches, linger even to this nineteenth century. Nay, some hold that our generation has seen more than a "survival" of Druidism, and trace in the Methodist revival a return to that ecstatic worship of the heathen Celt which only ecclesiastical authority restrained during the past ages.

From the people let us return to the place. The mining future of West Penwith, it is to be feared, is not so hopeful as the past; the fisheries, we trust, may prove inexhaustible. The growing demand for animal food, the improved modes of transit of our age, the systematizing of the fish trade increase, and must continue to increase the demand. It is to be hoped the progress of Ichthyology, and the art of fish-breeding, with our advancing knowledge of the habits of fish, may increase the supply. It would seem as if the ocean contained an inexhaustible mine of food for the rapidly increasing population of the world, and that the fisher's trade must yearly grow in importance as civilization advances, and population grows more dense.

No town in Cornwall would seem to have so bright a future before it as Penzançe. Decline of mining industry and even (what is less to be feared) the decay of fisheries need not affect it. Nature seems to point it out as one of the great watering places of Europe, and when art assists nature it must soon attain that position. When railway accommodation is improved, and capital employed for the adornment of the town, Englishmen will soon

x

learn that the Land's End district contains almost as many points of interest as any region of equal extent in civilized Europe. Other watering places also may arise with Penzance. Sennen and the North Coast offer far more natural attractions than many a wealthy and prosperous town of our eastern counties. Whether Mount's Bay ever is to be a harbour of refuge for the far west is a point which parliament may have to decide.

But we must not linger longer in dreams about futurity. My task is finished. If this little sketch of the past of Penzance and West Penwith has taught some of those born here to look with fresh interest on the familiar scenes of their native place, or to learn any "point a skians" (a piece of wisdom) from the history of their forefathers; or even if it gives the intelligent tourist a fresh charm to a visit to these "old world" regions, my trouble is repaid. I shall therefore conclude with the sensible Cornish motto of the "old men,"

An lavar kôth yn lavar gûr.
What's said of old is said in truth.

APPENDIX A.

COMPARISON OF CORNISH AND OTHER ARYAN LANGUAS.

NUMERALS.

	I. CELTIC				II. SANSCRIT	III. SLAVONIC (as pronounced)	IV. ROMANCE			TEUTONIC	
	Recent Cornish as pronounced.	Old Cornish.	Welsh.	Irish.			Latin.	French.	Italian.	German.	Dutch.
1.	On	Un	Un	Aon	Eka	Jeden	Unus	Un	Uno	Ein	Een
2.	Deu	Deu	Dau	Da	Dwi	Dwa	Duo	Deux	Due	Zwei	Twee
3.	Dre, tri	Try	Tri	Tri	Tri	Trzby	Tres	Trois	Tre	Drei	Drie
4.	Paj	Pedar, Peswar	Pedair	Cethora	Chatur	Chtery	Quatuor	Quatre	Quattro	Vier	Vier
5.	Pymp	Pemp	Pymp	Caig	Papch	Pientch	Quinque	Cinque	Cinque	Funf	Vijf
6.	Weth	Whe	Shwech	Se	Shash	Sheshch	Sex	Six	Sei	Sechs	Zes
7.	Seith	Seyth	Saith	Secht	Saptan	Shedm	Septem	Sept	Sette	Sielen	Zeven
8.	Eath	Eath	Wyth	Ocht	Ashtan	Oshm	Octos	Huit	Otto	Acht	Acpt
9.	Nau	Naw	Naw	Naoi	Nayan	Dzhieviench	Novem	Neuf	Nove	Neun	Negen
10.	Deig	Dec	Deg	Deich	Dasan	Dzhieshiench	Decem	Dix	Dieci	Zehn	Tien

COMMON WORDS.

	Recent Cornish	Old Cornish	Welsh	Irish	Sanscrit	Slavonic	Latin	French	Italian	German
Father	Da	Tas	Tad	Athair	Pia	Ojciec	Pater	Pe're	Padre	Vater
Mother	Ma	Mam	Mam (Mam a breast)		Ma	Maika	Mater	Mere	Madre	Mutter
Headend	Pedin	Pen (Penzance)	Pen	Ceann	Phan		Finis	Fin		
Man	Dean	Den (Dâns men?)	Dyn	Duinne	G'ana		Homo(inis)	Homme	Uomo	Mann(?)
Water	Dour	Douer (Chyandour)	Dwr	Dur	Var	Woda*	(Udor, Greek)			Wasser
Stone	Men	Maen (Men-scryfa)	Maen			Kamien	(†Maenia, walls)			
House	Chy ty	Ty	Ty	Tigh, teach	Teg	Dom (dach roof)	Tectum	Toit		

APPENDIX B.

PRIORS OF S. MICHAEL'S MOUNT.

1266   Ralph de Carteret.

1275   Richard Perer, collated by Bishop Bronescombe.

1283   Walfrid de Gernon, ruled 33 years.

1316   Peter de Cara Villa, or Carville; Prior at Bishop Grandisson's visitation.

1342   Nicholas Isabel.

1349   John Hardy, indicted at Launceston.

1362   John de Volant.

"   Richard Harepath (date dubious).

1385   Richard Auncell. His brass seal is extant.

1412   William Lambert, apparently the last prior; after him there were Chaplains of the Mount.

———:———

1537   Richard Arscott, Archpriest of the Mount.

1539   Dissolution of Sion Monastery. Mount leased by the Crown.

1611   Grant of Mount to Robert Cecil, Earl of Salisbury.

1640   Fee conveyed from Earl of Salisbury to Bassets, who sold it to Saint Aubyns.

APPENDIX C.

NORDEN'S TOPOGRAPHICAL ACCOUNT OF THE PLACES IN WEST PENWITH,

SLIGHTLY ABRIDGED, AND PUT IN MODERN ENGLISH SPELLING.

Armed Knight—A rock pointing into the sea at the Land's End, where is found a kind of stone that will attract iron.

S. Burien, (sic)—A great parish near the Land's End, where King Athelstan built a college for priests after his conquest of the Scilly Isles, which he vowed to do upon his victory, as did rash Jepthah. This church was consecrated to a holy Irish woman, one Buriena; so were most of the parish churches and chapels of Cornwall dedicated to some holy Saint, every church founder choosing his particular saint, to whose intercession they might address their devotions.

Bottalock—A little hamlet on the coast of the Irish Sea, mostly visited by Tinners, where they lodge and feed, being near their mines.

Castle Carninach (Castle Karnijack)—The ruins of an ancient castle on the very N.W. point of the Lands's End, upon a lofty craggy rock, where yet appear the ruined walls and forlorn trenches.

Castle-an-Dinas—A vast craggy rock (?) whereon in former times was a castle trenched about . . .

Castle-An-owthern—A craggy rock on the top of a hill, near Zennor, upon the North Sea, sometime trenched about and built of stone, as appears by the ruins of the walls.

Castle Hornocke (sic)—An ancient ruined castle, standing on a mount (?) near Penzance, and as it seems in former times of some account.

S. Erth—A parish near Hayle river.

Gulval—A parish standing in the bottom of Mount's Bay, near Penzans (sic).

S. Ithes or *St. Ies,* (sic) S. Ives—A poor haven (sic) town and a market. There is a Bay, but the sand has been very prejudicial to it, and made it insufficient to receive ships of any great burden; but fishing boats, being well employed, bring profit to the inhabitants, there being great quantity of fish on that North coast. The river Hayle runs into the Bay; it is also called Porthea.

St. Just or *St. Ewst*—A parish at Land's End. (That is all Norden gives).

S. Levan—A parish standing upon the S.W. point of land, having a little cove (Porthcumow) for fishing boats to shelter in. Near to, and in this parish, are many tin mines.

Lerworny (Lamorna)—A rock bending and pointing into the South sea.

Luggan (Ludgvan)—A parish near Mount's Bay, called in former times S. Illogan.

Mousehole (Medeleshole)—A little hamlet set within Mount's Bay, sometimes yet a market town; a harbour for fishing boats, and is called in the Cornish language Porternis, or rather Portinis, in Latin Portus Insalae. Near this place, as Hollinshed reports, certain tinners in the minerals found armour, spearheads, swords, battle axes, and such like, of copper, wrapt up in linen cloths, and weapons not much decayed. (What a pity they had no Archæological Societies in those days!) This little village, with others adjacent, was burnt by the Spaniards in 1595.

Maderne (Madron) called also S. Maderne—A parish situate under the craggy hills north of Penzance, near which is a well called Maderne Well . . . . . .

Morvath, Morveth (Morvah)—A parish standing upon the Irish sea; in a most cold seat in winter(?) It belongs to Maderne.

Mount St. Michaell's (St. Michael's Mount)—A steep and most craggy torr, called sometimes Dinsol in Ptolomy Ocrinum (?), in the Cornish language Careg Cowse, the grey rock; and in the Saxon tongue Michaelstow, Michael's hill or mount. It is at the full sea *Insula plena,* at low water Peninsula. The buildings that are on top of this Mount are ancient, all of freestone (?) very strong and permanent, whereof much was erected by William Moriton, nephew of William the Conqueror. (This statement, modern archæology leads us to regard as inaccurate). It was a cell of monks, but since fortified for defence. It has been much resorted to by pilgrims in devotion to S. Michael, whose chair is fabled to be in the Mount, on the S. side, of very dangerous access. The ascent to the Mount is steep, curving, narrow, and rocky, and that but one way, on the N. side. (Norden then gives the story of John deVere.) It is a place of no (?) importance, having small means to keep and defend it long. At the foot of the Mount is a stone pier, wherein boats are harboured, and from Marcajew there is a causeway or passage that leads to the Mount on foot at low water.

Mount's Bay—A great harbour (?) for ships, especially beneficial near the western shore, unless a forcible E. and N.E. wind disturb them.

Marcajew—Signifying in English "Market on the Thursday," is a very mean town opposite to the Mount; it was burnt by the French in the time of king Henry VIII, as of late its neighbours have been by the Spaniards.

Newlyn—A little hamlet within Mount's Bay, near Pensans,(sic) burned with others by the Spaniards, 1595. (Norden then gives an account which shows that he fell into the error so common in the Post office, of confusing Newlyn East and Newlyn West.)

Portcurno (Porthcurnow)—A little cove at the Land's End.

Pendene (Pendeen)—A hamlet upon the North sea.

Pendenevowe (vau)—A hole or deep vault in the ground, whereinto the sea flows at high water (?) very far under the earth. Many have attempted, but none effected to search the depth of it. The sea cliffs between this place and S. Ithes (sic) glitter as if there were much copper in them (?) Not far from thence inland is a great store of copper and copper mines, as about Morvah, Zennor, and Lelant.

Pawle Church—(sic)—Standing upon a hill above Mount's Bay, on the W. side; burnt by the Spaniards in 1595.

Pensans (sic) Penzance—It signifies the head of the land, and so stands at the bottom of Mount's Bay, adjoining the sand. Mr. Carew calls it the Saint's Head. It is a market town, but of late very much defaced, being also burnt by the Spaniards, in 1595. It is in Madern parish.

Sennan—The farthest parish westward in all the kingdom, situate at the very Land's End, in which and near it are many tin works.

Sener or *S. Sennar* (Zennor)—A parish upon the North sea, where are very rich copper mines.

Sancrete (Sancreed)—A parish situated among the hills.

Tringwenton (Trengwainton)—A house of Mr. Cowlynes.

Twydnack (Towednack)—A chapel to Lelant.

Uny juxta Lelant—Sometime a haven town (seaport), and of late decayed because of the sand, which has choked the harbour and buried much of the land and houses, and many devices they use to prevent the absorption of the church. Here are a great store of tin and copper mines.

Whitesand Bay—A bay at the Land's End.

APPENDIX D.

S. IVES.

There are abundant materials for a history of S. Ives, which might be worked up into a very interesting book. The archives of the borough, like those of Penzance and Marazion, are full of curious facts of the good old times. There is a MS. history of the town written by Hicks, in 1722.

It would seem that in the Stuart and early Georgian period the corporation of S. Ives enjoyed often feasts and fetes for all imaginable public occasions; these festivals were not without music. Two centuries ago the town possessed its band, and the payments for the drums, the fiddles, and the pipers figure in the borough accounts.

The borough appears to have been somewhat warlike, for it often spent money on purchase of guns, and powder, and shot.

Of the celebrated men of S. Ives there is not much to be said. In the last century there was an eccentric personage who certainly thought himself celebrated, and took curious means to impress the idea on the S. Ives folk. He was an East Cornishman, called John Knill, who served as an attorney at Penzance, and became the agent of the Duke of Buckingham, then very powerful in S. Ives. After a visit to the West Indies, he returned as collector of customs at S. Ives, and dealt in privateering. To permanently remind the S. Ives people of his services (?) to the borough he erected the curious pyramid so conspicuous on a hill over the town (now to be seen from the railroad), and left "certain property, with the monument, to the care and trust of the incumbent, mayor and collector of customs of S. Ives, and directed that every five years, on the feast day of S. James the apostle, ten pounds should be expended by them in a dinner, at some tavern in the borough ; each of them to invite two friends, making a party of nine persons. Five pounds to be equally divided among ten girls, every one not exceeding ten years of age, natives of the borough, and daughters of seamen, fishermen, or tinners, who shall, between ten and twelve o'clock in the forenoon of that day, dance for a quarter of an hour at least, on the ground adjoining the mausoleum, and after the dance sing the 100th psalm of the old version, 'to the fine old tune' to which the same was sung in S. Ives Church. One pound to a fiddler to play to the girls while dancing and singing around the monument, also before them on their return therefrom. The fete is still kept up, and so far as the funds will admit the poor are also remembered."

A more deserving person was a native S. Ives' man, *i.e.* Rev. Jonathan Toup, born in 1712, son of the lecturer of S. Ives, and Prudence Busvargus, of S. Just. He was ordained in 1736, having taken his degree at Exeter College, Oxford. He was curate at Philleigh, then of Burian, and afterward rector of S. Martin by Looe, and vicar of S. Merryn, and prebendary of Exeter Cathedral. He was celebrated as a careful and able Greek scholar. His chief work was his *Emendationes in Suidam*. He also edited *Longinus*, and aided Waston in his edition of *Theocritus*. He died in 1785, universally respected as a Christian scholar.

The old S. Ives pier was built in 1767-70, and a lighthouse established there; the new pier is quite recent.

The grammar school was opened in 1650; the master had an endowment of £30 per annum. It had at one time 100 pupils, but like many similar institutions, decayed, and has long ceased to exist. (Mem.: Why do not the S. Ives people try to restore it? They want a good public school for middle class education in the borough.)

The town hall, with market house, was built in 1832, for £1000.

Halsetown (the suburb of S Ives), is quite modern; it is so called from a Mr. Halse, who built it.

The ecclesiastical district of S. Johns, Halsetown, was gazetted in 1846. The pretty church of S. John was built in 1866, at a cost of £2,300.

APPENDIX F.

EVENTS IN WEST PENWITH CHRONOLOGICALLY ARRANGED.

XIth CENTURY.

Charter to S. Michael's Mount by Edward Confessor.
1070 Gregory VII confers charter on the Mount.
1085 Charter of Earl Moreton to the Mount ratified.
1087 Domesday Roll.
1090 (*circa*) Diploma of William II, Rufus, allowing Taillefers to assume name of Borlâs.

XIIth CENTURY.

1135 Church of the Mount, consecrated by Bishop W. Warlewest, and Abbot Bernard, of Mont S. Michel, Normandy.
1155 Adrian confirms the Mount on the Abbot of Mont S. Michel.
1190 Henry Pomeroy seizes the Mount, and is besieged.

XIIIth CENTURY.

1203 Thomas Chinelly, vicar of Madron.
1204 Henry de la Pomeroy (son of the captor of the Mount), repurchases his father's possessions.
1206 Investigation into the right of Presentation to Madron. Award to Knights of S. John.
1212 (?) King John lands in Sennen, from Ireland.
1234 Lelant granted to Tywardreath Priory.
1250 (*circa*) charter of S. Hilary, (Marazion,) by Richard, king of Romans.
1259 Arnold, prothonotary of Richard, king of the Romans, admitted in July Dean of Burian.
1261 Marazion vicarage endowed.
1265 Appropriation of Madron by Knights Hospitallers.

1266 Lanesley given Prior S. Germans.
" Ralph Carteret admitted Prior of the Mount.
1269 Stephen Hayme, Dean of Burian (by Richard king of the Romans).
1272 Bishop Bronescombe appropriates Lelant to Holy Cross Church, at Crediton.
1275 Richard Perer, prior of the Mount.
1276 Gyrard, " rector " of Madron.
1278 John Metingham, vicar of Madron, on presentation of prior of Knights Hospitalers.
1285 Itinerary of Solomon de Ross.
1290 Edmund, Earl of Cornwall, confirms the grants of his father Richard to the Mount.
1292 Mousehole market granted to Henry, Lord Tyes, by Edward I.
1294 Inquisition and taxation of Cornish benefices by bishops of Lincoln and Winchester.
1295 Lelant market granted by Edward I to William Bottreaux.

XIVth CENTURY.

1309 Marazion chapel, licensed by bishop Stapledon.
  John Metingham, vicar of Madron, succeeded by Nicholas Arthur de Tyntagel.
1313 Confirmation of vicarage of S. Hilary by Walter de Stapleton, bishop of Exeter.
  Mousehole market confirmed by Edward II.
1332 A market in Alverton. Penzance granted by Edward III to Alice L'Isle.
1336 Bishop Grandisson's official visits the Mount, and gives report ; charges prior Corville.
1336 Bishop Grandisson consecrates altar at S. Just, churches of Madron, Ludgvan, and Paul.
1340(?) Henry Lord Tyes, owner of Alverton, executed ; manor passes to the Berkleys.
1344 William York, vicar of Madron, exchanged for Redruth rectory.
1349 Ralph Roskasten, vicar of Madron.
1350 Richard Wolveston, dean of Burian.
1354 Dean Maynard appointed to Burian.
1356 Trial of John Hardy, prior of S. Michael's at Launceston, for treason.
1363 Henry Redour admitted vicar of Madron.
1381 Alan Stokes, dean of Burian.
1391 Lawrence Trewythgy, vicar of Madron.
1392 Quay built at Mousehole.
1394 John Boor, dean of Burian. Andrew Borlase, M.P. for Truro.
1395 S. Mary's chapel, Mousehole.
1397 Old S. Mary's chapel, Penzance, licensed by bishop Edmund Stafford.
1398 Kymyell acquired by S. Aubyns (who ever since retain it).

XVth CENTURY.

1404 Penzance market granted and confirmed by Henry IV, to Lord Berkeley.
1409 Morvah church consecrated.
1413 (?) S. Michael's Mount granted to Sion Abbey, by Henry V, and King's College, Cambridge.
1414 Bishop Stafford's appeal for rebuilding S. Mary's, Mousehole.
1421 John Hals, of Lelant, judge under Henry V.
1425 Marazion pier begun under patronage of bishop Edmund Lacy.
1427 William Morton, chaplain of S. Michaels, having begun the pier at the Mount, petitions king Henry VI for help in finishing it.
1428 S. Ives church dedicated.
1429 S. Gabriel and Raphael chapel, Penzance, licensed by bishop Lacy.
1430 Richard Beauchamp, vicar of Madron.
1432 Mark Borlas, M.P. for Helston.
1433 Fish tithe of Lelant and S. Ives made over to the canon of Crediton.
1435 Appeal for repairing Newlyn quay.
1437 S. Bridget chapel, Madron, licensed by bishop Lacy.
1439 John Nanfau's report on the Mount, sent to Henry VI. Adam Molyneaux (afterwards bishop of Chichester), made dean of Burien.

1440　Richard Beauchamp exchanges Madron with Ralph Drew.
1442　(*circa*) Sennen church consecrated.
1471　Trenwith manor (S. Ives) confiscated on attainder of Edward Beaufort, Earl Somerset.
1478　William of Worcester's visit and itinerary.
1483　Kerris granted to John, Duke of Norfolk. (v. Shakespeare's Ric III).
1485　John Vere returns to England with Henry VII.
1487　S. Ives market granted by Henry VII.
1490　.Market house S. Ives built.
1497　Perkin Warbeck landed in September, at Whitsand Bay.
1498　Benedict Trengoff, vicar of Madron.

XVIth CENTURY.

1512　Grant by Henry VIII of harbour dues to king's tenants of Penzance.
1514　Marazion burnt by French.
1521　Wolsey Inquisition into Cornish Benefices.
1529　Edward Baron Bray, of Brea, in S. Just, summoned to Parliament.
1536　Dissolution of Priories. Inquisition by Henry VIII.
1557　Archbishop Cranmer's dispensation to Rev. John Arscott, of the Mount.
1539　S. Michael's Mount dissolved; revenues to Arundell.
1542　Towednack cemetery consecrated by bishop Hippo, suffragan bishop of Cornwall, for
　　　 bishop Veysey.
1549　Cornish Rebellion.
1558　S. Ives first returns members to parliament 6 Mary I.
1567　Edward Pouter nominated vicar of Madron by Queen Elizabeth.
1574　Date of memorial in pew at old S. Mary's, Penzance.
1577　Existing registers of Madron commence.
1583　Ralph Harberts, vicar of Madron.
1592　Royal grant of market to Penzance by Queen Elizabeth
1595　Burning of Mousehole, S. Paul, Newlyn, and Penzance, by the Spaniards.
1595　Charter of Marazion, 37 Elizabeth.

XVIIth CENTURY.

1601　G. Hutchins, vicar of Madron.
1608　Date of font of old St. Mary's, Penzance.
1614　Charter granted to Penzance by James I. John Maddern, first mayor.
1615　Purchase of site of market-house by Penzance corporation.
1617　St. Mary (old) chapel, Penzance, enlarged.
"　　Book of record of minutes of corporation of Penzance commenced.
1634　Turkish pirates infest coast.
1635　A Turkish pirate ship brought in S. Ives as prize.
1639　Incorporation Charter granted to S. Ives (till then ruled by a portreeve), by Charles I.
"　　Great Storm at St. Ives.
1641　St. Ives rated for support of king's troops.
1642　The Mount seized by Charles I.
1644　S. Ives, Towednack and Zennor rebel against king. Revolt crushed.
1645·　Duke of Hamilton imprisoned in Mount.
1646　The Mount surrenders to Colonel Hammond.
1647　The Plague at S. Ives. 535 people die between Easter and October.
"　　The iron spire on the Armed Knight rock washed away.
"　　Great organ of S. Ives taken down and destroyed by Puritans.
1649　Great storm on Charles I Execution. Wreck at Godrevy.
1653　Oliver Cromwell proclaimed protector at S. Ives.
1656　Penzance quay let for £25 per annum.
1658　Thomas Westlake and Richard Myll elected M.P.'s for Marazion.

Y

1658   Remonstrance to the Protector from Penzance.
1659   Major Seely, governor of the Mount, by Richard Cromwell.
1660   Queen Catherine of Braganza visited Penzance. The Saint Aubyn's bought the Mount.
1662   Joseph Sherwood, vicar of S. Hilary, deprived for nonconformity. Imprisoned.
1663   Penzance made a coinage town by Charles II.
1665   Bishop Seth Ward's license to S. Mary's chapel, Penzance.
1670   Pendeen house built. Birthplace of Dr. Borlase.
1672   S. Mary's chapel, Penzance, enlarged.
1673   Fete at Penzance on proclamation of peace with Holland.
1676   Great aerolite struck the Mount. (vide Hals).
1678   New "caŭncing" of street to sea, at Penzance.
1680   Old S. Mary's, Penzance, consecrated.
1683   William Maddern indicted for assaulting mayor of Penzance.
1685   Fete at Penzance on proclamation of James II.
  "   Duke of Monmouth landed at S. Ives. Fetes at Penzance on defeat at Sedgemoor.
1685   S. Ives Charter forfeited. Penzance Charter also.
1686   New S. Ives Charter granted. Lawsuit on Penzance Charter cost £159.
1688   Alarm of French invasion at Helford. The Revolution.
1692   Fete given by Penzance to bishop and general Trelawney.
1695   Dr. Borlase, the antiquary, born at Pendeen.
1697   The sea broke in on S. Ives Church and destroyed a part of the roof, &c.
  "   Fete at Penzance on the peace of Ryswick.

XVIIIth CENTURY.

1702   Proclamation of Queen Anne. Fete at Penzance.
1704   Madron school (for poor) founded by Daniel.
1705   French privateer fires into S. Ives. John Borlase, M.P. for S. Ives.
  "   Carveth seizes mayoralty of Penzance.
1713   Jonathan Toup, the classical critic, born at S. Ives.
  "   Proclamation of George I. and Hanoverian dynasty.
1719   Dr. Borlase ordained priest.
1721   New regalia of Penzance mayoralty.
1722   Dr. Borlase rector of Ludgvan.
1727   New pier at the Mount.
1728   Enlargement of S. Mary's, Penzance. Riots at Marazion.
1730   Visit of Prince Chesroan to Penzance. Purchase and sale of advowson of Madron.
1732   Lawsuit between Penryn and Penzance in *re* coinage privileges.
1736   Visit of Prince of Canaase to Penzance and S. Ives.
1738   A gag and a maypole bought by Penzance corporation (relic of old times).
1740   Penzance battery built.
1743   John Wesley first preached on Hea Moor Rock.
1744   Enlargement of S. Mary's chapelyard.
1745   Penzance pier rebuilt. Fete after victory of Culloden.
1747   Rejoicings at victory of Belleisle.
1748   Fetes on peace of Aix-la-Chappelle.
1750   Borlase's Antiquities of Cornwall published; marks era in local history.
1751   Part of S. Mary chapel wall rebuilt by Corporation.
1753   Visit of bishop Lavington to Penzance.
1755(?) Convulsion of sea in the bay, on the day of the first great earthquake in Lisbon.
1756   Fetes at Penzance on victory of Rossbach. Famine in the winter.
1757   Reservoir at Penzance.
1760   Algerine Corsair wrecked at Newlyn.
1761   Agitation of the sea after second great earthquake at Lisbon. Trevethow house built.
1764   Dr. Oliver, of Ludgvan, the eminent physician, died.

1766 Dr. Borlase D.C.L. by University of Oxford.
1767-70 S. Ives pier built.
1768 Old Jews synagogue built at Penzance.
" Daines Barrington's visit, meeting with Dolly Pentreath.
1770 Sir Christopher Cole, K.C.B. and D.C.L., born at Marazion (June 10).
" Ladies' Book Club established at Penzance.
1772 Dr. Borlase, the antiquary, died.
1774 Tregenna Castle built.
1776 W. Bodenner's letter presented to Society of Antiquaries.
1777 Death of Dolly Pentreath, and perhaps of Cornish language as vernacular.
" Quakers (second) meeting-house built in Penzance.
1778 Sir Humphry Davy born at Penzance.
1779 The Mount batteries fire on Pirate ship. Last military action in the bay.
1780 Transport ship with famished troops from American war reaches S. Ives.
1782 Knill monument built.
1785 Rev. John Toup (the author), of S. Ives, dies. Penzance pier extended 70 feet.
1789 Baptist chapel built.
1790 Old Wesleyan chapel built. Price's Archæological Cornu Brittanica published.
1797 Longships lighthouse erected.
1798 Wherry-town submarine mine abandoned, reopened in 1838 for a short time.

XIXth CENTURY.

1801 Census of Penwith.
1803 Sir H. Davy elected F.R.S.
1807 Sir H. Davy discovers potassium. 300 Roman coins found near Land's End.
1809 Penzance public Dispensary instituted.
1811 John Knill died (author of the singular bequest at S. Ives).
1812 Sir H. Davy knighted.
1814 Royal Geological Society of Cornwall instituted at Penzance by Dr. Paris.
" Wesleyan chapel, Penzance, built.
1815 Lanyon Cromlech overturned.
1816 Breakwater begun at S. Ives, given up for want of funds.
1817 New tariff allowed by Act of Parliament for Penzance pier.
" Great storm, the Green flooded by sea (Jan. 19).
1818 Sir H. Davy made baronet.
" Penzance Library instituted (by Dr. Forbes chiefly) and Savings Bank.
1820 Sir H. Davy president Royal Society.
1824 Lieutenant Goldsmith overthrew Logan Rock.
1826 Herring fishery by Newlyn boats in Ireland begun (now an important industry).
1828 Morvah church rebuilt.
1829 Cemetery at S. Just opened. Sir H. Davy dies.
1830 First waterworks for Penzance.
1832 S. Ives deprived of a member by Reform Act.
" The present church of S. Mary's Penzance, commenced.
" Penzance made a polling place for West Cornwall.
1835 S. Mary's Penzance, dedicated. Municipal Corporation Reform Act affects Penzance.
1836 Western Cottagers' society instituted. Wherry-town mine re-opened.
1837 Penzance (present) market house built.
1838 Coinage privileges of Penzance abolished. Compensation to the town.
1840 New pier Acts.
1841 Bottallack mine nearly given up. Great discoveries and fortunes made.
1843 S. Paul's, Penzance, consecrated.
1846 Queen Victoria and Prince Albert visited the Mount.
" Hals-town vicarage gazetted, also Pendeen.

1848   S. Peter's, Newlyn, gazetted.
1849   Ancient smelting-house discovered near Marazion.   New by-laws enacted at Penzance.
"   Rev. R. Aitken admitted incumbent of Pendeen.
1850   Penzance reservoir works begun.
1851   Great monolith from Lamorna sent to the exhibition.
1852   Marazion school built.
1853   Old S. Hilary church burnt on Good Friday (March 25).
1860   Prince Lucien Bonaparte's visit.   Tomb to Dolly Pentreath.
1861   New church at Marazion built.
1863   Mr. R. Couch dies.
1864   Deanery of Burian abolished.   Burian, Sennen, and S. Levan rectories formed.
1865   Prince of Wales and Princess Alexandra visit West Penwith.
1866   S. John, Halsetown, built.   Restoration of S. Just-in-Penwith church.
"   S. Peter's, Newlyn, consecrated.
1867   Sennen church restored.
1868   S. John's Hall, Penzance, built.
1870   Towednack church restored.
1875   School Boards elected at Paul and Ludgvan.   S. Burian Church restored.
"   Art exhibition at Penzance.   Part of new churchyard at Towednack consecrated.
1876   Visit of British Archæological Association to Penzance.   Art exhibition at Newlyn.
"   G.W.R. purchases line to Penzance.
1877   Consecration of Dr. Benson to the bishopric of Cornwall, and restoration of the diocese.
"   Opening of S. Ives railway.

APPENDIX F.

PENZANCE NAMES.

The names of some of the ladies of Penzance in days gone bye must, to judge by the Madron registers, have been very peculiar.   Among those quoted by Mr. Millett in his valuable book are the following :—

Addama (feminine for Adam?), Anquite, Armanell, Duens, Earth (from S. Erth?), Eppow, Gratiana, Jaquelinah, Jaquite, Jellyan, Mellioner (S. Mellion?), Norow, Pasques, Porthesia, Syve, Tamer, Wany.   The gentlemen's names were not so singular.   Query was it that the ladies had such peculiar names from motives of vanity.   Some men's names were out of the common however, *e.g.* Emmet, Halenight, Madern, Morvah, Rowan, Udye.

Among the more remarkable Penzance and Madron surnames are Ammear, Angove, Angwin, Anhaye, Anhow, Argall, Asye ; Baragwaneth, Bazaw, Beckerleg, Benallack, Blazeria, Blewett, Bosavern, Bossence, Boskening, Bosava, Boswarthen ; Calenzo, Chinalla, Chirgwin, Clies, Connock, Crankan ; Dodo, Dunkyn ; Ethaw ; Friggens ; Gubbs, Gymball ; Holla ; Jacka, Jowan ; Lamyn, Lympany ; Madern (from Madron), Melyanneck, Mildren, Monallack, Mulfra (from the place) ; Nancothan ; Pedwell, Pendene, Pender, Penhellick, Pennaierick, Penalbean, Polhormal, Polsewe ; Reskorla, Rowen (?) ; Sacarya, Saloma, Scaddan, Sudgiow ; Teage, Tollvan, Treganhoe, Trelill, Trembah, Trenwith, Trereife, Tresies, Trevalles, Trewren, and (other *tres*) ; Udye ; Vean ; Wynselet ; Zackrey.

Mr. Millet's first book of the Parish Register of Madron is a most useful book to any who wishes to study the details of Penzance history.

Lightning Source UK Ltd.
Milton Keynes UK
UKHW050056090223
416726UK00017B/231